T0047526

THE KINDNESS AMBASSADOR
AND THE SUGARHOLIC PROSECUTOR

THE KINDNESS AMBASSADOR
AND THE SUGARHOLIC PROSECUTOR

KEYS TO LIVING THE LIFE YOU ARE MEANT TO LOVE

A Semi-Autobiographical Inspirational Novel
Written by

JOYCE M. ROSS

Inspired and Edited by

E. PATRICIA CONNOR

Co-founders of Kindness is Key Training Inc.
www.kindnessiskey.com

BALBOA.
PRESS
A DIVISION OF HAY HOUSE

Copyright © 2013 by Kindness Is Key Training Inc.

All rights reserved. No part of this book may be used or reproduced by
any means, graphic, electronic, or mechanical, including photocopying,
recording, taping or by any information storage retrieval system
without the written permission of the publisher except in the case of
brief quotations embodied in critical articles and reviews.

Balboa Press books may be ordered through booksellers or by contacting:

Balboa Press
A Division of Hay House
1663 Liberty Drive
Bloomington, IN 47403
www.balboapress.com
1-(877) 407-4847

ISBN: 978-1-4525-5749-6 (sc)
ISBN: 978-1-4525-5750-2 (hc)
ISBN: 978-1-4525-5806-6 (e)

Because of the dynamic nature of the Internet, any web addresses or
links contained in this book may have changed since publication and
may no longer be valid. The views expressed in this work are solely those
of the author and do not necessarily reflect the views of the publisher,
and the publisher hereby disclaims any responsibility for them.

The author of this book does not dispense medical advice or prescribe the use
of any technique as a form of treatment for physical, emotional, or medical
problems without the advice of a physician, either directly or indirectly. The
intent of the author is only to offer information of a general nature to help you
in your quest for emotional and spiritual well-being. In the event you use any
of the information in this book for yourself, which is your constitutional right,
the author and the publisher assume no responsibility for your actions.

Any people depicted in stock imagery provided by Thinkstock are models,
and such images are being used for illustrative purposes only.
Certain stock imagery © Thinkstock.

Printed in the United States of America

Library of Congress Control Number: 2012915703

Balboa Press rev. date: 01/02/2013

13 Keys to *Living the Life* YOU ARE MEANT TO LOVE

Personally, Professionally and Spiritually.

The 13 Kindness Keys

Key # 1: HARMONY
"Live in harmony within: mind, heart and soul." —Joyce M. Ross: Author, Teacher and Speaker.

Key # 2: GRATITUDE
"Be grateful for your shadows, light and dark, as they are your compass to the life you are meant to love." —Joyce M. Ross: Author, Teacher and Speaker.

Key # 3: LOVE
"Even after all this time, the sun never says to the earth, 'You owe me.' Look what happens with a love like that...it lights the whole sky." —Hafiz: 14th Century Poet.

Key # 4: INTEGRITY
"My word is my contract; my handshake, my seal; and, my conscience, my witness." —E. Patricia Connor: Ordained Minister, Author, Teacher, and Speaker.

Key # 5: FORGIVENESS
"You are loved, not for anything you did or didn't do; but because at Source, there is only love." —Anonymous

Key # 6: ACCEPTANCE
"My truth is but mine alone; as yours is yours. For this reason, I hear and see you free of judgment, fear, anger, and resentment.

This is my promise to you. This is my gift to me." —E. Patricia Connor: Ordained Minister, Author, Teacher, and Speaker.

Key # 7: EGO

"As a sense of self, ego is a great protector. As a sense of being separate from others, the universe and Creation, ego enhances the illusion that you are alone." —E. Patricia Connor: Ordained Minister, Author, Teacher, and Speaker.

Key # 8: LIVE

"Sing like no one's listening. Love like you've never been hurt. Dance like nobody's watching. And live like it's Heaven on earth." —Mark Twain: American Author and Humorist.

Key # 9: DREAM

"Dreams are the seeds still in the universal storehouse. To become a reality they must be chosen, planted, tended, and harvested." —Reverend Barbara Leonard: Author of *Don't Just Stand There Sucking Your Thumb.*

Key # 10: BELIEVE

"Belief in your dreams, yourself, others, and the guiding love of Source—chart the walkway to true meaning, the highway to greatness, and the flight path to the Life You Are Meant to Love." —Joyce M. Ross: Author, Teacher and Speaker.

Key # 11: ACTION

"Once I have mastered peace within, only then will I experience peace in my family, my community, my country, and finally, the world." —Ted Kuntz: Psychotherapist, Speaker & Author of *Peace Begins with Me.*

Key # 12: PROSPERITY
"There is no way to prosperity, prosperity is the way." —Dr. Wayne Dyer: Spiritual Teacher, Author and Speaker.

Key # 13: PURPOSE
"Everything in the universe has a purpose. Indeed, the invisible intelligence that flows through everything in a purposeful fashion is also flowing through you." —Dr. Wayne Dyer: Spiritual Teacher, Author and Speaker.

KINDNESS PLEDGE

First and foremost,
in reverence for life and Creation
I am kind to myself.
Life loves me and I love life.
Today and for always, I live...
Softly,
Passionately,
Compassionately,
and Forgivingly.
I seed Prosperity, Wisdom, Hope,
Love, Peace, and Kindness
by being the example.

Kind Welcome from Joyce and Patricia
AKA Joycelynn and Elizabeth

Fiction or Fact?
The truth about the real lives of our characters.

T*he Kindness Ambassador and the Sugarholic Prosecutor* is loosely based on the lives and experiences of the co-founders of Kindness Is Key (*KiK*) Training Inc., Joyce May Ross and Elizabeth Patricia Connor. The *13 Kindness Keys* woven throughout are the cornerstones to everything Patricia and Joyce believe and encourage in their seminars and inspirational authorship training. The spiritual awakenings of the characters are fact-based and meant to inspire you to explore your purpose-path—on earth and eternally—and bring greater meaning, abundance and love into your personal journey.

Patricia and Joyce have been close friends since they met in 1984 while retailing Mary Kay Cosmetics. Their friendship is based in: mutual respect; similar views, values and goals; and, a shared purpose-path. Discounting no one's religious or spiritual beliefs, throughout the book, our originating divinity is referred to as *Source.* Both women believe in what His Holiness the 14th Dalai Lama of Tibet espoused when he said, "My religion is very simple. My religion is kindness."

Patricia was raised in a Catholic family. Joyce's religious childhood education included: minimal teachings from the Protestant faith; influences from her mother's Catholic background; and, a brief time spent studying the Jehovah's Witnesses' book *From Paradise Lost to Paradise Regained.*

Mostly raised atheist, she affectionately recalls her father's colorful theories on aliens and spaceships.

Joyce's Purpose-Path

Joyce worked at the Victoria Youth Detention Home from 1974 until1980 and resigned as a result of the story you'll read. From there, she spent two years in Toronto and fell in love with writing. Her hands and manuscript covered in liquid White Out, she banged out her first romance novel on a well-used electric typewriter. Each evening she would read what she'd written to her five roommates gathered around the common-room table. All single women, Joyce soon discovered that when her hero did something the ladies disapproved of, they would chastise her! It was also when she discovered the sweetest joy of writing fictional romance—the hero eventually gets it right.

The heroine's afterlife communication with her unborn child's soul is an accurate recount of what was the most awe-inspiring experience of Joyce's life. Although heartrending, miscarrying provided Joyce with a glimpse into the afterlife, causing her to realize that all souls are eternally interconnected through a universal web of love-energy, or our *heartminds*.

Joyce's journey through gaming addiction is accurately portrayed in the book, including the divine *aha* message she received from her spiritual guides that led her to become an activist for gaming reform. Over three million Canadians and ten million Americans are severely, moderately, or in danger of becoming addicted gamblers. For this vulnerable segment of society, what begins as a fun activity slowly becomes a nightmarish addiction that destroys their finances, self-worth and families. Incorporating the 13 Kindness Keys into her life allowed Joyce to release shame and transform her shadows into a purpose-path of helping others.

Like the heroine, Joyce was married twice. Currently, she is unattached. For seventeen years, she ran singles dances for the over forty-five crowd. Her philosophy regarding the joys of living solo and the rewards of being coupled are reflected through the story characters.

Patricia's Purpose-Path

Patricia is an ordained minister and certified vision coach. She has studied with numerous brilliant masters, including many from Peak Potentials Training, Dream University and Experts Academy. She has a Bachelor of Arts from the University of British Columbia and speaks fluent Spanish and some French. For over twenty years, she has been married to Marek Kowalczyk. They live in North Delta, B.C. with their four-legged love-on-paws English Labrador, Charlie.

Since her early twenties, Patricia has moved forward and lived fully through what for someone else might have been debilitating depression. Her character, Elizabeth, shares some of her healing techniques in this book. Our next inspirational novel, *The Wooden Nickel Wellness Spa*, chronicles Patricia's life in deeper detail, and is a must read for anyone who suffers from this under-recognized and under-diagnosed condition.

Patricia's father, Robert J. Connor, who returned to Source in 2009 at the age of eighty-four, greatly influenced her humanitarian views. As a sales manager and later as the Vice-President of Canadian Airlines (now Air Canada), her father was the family Pied Piper, moving his loved ones throughout the world to Spain, Chile, Japan, and Mexico City.

A collection of early impressions led Patricia to become a heart-centered visionary. In Mexico City, she witnessed the pilgrimage of worshippers on their knees, suffering for miles to give their meager donations to the church—an institution abundant in riches while their flock endured poverty. Throughout the world, women were treated as second-class citizens, their subservient place marked by illiteracy, low-pay and undervaluation of their amazing contributions. Patricia's young mind questioned: Why the nuns weren't permitted to perform the same services as priests? Why class-distinctions existed at all? And why children throughout the world weren't granted the same privileges she enjoyed; especially, the basics of food, shelter, education, and health care?

From the delight-filled day when she taught the family maid to tell time by a clock, Patricia's recognized her inner-calling to inspire, educate and empower others. A spiritual giver by nature, her heart resonated with Meryl Streep's character in the movie *Out of Africa,* further fuelling her own desire to service our third-world brothers and sisters. The spiritual teachings of our past-day and modern gurus—Dr. Wayne Dyer, James Twyman, Mother Teresa, Mahatma Gandhi, the Dalai Lama, and Jesus—steeled her belief in the divine interconnection of all souls through all time.

Patricia's desire to propagate spiritual, as well as emotional and physical health for all, led her to become a practitioner of aromatherapy, herbology, Bach flower remedies, Reiki, and reconnective-healing. She has worked as a *Stop the Violence* Counsellor for Battered Women Support Services, was a Director of Development Resources for the Surrey Women's Center, and was a director of Berlitz School of Languages where she also taught English as a second language.

Heartmind Wisdom
Inspirational Anthology Collection

The *Heartmind Wisdom* anthology referenced throughout *The Kindness Ambassador* is a collection of inspirational stories from those who have been there. Part of Kindness is Key's divinely inspired mission is to help people heal through the life-gained wisdom of others. Each anthology contains twenty-one true accounts of the coauthors' individual journeys through a myriad of varying afflictions, including depression, addiction, health challenges, and loss.

www.heartmindwisdom.com

Kindness is Key's *Heartmind Wisdom*
Inspirational Anthology Collection

WRITING CONTEST

Our global brothers and sisters are invited to enter Kindness is Key's *Heartmind Wisdom* Writing Contest. For contest details please visit www.heartmindwisdom.com.

81% surveyed want to write a book.
Sadly, only 1% of wannabe writers are published.

Kindness is Key Training Inc. has greatly
increased the odds of being published!

Heartmind Wisdom Inspirational Authorship Course

Kindness is Key Training Inc. guides *new* and *published* writers through the joys of inspirational authorship. Graduates are published in *Heartmind Wisdom—An Anthology of Inspiring Wisdom From Those Who Have Been There.* All twenty-one coauthors with a submission in a *Heartmind Wisdom* anthology share equally in royalties. Each published *Heartmind Wisdom* coauthor benefits from a Personal Replicated Website that has blogging capabilities and is connected to *KiK*'s Online Library. Coauthors may 'co-link' other blogs/websites (of a healing or inspirational nature) and promote other published works (books, e-books, DVDs and CDs) on their Personal Replicated Website.

If you are interested in sharing your educational, healing or inspirational story with a global audience, please visit www. heartmindwisdom.com

Kindness is Key's
Annual 'Largest Human Peace Sign' Concert
and Guinness World Record attempt.

Gregg Braden in his book *The Divine Matrix* states that "the minimum number of people required to 'jump-start' a change in consciousness is the square root of one percent of a population." Known as the *Maharishi Effect*, this principle translates into ten people affecting one hundred thousand. To this end, Kindness is Key annually attempts the Guinness World Record for the 'Largest Human Peace Sign.' We invite you to help us seed global peace, hope, love, and kindness by challenging your neighborhood, business, organization or school to surpass our current Human Peace Sign participant numbers.

www.humanpeacesign.com.

Kindness is Key's
Annual 'Peace Sign Event' Contest.

Everyone is encouraged to enter *KiK's* annual 'Peace Sign Event' contest. To enter, simply host and video a Peace Sign Event or Project. Make certain that you include our sponsors' names and/or logos. Then, enter to win in one of the following categories:

- Outstanding Creative Peace Sign Event
- Outstanding Creative Inclusion of Sponsors
- Outstanding Creative Use of Nature
- Outstanding Creative Inclusion of Recycled Materials
- Outstanding Creative Entry from a Grade/ Elementary School
- Outstanding Creative Entry from a High School
- Outstanding Creative Entry from a University or College
- Outstanding Original Peace Song

Help seed worldwide peace—visit
www.humanpeacesign.com

HARMONY

"Live in harmony within: mind, heart and soul."
Joyce M. Ross

B randon Ashton stepped out of the funeral of his lifelong friend Terry Richards and into the soggy fall day. Disoriented and sullen, he fished in his pocket for his cell phone and turned it on. No calls. One text from his sister announcing that he had another niece: *five-pound, six-ounce baby Gabriela.*

Happy for his sister but disappointed for himself, he typed his return message: *Congratulations! I'll bet she's as pretty as you. See you tonight.* Having been hoping for a nephew, stuffing the phone back in his pocket he consoled himself with the adage that all children were a gift. Not that he'd know. He didn't have kids. An incredibly fat cat and a mangy dog with two legs in heaven were his immediate family.

Dropping his briefcase to the sidewalk, he waved both arms at an oncoming taxi, muttering obscenities when he saw that it already had a fare. Flipping the collar of his overcoat upward, he cursed the insouciant young forecaster who'd predicted sunshine. Vancouver's weather was bloody unpredictable. With mountains for a skyline and the Pacific at its feet, one might as well toss a coin as to whether to wear sunglasses or tote an umbrella. In the future, he'd carry both.

"Do you have far to go?"

Brandon jerked his head toward the sultry voice. Standing behind his left shoulder was a gorgeous woman with extraordinarily blue irises that he guessed were the result of colored contact lenses.

"Not far," he shouted above the downpour gurgling its way into a nearby drain. Ten blocks wasn't far, but it would seem like a thousand miles in this deluge. Going green by walking, biking or busing to work might be one of his dumbest ideas yet.

"Which way?" She glanced to her left and right as she bobbed her golf-sized yellow umbrella. "I'll walk with you." She smiled cheerily. "I carry my own sunshine."

"North." Brandon had no doubt that he was gawking as he scrutinized the purple-coated, midsized, middle-aged auburn beauty. Was she a lunatic or a Good Samaritan? Maybe she was like one of those homeless people who cleaned your car windshield while you were stopped at a light, then expected a handout.

Standing straighter and with her arm stretched skyward, Miss Sunshine positioned her umbrella so that it covered them both. "I saw you at the funeral."

Relieved that she wasn't just some crazy who earned her living escorting rain-drenched citizens to their destinations, he wondered if she'd also seen him sobbing his foolish head off. She hadn't been in the front rows, or he'd have noticed her. "You knew Terry?"

"I know his sister Dee. We met at a conference." She extended her free hand. "Joycelynn Rose."

"Brandon Ashton." Shivering as he shook her hand, he realized that he was soaking wet and likely looked as scruffy as his *Heinz 57* mutt. Hopefully he didn't smell as bad.

She took a small step forward, indicating that she wanted to get moving. "Your briefcase."

Stooping to pick it up, he bumped into Joycelynn, knocking the umbrella out of her hand and onto the sidewalk. "Sorry," he muttered, retrieving her portable sunshine, then his briefcase. Feeling like a dumb ass, in his mind's ear he heard Terry mocking him from beyond, *Not much of a ladies' man, are you, Bud?*

Ignoring his clumsy blunder, Joycelynn asked, "Don't you think we're rather spoiled living in Vancouver?"

The rain dripping from his nose, he contemplated debating her point. It was November, the first of four or five depressing months of grey skies and incessant rain. Except for rare times like today, which was supposed to be sunny and wasn't, winter in Vancouver was miserably dull. Not wanting to spoil her delusion of good fortune, he rolled his shoulders and said, "I don't think about it much."

"What do you think about?" Her curious blue eyes locked on his as though what he was about to say would be the most important thing she would hear today.

"Mostly work." His answer sounded trivial to him and likely lame to her.

"What do you do?"

"I'm a lawyer." He didn't elaborate. A lot of people detested lawyers, especially ones in his area of law. He couldn't count the number of times he'd been referred to as a bottom feeder, bastard or scumbag.

"What kind of law do you practice?"

Head tilted, her gaze uncomfortably intense, she awaited his answer with the attentiveness of a newly appointed judge. "I'm a crown prosecutor," he supplied, wondering if her reply would be a disapproving *I see.* She was a classy looking babe, but many well-to-do families were peppered with embezzlement, inside trading or tax fraud.

She continued studying him, her gentle manner reminding him of a picture he'd seen of Mother Teresa holding an orphaned baby. "You obviously like what you do, if that's what you think about all the time."

"I guess." Becoming more chilled by the minute, he shuddered. If they didn't soon start walking, he'd freeze to death. What would be even better was something hot to drink. "There's a Starbucks at the corner. Do you have time for a cup of coffee?" he asked, hoping that she did. He could use the company, and if the rain didn't let up he might still need her portable sunshine service.

"Coffee sounds great," she answered, seemingly delighted. "You must be cold."

"Frozen!" He considered offering to hold her umbrella, but fearing his chivalry might not be welcomed, he didn't. "What do you do for a living?" he asked as they headed toward the coffee bar.

"I'm a teacher."

"What do you teach?" Noting her flawless skin, he wondered if it was as soft as it appeared, and whether she was married or had a boyfriend. He'd earlier noticed that she wasn't wearing a ring, but that really told him nothing. For a fleeting moment he pondered what she might be like in bed, but having just left their mutual friend's funeral, his guilt kicked into overdrive. Instead, he pictured her in front of a blackboard.

"Kindness," she chirped as though it were an occupation one heard about every day. "Love in action."

Her captivating eyes roamed his face, then the space above and around his head. Knowing his hair was a mess, he shoved his fingers through it. *Kindness. Love in action.* Things were falling into place. On one of his many visits to see his dying friend, Terry had mentioned that his sister had befriended a kindness guru. This must be her! "You're the writer." Her career added a new dimension to her appeal. She and her partner taught writing, orchestrated inspirational anthologies and had written a couple of novels. Every book they published made the best sellers list. Until recently, Joycelynn had also run singles dances, which he remembered because Terry had jokingly suggested that might be the place where Brandon could find an endless supply of foxes in high heels.

"Guilty as charged." She laughed.

He was suddenly glad he'd booked the day off. Knowing he might need the distraction of work he'd brought along his briefcase, but it was his choice as to whether he went into the office. Terry's death, though expected and a merciful escape from suffering for his best friend, pummeled Brandon into a dark depression he didn't have the will to fight. Hearing Joycelynn's uplifting laugh ignited a reminiscent spark and he smiled. "We kicked up a lot of hell in our younger days." Chortling, he added, "I think our parents worried we'd end up in jail."

"Dee told me some of the stories." Joycelynn's laughter subsided, but her grin remained. "I think she referred to you as hooligans."

"*Hooligans!*" Recalling how Terry often joked that his sister was born with her halo attached, Brandon roared. "We weren't exactly *hooligans*, but we did get into our fair share of trouble."

"I don't know," Joycelynn teased, "I think being arrested for trying to outrun one of Vancouver's first female police officers is a bit *hooliganish*."

"Dee told you that story?" He roared louder. "I'm now guilty as charged." Visions played through his mind of himself and Terry trying to run full steam when they were laughing so hard they could barely stand. "We would've gotten away, if it weren't for her quick-witted partner sticking his leg out from behind a tree and toppling poor Terry, then me. The next thing I knew, we were sitting in the back of a cruiser with our hands cuffed."

"Why were you running away? What had you done?"

"We had a few beers that made us stupidly decide it would be fun to knock over a few garbage cans in Stanley Park."

"Serious stuff." Joycelynn feigned a frown as they reached Starbucks and he held the door.

"Serious enough to get us six months of probation and a hundred hours of community service work."

"Picking up garbage, no doubt?"

"Yeah," he answered absentmindedly, thinking that the incident had been more pivotal in his best friend's life than the judge had likely intended. Pulling out the chair facing the window, he waited for Joycelynn to sit in it before asking, "What can I get you?"

"A vanilla latte, please. I keep telling myself they're going to clog my arteries and be the death of me, yet I keep drinking them."

Ignoring the kick to his gut at the mention of death, Brandon brushed his bangs off his forehead while muttering, "We all have our vices."

While Joycelynn waited, she glanced out the window and spotted a small boy making friends with an English Lab puppy. They looked so cute together, the dog's guardian and the boy's mother smiling as the two young ones exchanged licks and hugs. The scene was a far cry from the somber one at the chapel. She'd seen Brandon sobbing in the front row, and thanks to Dee's stories, had a good idea about who he was before she offered to share her umbrella.

"I'm addicted to all things sweet," Brandon quipped as he plopped a gigantic pastry and two plastic forks on the table. "I eat one of these every day, and then after work, I run five miles to wear it off." Grinning, he placed her vanilla latte in front of her and his coffee on the opposite side.

"Yet, you're willing to share," she teased. "I guess if I eat half of this, you'll only have to run two and a half miles tonight."

"That would be the math." He sat across from her. "Tell me more about being a kindness guru." Forking off a chunk of the pastry, he popped it into his mouth.

"I'm not a guru, I'm an ambassador. I seed kindness." She lifted her cup and inhaled the sweet vanilla aroma. Too hot to drink, she placed it back on the table and waited while Brandon chewed. Dee was dead-on. The man was drool-on-your-shoes gorgeous. Clear vivid green eyes. Killer smile. Cocky confidence. *Was the rest of what she said true, too?*

"*Love in action,*" he repeated the phrase she'd used earlier. "How does one go about teaching kindness?"

"By encouraging people to be kind to themselves, and to lead by being the example. As Gandhi said: 'Be the change you wish to see in the world.'"

"It sounds more as though you're teaching people to be selfish," he commented. Then as if realizing his remark sounded arrogant, he expanded, "I mean, isn't the whole concept of kindness about being selfless and thinking of others first?"

"It is." Joycelynn nodded. "My *KiK* mission partner, Elizabeth, and I believe that *self*-kindness is the catalyst for *other*-kindness. Our premise is that when we are kind to ourselves personally, professionally and spiritually, we will naturally be kind to others."

"Spiritually!" Brandon's brow shot upward. "I'm not much for religion." He dumped three packets of sugar into his coffee. "There's too much suffering in this world for me to believe there's a God."

"Are you referring to Terry's battle with colon cancer?" she softly asked, her heart aching for him.

"Not just Terry. Cancer also took out my grandmother. All over the globe kids are starving to death." He wiped his mouth before crumpling his napkin and tossing it on the table. "The news is filled with stories about people killing each other because of territorial claims or differing religious beliefs. How can anyone believe in a loving Creator?"

"What do you believe in?" Joycelynn asked, ignoring his contemptuous tone and expression. Having just lost his best friend, it was understandable that Brandon was angry with Creation.

"My parents are devout churchgoers. When I was young, there was a lot of talk about Judgment Day and fearing God. Not my favorite topics."

"Don't you wonder about your soul's origin or life after death?" she asked, leaning forward and resting her forearms on the table.

"Nope! I think that we're born and then we die."

Brandon's cynical atheism didn't jibe with Dee's depiction of him as a holy godsend, whose quick laughter and attentive care made her brother's last days happier. "If you don't believe in a divinely intentioned universe, then what do you imagine motivates one person toward healing and kindness, and another toward hurting and criminality?"

"Free will, I guess." He grimaced, as though mentally berating himself for making a religious reference. "What I meant to say is that some people are flawed from birth. Perhaps some criminality is due to poor parenting, though that's debatable." Arms crossed, jaw jutted, he glowered at her.

More amused than intimidated by his assertive body language, she clamped her arms one over the other and glared back at him. "I can agree with your unfortunate parenting observation."

"At least we agree on something," he returned with a smirk.

Sitting upright, Joycelynn unlocked her arms. "When I was younger, I worked at Victoria's Youth Detention Center. Kids came in for everything from theft to murder. Many of them were raised in families where physical, emotional or sexual abuse was a common occurrence. Several of their parents were alcoholics or drug addicts."

Brandon's open palm jerked traffic cop forward. "If you're selling the *it's-the-parents'-fault* ideology, I'm not buying. There are many law abiding citizens who come from truly outrageous homes. Once we hit eighteen, we make our own choices."

"*Choices* with their roots in various advantages and disadvantages," she returned. "I can't imagine a psychopath being the byproduct of truly loving parents."

"Unless he or she was born mentally ill."

"That's true. People come into this world in all kinds of circumstances. Some are born into loving homes in fruitful nations; others into countries so poor that parenting takes a backseat to providing basic necessities. Some children are born healthy and others disabled." Saddened as she glanced out the window and saw that the puppy and boy were gone, she finished by asking, "Why do you think that is?"

"Why do I think what is?" Brandon's gaze drifted toward where Joycelynn had glanced, then back at her.

"Why do you think each person in this world is so unique? When you consider the various defining realms—physical, emotional, intellectual, spiritual, social, economic, and political—humans are as varied as they are plentiful."

"You've obviously thought about it more than I have. You tell me!"

"I believe we're born into the exact circumstances that we are meant to be born into, and that there is a divine reason for each individual's birth, life and death. As some philosophers have suggested, I think that we are *spiritual beings having human experiences,* rather than *human beings having spiritual experiences.*"

"Religion, again!" Brandon guffawed, stirring his coffee excitedly.

"I'm talking about spirituality, not religion."

"What's the difference? Same cloak, different color."

"Not really, though they are married through belief in a higher power."

"I rest my case. Next topic!"

"You can rest all you want, but *spirituality* isn't a particular dogma. It's about the spirit-self's individual relationship with our originating Source. What we teach in our Kindness is Key courses is that when you live in harmony within—mind, heart and soul—you're aligned with your intended purpose-path, and will naturally prosper financially, spiritually and personally. That's not religion. It's common sense."

Glee shadowed with apprehension flashed across his face before he said, "You might have misread your own purpose-path. With your debating skills, you'd be a fantastic lawyer."

"Thanks…I think." Joycelynn blushed. She wanted to help him deal with his loss by exploring the possibility of a divine rationale for human suffering. Brandon, however, seemed stuck in the thrill of courtroom style deliberation. "I'm beginning to wonder if I'm just wasting *my* time and *yours* by going on about my spiritual beliefs," she confessed, sounding more irritated than intended.

"Then I'll tell you what *I* believe," Brandon said, his tone triumphant, his expression smug. "I think our primary purpose on earth is to procreate. Everything on the planet just wants to reproduce and keep their species going."

"That's such a *guy* supposition." Crossing one leg over the other, she asked, "If our primary purpose is to procreate, then what's the purpose behind that? Why does it matter whether earth continues to exist? Why does it matter if people exist?"

"I'm a lawyer, not a priest. But off the top of my head, I'd say that people matter because we're the guardians of the planet. As for why it matters whether earth continues to exist, that's way too deep for me."

Regardless of what she said, Brandon was either going to debate or dismiss her point. Sharing her theories wasn't going to help him deal with Terry's death. He needed time. Slouching forward, she forfeited her objective. "I'm in the midst of writing an inspirational novel, so I sometimes get carried away. Let's talk about something that interests you."

"A female turning over the conversation reins, that's a first." Brandon pushed his bangs back and leaned toward her conspiratorially. "A woman I dated talked so much that I nicknamed her Motormouth. Of course, I was never brazen enough to call her that to her face." He laughed.

"I know that I sometimes get carried away," Joycelynn apologized, her cheeks sunburn hot.

Brandon studied her with the intentness of a kid happened upon fool's gold before saying, "You're different. You're not just talking to be heard, you're sharing beliefs close to your heart." His eyebrows wriggling above irises as bright as fresh grass, he added, "However, if I disappear into the men's room and I'm not back in ten, I've changed my mind."

"Thanks for the forewarning." Aware that Brandon was giving her a yellow light, not green, she again considered switching subjects.

"If we're going to be friends, I might as well get to know your spiritual beliefs. That's provided you don't attempt to convert me or save my soul." He closed one eye in an unhurried wink as he added, "Of course, my deal comes with the proviso that I can change my mind and the topic at will."

"As long as our next discussion isn't politics." Disregarding that Brandon's continued intense stare was prickling her nerves, Joycelynn switched tactics. "Let's consider spirituality from a scientific perspective."

"Science! I'm interested, keep talking."

"From radio waves and electricity, to computers, space travel and cloning, our terrific advances must be at least partially due to divine intervention, or guidance from the other side."

"Your spiritual manipulation theory is interesting, but have you considered that each scientific discovery propels the next?"

"I realize that accumulating knowledge expedites our advances. I am equally aware that many scientists report that what leads them to investigate or prove something, often begins as a feeling, which could very well be divine intervention."

"Let's assume you're right," he said, peering at her with concentrated interest. "Answer the question you asked me earlier. What do you imagine is the divine reasoning for the existence of people and earth?"

Fearing her response might detonate an emotional eruption he wasn't expecting, Joycelynn cautiously answered, "Like you, I was never comfortable with the fear-based motivation of some religions. Neither could I bring myself to accept an omnipotent, omnipresent Creator who idly permitted the degree of suffering Terry endured." Inwardly grimacing, she lowered her voice and glance as she surmised, "Unless there was a greater purpose or reason."

A windstorm of grief swept across Brandon's face. Although her words were intended as stepping stones across a healing pond, she'd said too much, too soon. Disconcerted by the ensuing silence, she contemplated conjuring an excuse to leave before her good intentions irreparably shattered the man's heart.

"When Terry told me he had cancer, I was scared—for him and me. When a biopsy confirmed he was terminally ill, I was terrified. Each time he was hospitalized, I tried to prepare myself for the inevitable. But I could never imagine life without him. I still can't." Swallowing hard, Brandon's eyes locked with Joycelynn's. "Terry was very brave. He concealed his pain and fear with humor, constantly making silly remarks about how well his Jenny Craig's diet was working, or telling stupid jokes that were supposed to make it okay that his life was shriveling away." Shaking his head, his voice flat, he cautioned, "You're going to have a very difficult time convincing me of a good reason for suffering."

"I know that I am." She smiled apologetically. "Terry meant the world to you, and I'm sorry if it seems that I'm making light of his suffering. That's not my intention."

Leaning back and resting his linked hands across his stomach, Brandon stared out the window.

After about a minute, Joycelynn nervously asked, "Are you okay?"

"I'm as fine as I'll be for a while," he said, nodding reassuringly. "No matter what we discuss, I'm still going to be thinking about Terry. Your theories might even be helpful." Head slightly bowed, he closed one eye and faintly smiled. "However, don't think by admitting this, I'm on board with *everything* you're speculating."

"I wouldn't dare be so presumptuous," Joycelynn responded, the edginess in her gut somewhat dissipating.

"Attractive and smart," Brandon returned, eyeing her lasciviously as he drummed his fingers on the table.

Seconds before, he'd been as gloomy as a moonless moor; now, he was flirting with her! Typical guy defense: mask what hurts with flirtatious overtures. Past that he desperately needed a haircut before his perpetual habit of huffily forking his hands through his hair became a permanent tic, the man was undeniably gorgeous. Normally, intimate interest from a man of his caliber would be flattering. Under the circumstances, it seemed borderline pathetic. "Do pick-up lines like that actually work for you?" she asked, knowing that they likely did.

"Sometimes," he said, brazen mischief afire in his eyes. "Obviously, they're not working too well today."

"No, not today." Joycelynn laughed self-consciously. If she hadn't already married and divorced two of his bad-boy compatriots, Brandon's devilish charm might have impressed her. "Been there, done that!"

"Me, too," Brandon admitted, sweeping his arm as if directing her toward a witness box. "The floor's all yours. Explain why you *speculate* that there might be a divine reason for suffering."

Knowing it would be infinitely easier on her nerves to walk away from his skepticism and juvenile bantering, Joycelynn considered passing on his offer to continue their conversation.

"You were saying...," Brandon encouraged, twirling his hand in the air, his pouty simper again dialing his charm into the danger zone.

Somewhat irritated by his extreme confidence, and her attraction to him in spite of it, she ignored his penetrating stare as she asked, "What if we are souls having human experiences, and each of us actually *preselected* our life purpose?"

"I'd say, what was I thinking?" Brandon chortled. "Why didn't I choose to come to earth as Richard Branson or Bill Gates?"

Encouraged that he hadn't immediately dismissed her theory as dubious hogwash, she further speculated, "What if earth is a school for souls?"

"A *school for souls*. Uh-huh." Brandon took a mouthful of coffee, nearly choking on it as his eyes sprung wide.

Joycelynn followed his anxious gawk to the sweaty muscled back of a huge man wearing a wifebeater tank top. "Who's that?"

"He's the dimwitted brother of a murderer I helped convict last week. He was furious at the sentencing. Said if he ever laid eyes on me again, he'd kill me."

"The guy's big enough to break a bear in two! Do you want to leave?" she asked, already reaching for her umbrella and coat.

Shaking his head as the gigantic oaf collected his coffee and headed toward the door, Brandon muttered, "Keep going, you jerk. Just keep going."

Joycelynn was about to settle back in her chair, when she heard a syrupy female voice loudly declare, "There you are, baby."

"Diane!" Brandon's jaw dropped in unison with the blood rush to his head.

"Aren't you going to introduce me?" Donning a pout, the stylish woman tilted her head sideways.

Brandon pasted on a polite smile. "Diane Rogers, this is Joycelynn Rose."

Amused, Joycelynn nodded her hello. Apparently, the bear-like man wasn't the only one trailing Brandon's tracks. This just wasn't the poor guy's day.

"Do you two work together?" Diane asked in a timbre that demanded an explanation if they didn't.

"We just came from a friend's funeral," Brandon answered tersely.

Diane further studied Joycelynn. Then, as if suddenly too bored to care, she turned on her four inch heels and wiggled toward the exit. "Ta ta!"

"Ta ta!" Brandon mimicked her.

"One of your harem?" Joycelynn asked, delighted when he squirmed just enough to make teasing him worthwhile.

Brandon's lips curled at one corner. "Are you referring to the big sweaty oaf or the blonde on stilts?"

"You choose?"

"I'm not answering on the grounds that it might incriminate me."

"You're a man of many women and many clichés."

"Ouch!" He clapped his hand against his chest and chuckled. "Dee's obviously been telling you that I'm a ladies' man." Looking downward, he rubbed his bare ring finger. "Since my divorce, I've been out with a few women. Nothing serious. I dated Diane three times. She's as dull as she is self-centered."

"She seems to think you two are an item."

"That's my fault." Brandon picked up his stir stick and spiked it into his empty cup. "I've been deliberately slow to return her calls and emails. I thought she'd take the hint. Apparently, that might have been a mistake."

"Do you think?" Glancing at her watch, Joycelynn laughed. "As much fun as it is watching your circus of exes and criminals, I need to get going. I have a marketing meeting with Elizabeth."

"One criminal's brother and one ex-girlfriend," Brandon defended himself. "Being a crown prosecutor presents the occasional problem."

Standing and putting on her coat, Joycelynn taunted, "Your dating life seems to present problems, too."

Seemingly unscathed by her last jibe, Brandon said, "I guess that if I want to know more about your theories, I'll have to buy one of your books."

"If you're seriously interested, I'm speaking at the Inner Garden Chapel in Surrey this coming Sunday morning."

"Church!"

"Our chapel is a fellowship center, not a traditional church. Elizabeth is one of our ministers and I think you'd enjoy the service." Lowering her head, she buttoned her coat.

"It's not likely that I'll be there."

"If you change your mind, we start at eleven." Retrieving her yellow umbrella and resting it on her shoulder, she gave Brandon a moment to decide if he wanted the chapel's address.

Brandon briefly held her gaze before shaking her hand and saying, "It was nice to meet you."

"It was nice *and* entertaining to meet you."

"Have fun at your marketing meeting," he called after her as she headed for the exit.

"Thanks!" *Have fun with harem girl.* Stepping into sunshine and rain-fresh air, Joycelynn beamed. Bantering with the sexy and charming Brandon Ashton wasn't how she'd expected her morning to unfold. Thank goodness he was emotionally unavailable, or so Dee had said. Thank Source she knew better than to take his unabashed flirting seriously.

Joycelynn was still feeling light and cheery when she walked into Elizabeth's house.

"You seem incredibly happy for a woman who spent the morning at a celebration of life," her best friend commented as they exchanged hugs and then headed down the stairs to the entertainment room.

"I'm always happy," Joycelynn answered. "The service was beautiful and poignant. Afterward, I had coffee with Dee's brother's best friend, Brandon Ashton."

Elizabeth's expression contorted confusedly as she vacillated between minister consolation mode and best-friend matchmaking frenzy—per usual, the latter ruled. "Tell me more! Is this Brandon single, cute and rich?"

"There's nothing much to tell. He's a divorced prosecutor and seems nice enough. It was raining when we left the service, so I offered to share my umbrella. He invited me to coffee at Starbucks where we bantered about spirituality for an hour, and then I left to come here." She shrugged. "I invited him to Sunday's service, but as he detests churches he likely won't show."

"If he's single and available, he'll show," Elizabeth assured her as she popped the first CD from Brendon Burchard's co-marketing video series into the player. "You might be getting closer to Source, but you're still hot!"

"If he shows, he shows," Joycelynn said, determined to get her friend off the pair-'em-and-marry-'em trail she so loved to wander. "Let's just watch Brendon Burchard's marketing partnership video."

"Okay, but you're going to have to start dating again someday," she acquiesced, picking up the pot of tea she'd earlier prepared and filling their cups.

"Someday," Joycelynn agreed noncommittally as Brendon Burchard appeared on the television screen and Brandon Ashton faded from her mind.

Reviewing Brendon's *Nonprofit & Corporate Partnership Seminar*, Joycelynn was reminded of how much of *KiK's* success was due to their having followed his roadmap for teaming with nonprofit and Fortune 500 companies. Elizabeth had purchased the series after hearing Brendon speak at a Peak Potentials Training course in California. With roots in his own near-death experience, Brendon's teachings and his book about second chances, *Life's Golden Ticket,* beautifully portrayed his humanitarian message—*"Did I live? Did I love? Did I matter?"*

Between kindness rallies, writing, teaching, and editing *Heartmind Wisdom* coauthors' submissions, she was definitely living life to the fullest. Which made her confident that she was now following her purpose-path and that her contribution to global peace and kindness mattered. It was the *"Did I love?"* component of Brendon's life-purpose trilogy that caused her to wonder if Elizabeth might be right that she should again date. Family and friends wise she was rich. Romantically, she'd failed twice. *Would she one day regret the latter?*

"Let's make the Mercy Ships Charity Hospital Foundation the recipient of our five percent donation from *KiK's* online library sales of *Heartmind Wisdom*," Elizabeth suggested, pausing the video and refilling their teacups.

"That's a great idea," Joycelynn agreed, her mind turning to the floating hospital that delivered medical and dental care to some of the world's poorest people.

"It *is* a great idea, but not entirely mine," Elizabeth confessed with a laugh. "The other day after writing class, Arnold Vingsnes said he was going to donate a portion of his *Heartmind Wisdom* co-authorship royalties to Mercy Ships, so I researched their foundation on the internet."

"Arnold's a certified ship's captain, so it makes sense that he'd have a kinship with that organization," Joycelynn commented, thinking of what an amazing asset their coauthor was to *KiK's* mission of seeding global peace and kindness.

"Mercy Ships' volunteers not only provide medical and dental to poorer nations, they also empower communities by putting in irrigation systems so the locals are agriculturally self-sufficient. To reduce disease they teach hygiene, dig fresh water wells and erect latrines."

"Wow!" Joycelynn said, shaking her bowed head in admiration and gratitude for the Mercy Ships' earth angels and their selfless work. "I'm impressed."

Smiling her concurring sentiments, Elizabeth settled back on the chesterfield and pushed the remote control video 'start' button. "I'll ask Marcus to update the *KiK* Library Charity Donation Page."

"We're fortunate in so many ways," Joycelynn said with sincerity. "With the *Heartmind Wisdom* coauthors' heartfelt reach into our global community, and Marcus's web wizardry, *KiK's* mission just keeps expanding." Then holding Elizabeth's wistful gaze, she asked, "When we started Kindness Is Key, did you know we'd be so blessed?"

"I'm the queen of manifesting, so, yes," her best friend answered sassily. "But we'd better get back to watching Brendon Burchard or we won't be prepared for our sponsorship meetings next week. Without sponsors to provide water for our 'Largest Human Peace Sign' Concert and Guinness World Record attempt, we could have nearly six thousand dehydrated school kids fainting like dominos in a circle."

"Uh-huh," Joycelynn retorted as a jolt of excitement hit her mid-center. It was only four months until they attempted the record. The idea of actually securing the record was fun. But what thrilled her to the bone was how excited people were about helping to seed hope, love and kindness. Whether they hit the magic number of 5,815 participants didn't matter. What did matter was that businesses, organizations, authorities, politicians, and communities were gathering together in the name of peace.

GRATITUDE

—❧—

"Be grateful for your shadows, light and dark,
as they are your compass to the life you are meant to love."
Joyce M. Ross

Sunday was the day Joycelynn reserved for enriching her spirit and staying connected with friends and family. There wasn't much sense in trying to work, because she was generally exhausted by the end of the week, sometimes falling asleep during the meditation portion of the service. Today, she was scheduled to speak, so was on a bit of an adrenaline high and wide awake.

"Good morning, angel," Reverend Barbara Leonard said, reaching upward and wrapping Joycelynn in a heartfelt hug. "How did your week go?"

"Busy and rewarding, as usual." Peeking over the minister's shoulder at the freshly baked goodies, she asked, "Are there any nuts in those cookies?"

Releasing her embrace, Barbara assured her, "No nuts. I know you're allergic."

"You do realize that your baking is why I attend church," Joycelynn chirped as she folded an oatmeal cookie into a napkin, and then poured a coffee.

"The Lord gathers His flock in mysterious ways," Barbara returned, a glint in her blue eyes.

Taking a seat in the healing area adjacent to the entrance, Joycelynn watched their senior minister welcoming each guest with a brilliant smile, songbook and kind words. Curly silver strands bouncing around her pretty face, she seemed infinitely younger than the seventy years she wore with honor. Undoubtedly, the cornerstones that propelled the Inner Garden Chapel's ever-increasing popularity were Barbara's mothering nature and her teaching that *all spiritual pathways lead to one God.*

"There you are," Elizabeth said after greeting dozens of people. "I thought I might find you sitting here filling your face."

Swallowing the last of her cookie, Joycelynn stood to embrace her best friend. "You're limping. Is your hip sore this morning?"

"A little," Elizabeth admitted, masking her pain behind a bright red smile.

Retaking her seat, Joycelynn's brow furrowed as she sympathized, "I'm sorry that you're hurting. If it helps, you look beautiful."

"Thanks." Sitting next to Joycelynn, Elizabeth asked, "What are you speaking about this morning?"

"Re-intending your life-path."

"Good! Your talk will lead into our upcoming *Heartmind Wisdom* authorship call." Glancing about, she asked, "Did that Brandon fellow show up?"

"Not yet." Joycelynn guarded against sounding disappointed, just as she had guarded against sounding too interested when she mentioned having had coffee with Brandon. Married and madly in love with her husband, Elizabeth was continually on the lookout for potential mates for her single friends. "Are you chairing the service this morning?"

Elizabeth nodded as Celia, their pianist, began playing and Barbara indicated that it was time to get started. Following their minister to the rostrum, Joycelynn listened with delight as the congregation belted out the first song—off-key, out of sync, and loud enough to collapse the sky. At the Inner Garden Chapel, perfectionism was prioritized light-years behind love and acceptance.

"Good morning, everyone," Barbara said, beaming. "What a glorious day this truly is. The sun is shining, and you are all here." She opened her arms wide. "I want you to turn to your neighbor and tell them you're glad they're here!"

The room buzzed as people welcomed and hugged one another. When the commotion settled, Barbara continued, "Reverend Elizabeth Connor is chairing for us today. For those joining us for the first time, Elizabeth is my right-hand woman. Without her generous help and steadfast commitment to our chapel, we wouldn't be able to offer half of the programs that the bunch of you so thoroughly enjoys. Please help me give her a warm welcome."

After briefly hugging Barbara, with her palms together in front of her heart, Elizabeth led the group in a gratitude prayer. When everyone was seated again, she said, "Our guest speaker this morning is Joycelynn Rose, my best friend and mission partner. Her life today is filled with good fortune, but it wasn't always that way. Joycelynn is a recovering gambling addict. In just a few short years, she went from having a comfortable nest egg to financial ruin, and from owning a house in White Rock to living in the basement of our home."

"My good friend didn't stay down for long. Instead, she did what she is going to share with you today—she re-intended her life-direction. Determined to protect others from an addiction that almost ruined her life, she became a gaming reform activist. You may have read or heard about her legal action against the British Columbia Lottery Commission and their casino service providers. Although there is a dollar amount attached to her lawsuit, her main goal is to see some teeth put into our provincial government's Voluntary Self-Exclusion Program—a program that desperately failed her." Admiration shining in her hazel eyes, she turned so that she was facing Joycelynn. "Please help me welcome her to the rostrum."

When the applause subsided, Joycelynn began, "Elizabeth is right. A few years back, my life looked very different than it does today. From my finances to my soul, gambling had overtaken my entire being. Having misled or lied to most of my loved ones, borrowed money I couldn't repay, and made promises to quit gambling that I couldn't keep, I was filled with remorse and shame. Desperate and disgraced, I signed out of all provincial casinos via the government's much touted Voluntary Self-Exclusion Program. Unfortunately, I was still permitted to enter and gamble. It didn't take long to realize that the VSE Program wasn't being enforced."

Brandon slid into the room, leaned against the doorway, crossed his arms, kicked one ankle over the other, and grinned. Annoyed by her weak-kneed response to the bugger's cocky charm, Joycelynn nodded her hello, looking away as she continued her presentation, "About a year later, deeper in debt, still gambling and without a clue how to help myself, I turned to my spiritual guides and asked the question that would forever change my life: *What is it that I really need?*

Glancing around the intent crowd, she smiled. "The human conditioned response that I was expecting to receive was: *You need a swift kick in the butt or to win the lottery.* That wasn't the message I was given. The answer I *did* receive was—*you need kindness.*"

Inhaling deeply, palms upward, she raised her spread-eagled arms waist high as she said, "Following my kindness *aha* moment, for the next several seconds, a magnificent numinous energy fused with my being, shrouding me in radiating celestial love." Exhaling as though blowing a feather, she lowered her arms. "My self-recrimination, angst and regret gave way to inner-peace and a sense of well-being, as I realized the divine key to healing and moving forward—self-kindness." Her heart brimming with gratitude, she reiterated, "Kindness *was* and *remains* the key to my recovery."

Peering into the green eyes staring at her from the back of the room, she wondered what Brandon must be thinking. After returning his quarter smile, she continued, "Most of you know that Elizabeth and I teach that *kindness is key to living the life you are meant to love—personally, professionally and spiritually.* Now you know why. We believe that kindness is the key to healing a myriad of societal ailments, including poverty, addiction and depression. Everyone needs and benefits from kindness. And the place for you to begin a kindness healing journey is with yourself."

"When I first received my kindness aha message, I eagerly shared my vision with everyone. One day I was talking with a business associate about the premise that the first step toward being kind to others is being kind to one's self. I'll never forget what happened. This woman started to cry as she said, 'I'm not very kind to myself.' She was at her place of work, and fearing that she might lose control, instead of asking her to elaborate, I suggested that if a friend treated us with the same lack of regard, or lack of kindness, that we sometimes afford to ourselves, that person wouldn't be our friend for very long."

Joycelynn walked across the platform in silence, before saying, "Self-kindness is the key to global kindness. It's also the key to re-intending your life so that you're living in alignment with your divine purpose. If you feel your life is already divinely inspired and purpose driven, then congratulations. You're the example of what Mahatma Gandhi meant when he said, *'Be the change you wish to see in the world.'* For those of you who feel you might be off track, I invite you to start making positive changes and taking steps toward *your* purpose-path."

Pausing momentarily, she expanded, "The steps you take don't have to be huge, but they need to be constant. Life is filled with both compassion and *compassion-distraction*. Which is why it's important for those of us who see ourselves as *light-workers* to stay focused on the contributions we want to make. To help stay on what I believe is my intended path, I read spiritual books, listen to inspirational music, and associate with likeminded people such as the group of you."

Noticing the congregation's youngest member, a freckle-faced lad named Lucas, busily kicking his feet under his chair, she glanced at the clock. Her allotted time was up. "The final message I'll leave with you this morning, is that no matter where you are on your purpose-path, whatever personality traits and gifts led you here, are the same personality traits and gifts that will lead you the rest of the way. My *determination* led me to be successful in business, and was a factor in my gaming addiction. When difficulties arise in business, I determinately find solutions. When I lost at the casino, I went back determined to regain my losses. My *love for people* led me to become an organizer of singles dances, which I did for seventeen years. Love of people also explains my attraction to the never-ending party at the casino. Currently, our mutual love for humanity is why Elizabeth and I encourage others to seed global kindness by sharing their healing experiences in our *Heartmind Wisdom* anthology collection."

Everyone giggled as young Lucas stopped kicking, jumped from his chair and bolted toward the room with the refreshments. "I'm guessing that's my exit cue," Joycelynn said, smiling as she brought her hands together in prayer formation. "My gambling addiction is the shadow that led me toward the divine light of kindness. "Be grateful for your shadows, light and dark, as they are your compass to the life you are meant to love." Bowing her head, she ended with the Sanskrit inspired yoga salutation, "Namaste."

"Thank you, Joycelynn," Elizabeth said as she addressed the congregation. "If you're interested in coauthoring one of our inspirational *Heartmind Wisdom* anthologies, there are Kindness is Key pamphlets on the front entrance desk." Smiling, she announced, "It's time for our healing meditation. Those of you who would like hands-on healing, please take a seat in the adjoining room. The rest of you can just relax where you are as I start the meditation CD."

Bending over the CD player, Elizabeth whispered to Joycelynn, "Is that Brandon standing at the back of the room?"

"Yes, it is. I'm going to take him outside. I don't think he's the meditating kind."

"You're probably right," Elizabeth concurred. Eyebrows raised and donning a countrywide grin, she added, "Brandon's a hunk! I'd have offered him my umbrella, too!"

"What woman wouldn't?" Joycelynn agreed, as she noticed Brandon exchanging extended glances with every female filing past him on the way to the healing circle.

Ignoring the fluttering in her stomach, Joycelynn greeted Brandon with a friendly hug. Feeling how fit he was, surprised her. Noticing that he smelled like chocolate, amused her. Stepping back, she whispered, "I'm glad you came."

"Don't get too excited...." His lips curled at one corner as his gaze held hers. "I'm on a self-serving mission."

"And what would that be?" she asked, guiding him outside so that the rest of the group could meditate in peace.

"I'm hoping to convince you to come to my Aunt Katharine's family barbecue."

"Would that be today, or next summer?"

"This afternoon," he supplied, bowing his head as though half-expecting her to refuse his invitation.

Shivering, Joycelynn wished she'd thought to bring her coat outside. The sun was shining and the sky was clear, but it was freezing cold. "Is your family in the habit of eating outdoors in the middle of winter?"

"It's fall, not winter," he countered.

"You didn't think to call ahead?" Her eyes still on his, she crossed her arms to lock in her body warmth.

Batting his eyelashes as though trying to take flight, Brandon cajoled, "I thought I might be more persuasive in person."

"Definitely *persuasive*." She laughed. "Unfortunately, I promised Elizabeth that we'd spend the afternoon searching the Internet for a suitable location in Costa Rica to build a healing retreat."

"Can't you do that another time?"

"I'm not exactly dressed for a barbecue, and it wouldn't be very *kind* of me to cancel on Elizabeth at the last minute."

Brandon quickly glanced down and then up Joycelynn's frame. "You look fine to me!"

"I'm wearing high heels!"

"So?"

"They'll sink into the ground."

"Why would they do that?"

"Aren't we going to be walking on grass?"

"No, my aunt lives in a condo. We'll be on a concrete balcony."

Feeling colder by the moment, Joycelynn turned and peered through the chapel window. The meditation session was still in progress. Her best friend was standing with her hands on the shoulders of an elderly gentleman who had recently been diagnosed with Alzheimer's. He and his wife often attended their Sunday sessions, and he always wanted Elizabeth to do his hands-on healing.

Brandon cupped his hands around his eyes as he joined her at the window. "What are they doing in there?"

"Hands-on healing."

"Does that work?"

"If both the healer and receiver believe it will, it does."

"Have you had any miracles?"

"Small ones." She recalled her own healing experience when she'd been a Guinea pig for Elizabeth's aromatherapy massage course. After the session, the disc in her back that had been out of place for years, was miraculously realigned and had remained so since.

"My Aunt Katharine reads tea leaves, and her best friend, Georgina, predicts the future through tarot cards."

"You're just sweetening the pie so that I'll go to the barbecue," Joycelynn responded with a light laugh.

"Could be," he retorted, a devious grin brightening his eyes as he swept his bangs back.

"How do your parents handle your aunt and her friend reading tea leaves and tarot cards?"

"They refer to them as being eccentric."

"Are they eccentric?" she asked, thinking that a fall barbecue was a little left field, but not totally off the sanity grid.

"They're eccentric and wonderful, which you'll see for yourself, if you come with me."

"I'll talk to Elizabeth after the service." Playfully shaking her head as she opened the chapel door, she added, "If she never again speaks to me, it's on you."

Brandon followed her inside, this time taking a seat in the back row. Only half listening as Elizabeth read out the announcements, he surveyed the room. The crowd seemed normal and nice enough. He detested church, but could easily see what attracted people to the Inner Garden Chapel. The service was uplifting and informative. The place felt more like a home than a church, unless you counted the plum colored rostrum, purple curtains and angel theme. Although he hadn't been introduced to her, Reverend Barbara Leonard seemed very approachable and motherly. He was feeling surprisingly relaxed, when everyone suddenly started standing and he heard

Elizabeth announce, "Let's form a circle and sing our closing song, 'Let there be love.'"

Brandon was about to head out the door, when Joycelynn appeared at his side and reached for his left hand. Reluctantly, he extended his other hand to the woman on his right. Within seconds, the pianist was playing and everyone was singing as they held hands and swayed from side-to-side. Most of the congregation obviously knew the song, because except for himself and another guy who seemed equally uncomfortable, everyone else was exchanging glances and smiling as they sang their hearts out.

He rested his eyes on the freckle-faced boy, who looked to be about nine. When the group went left, the kid raised his straightened right leg and tipped left. When the group went right, the kid raised his straighten left leg and tipped right. Catching the young lad's eye at the end of the song, Brandon winked, delighted when the boy grinned before shyly tucking his head under his mother's arm.

"You survived the service unscathed," Joycelynn said, releasing his hand, her bright blue eyes amused.

"You look pretty." She was wearing a flowing brown calf-length skirt, topped with a beige cashmere sweater, and had straightened her auburn hair. Joycelynn was definitely classy, with just enough foxy to stimulate a man's libido.

Lightly blushing, she sassily asked, "While I disappoint Elizabeth, do you want to wait here or in your car?"

"I'll wait here," he answered guiltily, berating himself for asking her out at the last minute. He hadn't invited her when they were at Starbucks, because he wanted to make certain her spiritual theories were at least sound, and that she wasn't going to start babbling about aliens and flying saucers. After hearing her speak, he was fairly certain she wouldn't say anything that would shock his Aunt Katharine or her girlfriend. For those two, a discussion about aliens would likely be a welcomed addition to the usual *You'll never guess what I saw in so-and-so's cup.* Which was generally topped with *Is that so? Well, you could have bowled me over with a feather when the cards predicted whatever.*

He'd never taken any of it seriously, simply viewed their predictions as harmless amusement for a couple of old fuddy-duddies he loved. His parents, however, were another story. Fearing either being painted with the same brush as his mystical aunt or his religiously fanatical parents, he normally didn't invite anyone to their family gatherings. Joycelynn was different. She would accept and fit into both realms.

As she'd anticipated, Elizabeth was glad to forfeit their time together. Obviously hoping for a match made at Source, she snatched onto Joycelynn's hand and excitedly led her back to Brandon's side. After saying how much she enjoyed meeting him, she nearly pushed them out the door.

Brandon held the door for Joycelynn as she tucked inside his car. Climbing in the driver's side, he commented, "Your partner seems very nice."

"She is," Joycelynn agreed. "We've been friends for over a quarter of a century."

"You must have met when you were babies," he flattered her.

"We must have," she returned, not admitting that they'd met during their mid-twenties. Judging by Brandon's unruly thick brown mane, he was a few years her junior. But with hair dye and implants, one could no longer be certain of anyone's age.

"I'm a lot older than the blonde bombshell who dropped by our table yesterday," she baited, trying to see if her own age would be a dating deal-breaker.

"Diane?" he asked, sounding as though it were possible Joycelynn was referring to someone else. "Who cares how old she is? She's the most boring superficial person on the planet." Starting his car, he thrust it into gear and headed out of the parking lot.

Realizing that Brandon assumed she was checking out the competition, not whether he thought she might be too old for him, Joycelynn pointedly asked, "I'm fifty-six, is that a problem for you?"

"I know how old you are." He pulled into the traffic, shifted gears and accelerated his BMW. "I Googled you."

"You Googled me!" Joycelynn blurted, inwardly chastising herself for not having thought to research Brandon on the Internet. She hadn't expected to hear from him, so it hadn't mattered. But it did now!

Chuckling, he gleefully expanded, "I found a number of archived articles regarding a fifty-four-year-old gambling addict, followed with about a zillion more with the headline: *Gambling Addict turns Kindness Ambassador.*"

Feeling disadvantaged, she asked, "When I Google you, will I find out how old you are?"

"I doubt it," he retorted with apparent self-satisfaction.

"Then, I'm asking."

"Asking what?" he teased, pulling onto the highway toward White Rock.

"Asking you to marry me," she shot back.

Brandon chuckled. "I'm fifty-two. I was married once. It lasted ten years. I'm not in a hurry to do it again."

"Do you have children?"

"No kids, just a dog and a cat." He glanced her way, then back at the road. "How about you?"

"Google didn't tell you that?"

"Nope!" he supplied with a snicker.

"I was married twice: once, when I was quite young, and a second time when I should've known better." She sighed. "Both marriages dissolved before we had kids."

"Would you do it again?"

"If I met the right person, I might." As a result of her own painful experiences, and the equally traumatic breakups of some of the singles who'd attended her dances, she'd become relationship wary, but she wasn't against marriage.

"Are you sorry you don't have children?"

"Sometimes, I guess. But you can't miss what you never had." Memories of her miscarriage tugging at her heart, she asked, "Would you like to have children?" Kids were no longer an option for her, but they were for Brandon should he marry a younger woman.

"I have a few nieces I thoroughly enjoy," he said, rolling his shoulders dismissively.

Recalling his comment that procreation was the primary human purpose, she imagined fathering children would top Brandon's priority list. "You still haven't answered whether you wish you had children."

"It's like you say, you can't miss what you never had." Brandon pulled off the highway and onto the road that led toward the beach. "When my marriage fell apart, I headed to the local pound, picked out the ugliest mutt I could find, added a stray kitten to the mix, and decided that would be my family."

He half sniggered, half scoffed. "Pets are less complicated and infinitely less painful."

Joycelynn understood his *less complicated* comment, but not his *infinitely less painful* conclusion. Having lost her golden retriever, Robin, to cancer when he was only eight, she was reluctant to get another pet. Animals were undoubtedly the universe's gift of unconditional love. But unless a stray dog or cat came her way, she was avoiding the inevitable heartbreak. "I love animals, too," was all she offered as she looked out the window and sighed.

LOVE

~❦~

"Even after all this time, the sun never
says to the earth, 'You owe me.'
Look what happens with a love like that...
it lights the whole sky."
Hafiz, 14th Century Poet

Purple chiffon flowing from her arms like angel wings, Brandon's aunt threw open the door and scooped her nephew, then Joycelynn, into a rose scented pillowy embrace.

"Who's *this*?" she asked, stepping back, her shimmering red smile as welcoming as her happy expression. "Pretty little thing, aren't you?"

"Joycelynn Rose, meet my father's sister and my favorite aunt, Katharine Mortin."

"Come in. Come in." Aunt Katharine looped one plump arm through Brandon's and the other through Joycelynn's. "Everyone's here." Taking quick, short steps she led the way to the sunny balcony, where she hurriedly introduced Joycelynn. Then she flew out of the room, muttering something about someone needing to behave better, and that she needed to reheat the apple cider.

"What a beautiful view," Joycelynn commented as she sat down next to the second most colorful woman at the party, who had been introduced as Aunt Katharine's lifelong friend, Georgina. Like octopus arms, backcombed magenta-hued hair played about her sun-creased face, frequently getting trapped in her heavy coral lipstick. She was also draped in chiffon, but had chosen teal over purple.

Brandon's parents were far less colorful. Mrs. Ashton was wearing a grey winter coat that was buttoned closed, and sitting with her back as straight as a streetlamp. Her hands were tightly clasped on top of the wool blanket wrapped around her legs. Expressionless and appearing very stern, her husband sat next to her as though guarding royalty.

Grateful for the three propane heaters that made it feel somewhat like summer, even though there was a cold breeze sweeping in from the ocean, Joycelynn unbuttoned her own coat.

"Joycelynn's a writer and seminar leader," Brandon said. "She teaches people to be kind to themselves as a way of encouraging them to be kind to others."

"Oh, that's very nice, dear," Georgina offered, before taking a sip of her cider. When no one else offered a comment, she proudly added, "I read tarot cards."

Brandon had said his parents were extremely religious, and that his aunt and her friend were tolerated as being eccentric. Rather than risk igniting a debate about the evils of black magic, Joycelynn nodded without commenting.

"Would you like me to read your cards?" Georgina asked, retrieving a deck from her large peacock covered bag. I carry these with me everywhere. You never know when someone might need a little guidance from the angels."

There was some mumbling from Mr. Ashton, which was silenced when his wife placed her hand on his knee. Joycelynn glanced at Brandon for a clue as to how she should respond. His slight shoulder roll accompanied by a silly smirk, let her know that she was on her own.

Georgina carefully removed the cards from their packet and set them on the small plastic table in front of Joycelynn. "You cut the cards, dear."

Joycelynn reached out and did as instructed, choosing to cut the cards midway. Everyone watched as Georgina carefully laid down the first card, revealing a picture of a regal woman sitting on a throne, and two rather odd looking wildcats parked by her feet.

"That's a very good first card. It's the Chariot. You'll continue to overcome diversity and to have financial success." Georgina was reaching for a second card, when Aunt Katharine came back. Carrying a silver platter with two fine China cups decorated with violets, she frowned when she spotted the tarot cards.

Aunt Katharine held the tray while Joycelynn reached for the cup that wasn't filled to the rim. "Now Georgina, you know Irene and David don't approve of the cards. Please put them back in your purse." She moved the tray toward Brandon, waited while he gingerly picked up the brimming cup of apple cider, and then went to stand in front of her good friend.

With Aunt Katharine watching over her, Georgina reluctantly gathered the cards and put them away. "I don't know what the big deal is all about. People have been reading cards since the thirteen hundreds."

"That may be true, but some people believe that reading cards is the devil's work. We must respect that, don't you think?" She sounded stern, but her kindly smile relayed her apology for having to force her good friend to do something she clearly didn't want to do.

"Then somebody better think of something to talk about, because it's too darn cold to sit out here in this bone chilling hurricane and pretend like nothing is wrong, when it is!" Georgina grumbled huffily as she clamped her arms over her bosom, and then pushed her bottom lip out so far she looked comical.

"What's wrong?" Brandon's torso jerked straight. "What are you all trying not to talk about?"

"Your Aunt Katharine and Georgina bought themselves a gypsy van," Mr. Ashton griped as he suddenly came to life. "They're planning on spending the winter traipsing across the southern United States reading tea leaves and tarot cards." He slammed his fist on the plastic arm chair, seemingly more miffed when it didn't produce a thundering sound. "They're a couple of damn fools!"

Brandon flopped back, obviously relieved that no one was sick or dying. "So it's just the same old fight. Aunt Katharine wants to do something adventurous, and you're trying to talk her out of it." He glanced back and forth at his parents. "Life is short. Maybe she and Georgina should go. It makes me sad that Terry died before he realized his dream of spending the summer hiking the Grand Canyon with his wife and kids." Leaning forward and resting his forearms on his knees, he bowed his head and lowered his voice as he continued, "I never interfered when you two quashed Aunt Katharine's dream of moving to Hawaii. I said nothing when you scared the daylights out of her about backpacking around Europe. I now wished that I had."

"You see, Brandon thinks it's a good idea," Aunt Katharine bubbled enthusiastically. "And it's not dangerous. We purchased a brand new class-A motorhome from a reputable dealer in California. Georgina used to drive a semi-truck, so she can handle a little thirty-foot home on wheels. We meet up with the RV Club in Anaheim, so there'll be lots of other people with us. In the spring, when the mountain passes are safe, we'll drive back home."

"Yes, and they won't make me put away my tarot Cards," Georgina mumbled as she refolded her arms across her chest and harrumphed. "And there won't be any dumb talk about the devil every ten seconds."

"Hush!" Aunt Katharine quieted her friend, then facing her brother, rationalized, "We've already joined the club and paid our fees. We leave next weekend, so there's not much point in discussing it further."

"Then, we're going home!" Mr. Ashton stood, and like a duty-bound underling, his wife popped up next to him, and began folding the blanket that had been draped across her legs.

"Dad, don't be like that." Brandon bolted upright and stepped toward his parents. "Can't we just have a nice family barbecue? They're grown women. They have a right to make their own decisions."

"She's nearly seventy years old, for God's sake!" His father snatched the blanket out of his wife's hand and threw it on the chair. "People your aunt's age shouldn't be running all over the planet with a bunch of gypsies and hippies."

"The people we're traveling with are hardly gypsies or hippies. They're retirees with motorhomes," Aunt Katharine defended her decision.

"Dad, this is ridiculous." Brandon followed his father into the living-room.

"What if she gets sick in some little town where there's no hospital?" Mr. Ashton bellowed, vehemently shaking his head. "Damn fools!"

"What if she doesn't? What if she goes to California and has the time of her life?" Brandon countered, sounding frustrated.

"Don't bother sending us any postcards," was Mr. Ashton's final barb as he stomped toward the exit, his wife traipsing after him.

"Mom, try to talk some sense into him," Brandon pleaded as the condominium door shut.

"Don't worry, dear. He's just concerned," Aunt Katharine rationalized as she flittered about the balcony collecting empty cups and saucers. "It'll take a bit of time for him to adjust."

Proud of her for standing up to his father's bullying ways, Brandon walked over and kissed the top of her silver-haired head. It was the first time he'd witnessed his aunt fighting back, which now struck Brandon as being odd. Why had she caved in to his father's oppressive fear-driven demands all these years? When they were younger, his father had helped finance his aunt's book store, but she had paid him back with interest. A few years ago, when she sold her store, she tried to give his father a portion of the proceeds, saying that she owed her success to him. He'd refused to take it, explaining that he was just happy that she'd done well. When she continued on about the reasons why she wanted him to have the money, peering adoringly into her grey eyes and with his big hands cupping her slight shoulders, his father had quoted something that he often did—a proverb coined by the fourteenth century poet, Hafiz:

"Even after all of this time, the sun never says to the sky, 'you owe me.' Look what happens with a love like that...it lights the whole sky."

"Now you go and visit with your nice friend, or the poor girl will think that we're all boorish," Aunt Katharine said, motioning for Georgina to follow her. "We'll be in the kitchen."

"How do you like us, so far?" Brandon quipped as he went to stand beside Joycelynn, who was poised against the railing as she stared out at the Pacific.

"You have a very colorful family." She smiled. "I like your aunt and her friend."

"But not my parents?" At the moment, he didn't much like them either.

"Your parents were upset. There was nothing to like or dislike." She shrugged. "Your father obviously wears the pants in the family, but when I was young, it was the same with my parents. Their generation's values are quite different than ours."

"Dad can be a very stubborn man. Mom never stands up to him in a big way, but she can be very persuasive when she wants to be. I hope she doesn't back him up this time, but she likely will. Neither of my parents is very adventuresome."

"My mom's traveled all over the world. Dad prefers to stay home in the house he built on a lakefront just outside of Victoria," Joycelynn offered cheerlessly. "They're divorced."

"Did they get divorced because your mom wanted to travel and your dad didn't?"

"No, it was more complicated than that."

A faraway focus dulling his usually bright eyes, Brandon shared, "Sometimes I worry about the fact that my family is aging and one-by-one will leave this world, which makes me feel like a heel for arguing with Dad."

Joycelynn moved closer and placed her hand on his arm. "People who love each other sometimes argue; especially, when they differ on important issues."

Brandon glanced at Joycelynn's hand on his arm and then into her eyes. In the sunlight, he could see that her unnaturally brilliant blue irises were nature's work, not because she wore contact lenses. A strand of her copper hair lifted in the breeze and settled across her partially parted lips. Reaching over, he tucked the errant hair behind her ear. Noting desire flicker across her face and then quickly vanish, he wondered whether she was afraid of him or all men. Regardless, intimacy obviously frightened her.

Turning so that they were standing side-by-side, they stared out at the ocean. The wind had kicked up, and a couple of small boats were fighting their way through the rough water. As they watched, one boat lost power, disappearing every few seconds as it dipped behind a swollen wave.

"That boat seems to be in trouble." Joycelynn pointed toward the bobbing craft. "We should call the coastguard."

"I will, if they don't get the engine restarted in the next few minutes."

Locking her arms waist high, Joycelynn's raised-brow glance focused heavenward and then back at the ocean.

As much as he hated to admit it, his dad was right. Things sometimes went awry, as they had for the boaters bobbing about in the perilous water—as they had for Terry and his family. Brandon suddenly regretted that anxious fear had prevented him from being fully present during his best friend's final days. That his own fear of intimacy was clouding his joy, as it had Joycelynn's vivid blue eyes. Left at the helm, fear could swallow your heart, dreams and precious moments—it could sink your life.

"Look!" Joycelynn screeched excitedly, again pointing toward the ocean. "That bigger boat's rescuing the smaller one."

They silently watched as the skipper of the larger boat tossed out a rope. When the smaller boat was under tow, Joycelynn shouted, "They're safe! Thank you, Source."

"You're amazing," Brandon remarked. "I'll bet if need be, you'd have swam out there and pulled that boat in with a rope between your teeth."

"I don't think so," she said, still grinning. "I need these teeth for eating one of those juicy steaks your aunt just plopped down beside the barbecue. I'm starving."

"Since Dad's gone, I'll be your grill master." Ignoring a powerful urge to kiss her, he tweaked Joycelynn's nose. "Mom usually does the dishes. I guess that's your job today."

"Lucky me," Joycelynn chirped.

"No, *lucky me*," Brandon quipped. "There are two extra steaks, and at least one of them has my name on it."

Glancing out the window on the drive to collect her car from the chapel parking lot, Joycelynn felt a familiar melancholy. She enjoyed living in Vancouver, but still sometimes missed the quaintness of the small seaside community. White Rock had been her home for a decade, until her gambling debts forced her to sell the house she'd spent a year renovating with the help of her father. She'd long ago released the shame associated with her addiction, but occasionally still became mired in regret.

Brandon was the first man she'd spend time with since she'd declared herself an addict and become a gaming reformist. *Water finds its own level,* and when her level of self-worth became marred by her recent divorce, the threat of bankruptcy, and the emotional seesaw of addiction, she felt she had little to offer someone else. Plus, pursuing Kindness is Key with Elizabeth, writing, teaching, and editing kept her so busy she didn't have time to socialize.

Although she enjoyed working with her lawyer, Jim Hanson, her case consumed a fair share of her time, too. From their initial meeting forward, Jim treated her with respect and offered her encouragement. Most importantly, he shared her desire to see the lottery corporation make the changes necessary to protect addicts.

"You're a million miles away," Brandon said as he pulled onto the highway.

"I was thinking about how much I admire my lawyer."

"Jim Hanson? He's a brilliant man with loads of class action experience. His firm, *Hanson, Matheos and Warsig,* is well respected in the law community. They have a great track record with personal injury and disability claims; especially, regarding the Insurance Corporation of B.C." He smiled. "From what I can tell, BCLC's Voluntary Self-Exclusion Program, although purported as a responsible approach to gambling addiction, is merely a strategic solution to potential duty of care litigation—a legal defense which is greatly weakened by the lackadaisical enforcement of the program."

"Do you know all of this because you're a lawyer, or because you Googled the court filings for my law case?" she asked, still somewhat miffed that he'd researched her on the Internet, and she hadn't thought to do the same.

"From work *and* from Googling your case filings." He laughed. "For a woman who deliberately went public with the intention of drawing attention to much needed gaming reform, you're pretty sensitive." He glanced her way and she sneered at him, which made him laugh harder. "At the risk of sending you into a complete tizzy, how did you manage to lose over three-hundred-thousand dollars gambling?"

It was a question she'd been asked a hundred times, so she wasn't offended. "I lost that money over three years, not all at once. My losses per visit were usually between five and fifteen hundred dollars. Multiply that by three or four casino visits a week. It adds up fast."

"When you do the math, things always make more sense. I've known guys who've blown that kind of money in a friendly poker game." He paused while changing traffic lanes. "It was brave of you to go public with your lawsuit. I read some of the online news articles. The editorials supporting your case far outnumbered those that didn't, but some of their readership's comments were brutal."

"Controversy keeps my case in the news." She wasn't surprised that some people accused her of being self-serving. Apparently, they didn't realize that without a dollar amount attached to a lawsuit, there would be no media attention, and no public pressure on the government to enforce their Voluntary Self-Exclusion Program. Recalling a quote by American author Lois McMaster Bujold, which had helped her with the sometimes negative comments her case invited, she shared it with Brandon, "*Reputation is what other people know about you. Honor is what you know about yourself.*"

"That's a great quote," Brandon said, then asked, "Do you ever get the urge to go back to gambling?"

"Every now and then when I'm stressed, part of me wishes I could go back to numbing at the casino. I may no longer be robotically compulsive, but I'm still an addict."

"*Robotically compulsive?*"

"Addicts aren't rational. Even though I wanted to quit, several times a week, I'd climb into my van and head for the casino. All the way there, I'd reproach myself for being so stupid. I knew the odds were I'd lose and that I could no longer afford to gamble. But like one of those robotic women in the *Stepford Wives* movie, I'd just keep driving."

"I suppose it doesn't help that print, radio and television ads continually depict casinos as exciting carefree fun. Seeing those advertisements must repeatedly provoke your addiction."

"What the ads *don't* show is the suffering casinos breed— the guilt, self-loathing, anxious desperation, and gut-wrenching fear following a big financial loss. Losses I could ill afford, and which on many mornings had me bolting awake and clutching my stomach like I'd been slugged in the solar plexus. I swallowed so much dignity borrowing money from friends and family, I nearly drowned in shame."

"This might be a naive question, but before you got to the stage where you were robotically compulsive, if losing made you feel bad, why did you keep gambling?"

"Gambling is a two-edged sword. When I won, convinced I was on a winning streak, I'd try to capitalize on my good fortune. When I lost, I'd desperately try to regain my losses."

"Why didn't you cut your losses a lot sooner? You must have known you were becoming addicted. Your bank account must have been a huge red flag."

"Whose side are you on?" she quipped, crossing her arms protectively. "I hope that BCLC and the casinos don't hire a lawyer with your machine-gun questioning skills, or I'll be sunk during discovery and never see the inside of a courtroom."

"Oh, I'm certain that they've already hired a *team* of machine-gun questioning lawyers." Brandon became quiet for a moment, before saying, "I hope you don't mind me asking so many questions, but I find your case intriguing."

"Talking about my addiction is a necessary evil if I want to evoke gaming reform," Joycelynn said matter-of-factly.

Brandon pulled into the chapel parking lot and cut the engine. "I can't imagine being that addicted."

"You're addicted to sugar!" Joycelynn quipped, rummaging through her purse for her car keys. "This afternoon, after eating both yours and your father's steak, you gobbled down two heaping servings of your Aunt Katharine's pumpkin pie, which was smothered in whipped cream. When we were at Starbucks, you wolfed down your pastry and chased it with a cup of coffee loaded with three packets of sugar. She grinned. "I'm not a doctor or psychiatrist, but I'd say that you, my friend, are a *sugarholic*."

"You're accusing me of being addicted to sugar! How can you be addicted to sugar?"

"Considerable participation in an activity, or over consumption of a substance that can harm you, is addiction."

"Now you're just starting to tick me off."

Joycelynn laughed as Brandon tucked in his chin and scowled. "It wasn't my intention to insult you." Smiling, she added, "If I were still a gambler, I'd bet that you had something chocolate for breakfast today."

Brandon's jaw dropped as he jerked his head sideways. "I had a chocolate donut on the way to the chapel. How did you know that?"

Joycelynn roared. "Don't worry, I'm not psychic. I smelled chocolate on your breath when we hugged."

Chortling, Brandon narrowed his gaze. "I hope you realize that you've taken on a Goliath-sized challenge. You're a gutsy lady."

Noting the same amorous gleam she'd seen in his eyes when she'd touched his arm on the balcony, Joycelynn blushed. There was no denying their shared sexual attraction, but he was too much like husband number one and two—a dash of debonair mixed with good looks, and an undeniable preoccupation with long-legged babes on stilts. She'd promised herself that the next man she dated would be more introspective and spiritually minded. And definitely a little less eye candy.

Glancing toward the floorboard, she confessed, "Nothing associated with my gambling addiction has been easy. Accepting that I was addicted was tough. When I first signed out, I experienced a myriad of emotions from relief that I wouldn't be allowed to gamble anymore, to a sense of a loss and sadness because I'd given up my social network of fellow gamblers. Casino dealers and floor staff are very friendly, so I missed them, too."

"I can't even imagine what you went through."

"Any type of addiction is difficult to understand, unless you've lived it," she said, while playing with her car keys. "From what I've read, when you win a large jackpot, or the first time you get high on a street drug, the extreme thrill, or pleasure of it stimulates the production of adrenaline, endorphin and dopamine—a *feel-good* chemical cocktail. In the case of gamblers, we soothe our losses and justify our gaming by recalling our wins; which is clinically known as *euphoric recall*." Sighing heavily, she confessed, "Going forward with the lawsuit is difficult for me, because what I really want to do is seed global kindness."

"Encouraging elected officials to take care of the citizens who put them in office is an act of *kindness*," Brandon argued.

"I guess," Joycelynn agreed with a shrug.

"There's so much wrong with government participation in gambling, at the *very least*, they should protect addicts," Brandon said, his brow puckering. "I wouldn't want to fathom a guess as to what gambling addiction is costing taxpayers in terms of increased mental health care and hospital costs."

"And employers in terms of work days lost." Joycelynn checked her watch. She was exhausted and had promised to call Elizabeth before she went to bed. Knowing that her girlfriend would request a minute-by-minute account of her time with Brandon, the call would undoubtedly last for at least half an hour.

"Do you need to get going?" Brandon asked, gazing at her as though a goodnight kiss was on his agenda.

"I can talk for a few more minutes." Flattered but unnerved by his romantic interest, Joycelynn glanced past him and out the driver's window. It seemed a million years ago that she'd last kissed someone, and the idea of it was a trifle terrifying. Kisses led to promises she could no longer make, and to commitments she no longer trusted.

"What about online gambling, are you against that, too?"

"Online gaming is incredibly addictive and too easily concealed. Addicts are free to gamble anywhere they can find a computer, and never have to explain their absences to loved ones." Joycelynn's attempted smile stretched into a yawn.

"You're tired," Brandon said before leaning forward and throatily murmuring, "I like you, Joycelynn Rose."

There was a sparkle in Brandon's striking green eyes that indicated trouble. Trouble she wasn't ready for, and definitely didn't need. Turning away, she placed her hand on the door handle and cheerful chirped, "I like you, too." Opening the door and swinging her feet onto the pavement, she peeked over her shoulder and added, "Thank you for taking me to your aunt's barbecue. I had a nice time."

Brandon leapt out of the driver's side and followed her toward her car. "I'm glad you decided to come. Although, when I invited you, I didn't expect that it was going to be a dinner show."

As they reached her car, she briefly hugged him before unlocking her car. "I enjoyed your family."

"I enjoy them, too. Mostly, anyways," he said, unconvincingly. "Dad can be a bear sometimes."

Smiling her understanding, she got into her car.

"I'll call you!" Brandon hollered as she shut the door, started the engine and waved goodbye through the closed window.

INTEGRITY

"My word is my contract; my handshake, my seal;
and, my conscience, my witness."
E. Patricia Connor

Strolling along English Bay with Brandon and his appropriately named dog Scruffy, Joycelynn smiled reminiscently. "When Elizabeth and I lived here in our late twenties, we walked this beach nearly every morning."

"After the fiasco at my Aunt Katharine's, I wasn't sure you'd want to come." He stooped to pat his dog's head. "Though he means well, my father can be somewhat controlling."

"Is that why you asked me to join you and Scruffy, because you're trying to make up for what happened at your aunt's place?" she kibitzed. "When you invited me, you claimed you were interested in hearing more about my book."

Brandon threw a stick into the water and Scruffy took off after it. "I wouldn't want to come up against you in court." A countrywide grin lit his green eyes with mischief.

"Oh, I'm sure." Joycelynn laughed. "Regardless, I'm holding you to your offer to be my sounding board. 'A promise made is a debt unpaid,'" she quoted a line from Robert Service's poem *The Cremation of Sam McGee.*

The dog returned with the stick, his tail madly wagging as he dropped it at his master's feet.

Scruffy's well trained, was her initial summation. Then as Brandon rewarded him with a biscuit, she realized his dog was more *treat* trained, than *well* trained. She'd trained her golden retriever, Robin, the same way, and had often been criticized for not having had more command over him. Eventually, she grew tired of explaining that she loved her pet's high-spirited energy, and that if she'd wanted a puppet she'd have bought a puppet, not a dog. Sometimes she could sense Robin's presence, and once she heard him barking by her bed, so she'd dubbed him her *spirit dog*. Feeling his essence nearby helped a little, but a year later, she still grieved for him.

Oblivious to her melancholy, Brandon suggested, "Let me tire this guy out a bit and then we can talk." He tossed the stick again and Scruffy took off after it.

Fetch was a game for two, not three, so Joycelynn went to sit on a nearby log. Backdropped by a gigantic crimson sun, the silhouetted ocean liners appeared much smaller than they were in actuality. Eminent nightfall had tinged the water blueberry, adding brilliance to the white-capped waves splashing against the shore. Down the beach, the gulls were carrying on their customary fuss as someone tossed morsels of food into the air. A kid wearing a red hoody buzzed by on a skateboard, followed by a cyclist and two joggers. Even in late fall, Vancouver's West End beach was as lively as it was beautiful.

"You warm enough?" Brandon asked as he sat next to Joycelynn, and a panting Scruffy flopped down at his feet.

"Getting a little chilled," she confessed. "It gets cold quickly when the sun fades."

"I've got hot chocolate."

"Where?" She glanced about for a thermos.

"At my place."

"Sounds perfect." When she'd arrived at Brandon's earlier, he'd buzzed her into the lobby, telling her that he'd be right down. At the time, she'd wondered why. Relieved that his not inviting her up wasn't a part of some commitment phobia, she savored the fresh air and took another long look at the ever-changing ocean. "It's so beautiful here. I get so busy with writing and teaching, I sometimes forget to enjoy the simplicities of life." She laughed lightly. "One of our thirteen kindness keys centers on maintaining balance in your life. I should learn to do what I preach."

"We're all sometimes guilty of needing to take our own advice," Brandon offered, then changed the topic to the one he'd promised they'd discuss. "Before we were so rudely interrupted at Starbucks, you said something about earth being a school for souls."

"You remember me saying that?"

Brandon stood and held her hand long enough to help her up, then released it. "I remember, and I thought about it."

"I'm listening," she encouraged him, as they started walking toward his condo.

"If, as you say, humans are spiritual beings temporarily housed in physical bodies, and earth is a school for souls who preselect their life purposes, then I have some questions." He stopped to clip on Scruffy's leash. "Why do souls need a school? Why would a Source emanating soul agree to become one of the dirt-bags I've prosecuted, or to suffer the way that Terry did? The guy was so skinny when he died his cheekbones looked like mountains against his hollowed face." With a dismal shake of his head, he finished with, "I can't see any *logical* or *divine* reasoning for anyone's cruel fate."

Realizing that when people lose someone close, especially after a painful illness, they often ended up with more spiritual questions than answers, Joycelynn chose her words carefully as she said, "It took me a long time to get my mind and heart around why some souls would opt for a life that included suffering, being shunned or punished."

Frustrated by the way the wind was whipping her hair about her face, she quit talking while she put on the toque that had been tucked in her coat pocket. "But think about it. If earth is a school for souls, some souls would have to agree to become *sacrificial teachers.*"

"*Sacrificial teachers?*"

"Just as experiencing love requires an object of affection, experiencing hate requires something or someone to hate. Perhaps some enlightened souls agree to an earthly experience that includes being shunned or punished, so that younger earthly souls can learn compassion and love."

"Your theory seems a bit farfetched," Brandon countered, skepticism etched in his forehead.

"Is it farfetched to believe that we each have a purpose?" she prodded, her tone feathery soft.

Brandon untangled the leash from where it had slipped under Scruffy's left hind leg, before answering, "I knew I had to become a lawyer, if that's what you mean? Originally, I planned to practice criminal law."

"That's precisely what I mean," she returned, encouraged by his response. "How did you end up on the other end of the spectrum, prosecuting instead of defending?"

"Prosecuting isn't opposite to defending; not if true justice is your goal. I see my role as a *protector* of society, not as a *prosecutor* of criminals."

"What if before you were born, your soul chose to come to earth as a defender of justice?"

When Brandon didn't immediately respond, she reasoned, "You said you knew you had to become a lawyer. That's what happened for me, too. I've always known I was born to help others, and I've tried to do that. What I didn't see coming was my gaming addiction, which thanks to my aha moment, led me to become an inspirational author and champion of kindness. I think that's how it is for many of us. Either from when we're young or through life choices and circumstances, by listening to our inner-knowing, each of us becomes aware of our earthly calling—our Source emanating purpose."

"If you apply that logic, then criminals must be answering their callings, too. What about mass murderers, are they following their soul chosen purpose-paths?"

"My belief that *love* is the only emotion expressed and registered at Source, keeps me from being harshly judgmental of myself and others."

"You're purporting that God loves everyone, no matter what?" Brandon interjected, with a slight rise to his brow.

"Exactly! God loves us because of who He is, not because of who we are or aren't."

"Keep talking," he said, obviously unconvinced.

"I also believe each of us has a purpose that we chose before coming to earth. For some, that's a calling into a special field or to accomplish something specific. For others, that purpose might be to provide the opportunity for the rest of us to *learn* and *be* and *do* what we are intended to learn, be and do. Assuming my theory is true, criminals are our sacrificial teachers, and are deserving of even greater blessings than those of us who suffer less."

"Blessings!" Brandon bellowed, staring at her as though convinced she'd completely lost her mind. "Monday, I'm prosecuting a scumbag who raped and killed a thirteen-year-old girl. The DNA results prove he's guilty. I can hardly wait to send that sick bastard away for life! *Blessing him* is the furthest thing from my mind."

Unnerved but not derailed, Joycelynn lowered her tone and slowed her delivery as she explained, "I'm not saying that murderers should get off scot-free. I accept that there is a need to keep criminals out of the general population. Past incarceration, though, I can't see any benefit in punishing anyone."

"There's no *eye for an eye* in your philosophy. You just bless criminals and go on about your life as if nothing happened." He raised his free arm and whirled it in the air. "Victims don't matter. It's the criminals you're concerned about."

Guessing helicopter-style arm circling was one of Brandon's courtroom theatrics, she almost snickered. "Mahatma Gandhi said that *'An eye for an eye only ends up making the whole world blind.'*" She twisted her mouth sideways and narrowed her gaze, before saying, "I think that's also what Jesus was referring to when he said we should love our enemies, and pray for those who persecute us. And what Lao Tzu meant when he said, *'If a person seems wicked, do not cast him away. Awaken him with your words, elevate him with your deeds, and repay his injury with your kindness. Do not cast him away; cast away his wickedness.'*"

"You quote anyone that makes you happy. But when you work with the lowest of the low, hear the stories and see the faces of their victims, your philosophy becomes the Criminal Code of Canada. If you do the crime, you better damn well be prepared to do the time!"

Bending forward, he snatched up a piece of driftwood and tossed it as far as he could. Leashed and unable to chase after it, Scruffy glanced at where the stick had flown, plunked his butt in the sand, and looked up at his master. Brandon reached in his jacket pocket and gave his dog a treat, causing Joycelynn to smile.

"I may have a prejudiced view because I work in the judicial system," he admitted as they started walking again. "And I'm not in favor of vigilantism or the death penalty, but neither am I keen on your Mother Teresa philosophy of forgive, forget and bless."

"I can accept that." The sorrowful faces of some of the teens she'd worked with at the Youth Detention Center popped through her mind. Working with them, she soon realized that at soul level all people are good. Her hope was that Brandon and those who read her books, would at least consider the possibility that criminals were sacrificial teachers—caring, evolved souls who came to earth to provide others with opportunities to choose *forgiveness* and *compassion* over the self-protecting emotions of *fear* and *anger*. But it wasn't her place to shove her beliefs down anyone's throat, so she let the matter drop and enjoyed the rest of their walk in silence.

"I have another question for you," Brandon announced with a smirk as they entered his condominium, and they both removed their footwear and coats. "If we're all souls having an earthly experience, why wouldn't we just off ourselves, and go back to Heaven, the Universe, Source, Nirvana, or whatever you want to call it? Why should we stay here, where there's so much pain and suffering?"

"Because we're in school, and meant to fulfill our life purposes before we return to our originating Source," Joycelynn answered as she followed him to the living-room.

"Are you saying that if you became terminally ill, and were suffering the way that Terry did, you wouldn't just kill yourself?"

"I don't know. I haven't been in that situation. Some people believe in euthanasia for all beings. Followers of the Tao believe we shouldn't take anyone's life, including suffering animals."

Brandon's expression drained sober as he said, "When Terry was sick, I sometimes wished euthanasia were legal in Canada. Of course, I understand all the reasons why it isn't, but still…." Folding his lips against emotion too raw to process, he murmured, "I'll be back in a minute." Making an about face, he headed for the kitchen.

Knowing he needed a moment to himself, Joycelynn didn't follow him. Glancing about his living-room, she noted the brown leather furnishing, an enormous flat-screen television, and a surround-sound stereo system. Except for the two walls brimming with books, Brandon's place was definitely a bachelor's pad. Seeing that his fireplace mantle was lined with cards, she walked over to look at them. They were birthday cards. The first one she picked up was from his Aunt Katharine, who had added a note promising that she'd send him dozens of postcards from California. Predictably, the one with a small boy sandwiched between and holding hands with a man and a woman as they walked along the beach was from his parents. There was also a silly joke card from Diane, who Joycelynn assumed was the woman she'd met at Starbucks. The last one she picked up was from Terry's sister, Dee. There was a handwritten letter tucked inside. Guessing that it was from Terry, and the last communication between two lifelong friends, without reading it, she carefully placed the card and letter back on the mantle.

A few seconds later, Brandon returned with two huge cups of cocoa, heaped with melting marshmallows. As he carefully positioned the cups on coasters, Joycelynn commented, "You didn't tell me it was your birthday."

"You didn't ask," he retorted with a flippant grin. "I'm almost as old as you now."

Reminded of their age difference, and still feeling a bit chilled, Joycelynn folded her arms across her chest and quipped, "As your elder, I guess I'm entitled to more respect." Why so many men in midlife went for younger women, she'd never know. The idea of dating younger men made her uneasy. Perhaps men had virility issues.

"You have my respect, don't worry about that." Brandon walked over and turned up the thermostat, then headed down the hallway.

Joycelynn reached for a cream-colored blanket on the far end of the sofa, and draped it over her knees.

Brandon returned with a sweater in hand, grinning when he looked at her. "That's Scruffy's blanket. You're going to be covered in dog hair."

Joycelynn lifted the blanket, laughing when she saw that bits of grey fur had already adhered to her pants.

Tossing the sweater onto an armchair, Brandon went to sit beside her. "What were we talking about?"

"Birthdays, euthanasia...life purpose," she answered wistfully. "You choose the next topic. I'm fairly certain that you're tired of listening to me."

"Not at all," Brandon assured her, seemingly sincere. "It's hard for me when what we talk about touches on subjects I struggled with when Terry was ill. But aside from that, I find *you* and our conversations thought provoking." Shifting so he was facing her more directly, he rested one long arm along the back of the couch, and then said, "I want to go back to your theory that we choose our earthly purpose. Does that mean you believe that our entire lives are fated, and that there's no such thing as freewill and choice?"

"To a degree, I think that's true. However, I believe we're free to choose *how* we accomplish our divine calling or purpose. Some people might spend the majority of their lives off their intended pathways. Some souls may even be summoned back to our originating Source before they fulfill their earthly purposes."

"Are you saying that souls can fail life school?"

"For me, failure equates with experience, in the same way that success equates with experience. Not succeeding a hundred percent of the time is part of the journey, and how we learn and grow."

"I don't know if you're the wisest or wackiest woman I've met." Brandon took a sip of his chocolate, smiling faintly as he placed it back on the coffee table.

"I'd prefer to go with *wisest*, although *wackiest* makes me sound far more interesting," Joycelynn joked good-naturedly. Setting the comforter aside, she asked, "Where's the bathroom?"

"First door on the right."

Brandon watched Joycelynn walking away. Even in sock feet she had a cute wiggle. If she were anyone else, by now he'd have put much more effort into scoring a kiss, or seducing her. He hadn't progressed through his usual advances, because assertively hitting on a kindness ambassador, who confessed her deepest secrets in church, seemed somewhat sacrilegious.

To distract himself, he picked up Scruffy's blanket, and shook it over the balcony. Hearing laughter echoing up from the beach, he thought of how easily Terry had laughed, and about Joycelynn's life-purpose suppositions. His best friend was extremely well read, yet he worked as a garbage man. *What kind of divine mission was that? And how could there be any purpose to his suffering?* Terry deserved to die with dignity, not writhed in pain and with tubes coming out of every orifice.

"You look upset," Joycelynn commented as she sat down, and Brandon draped Scruffy's blanket across her legs.

"I am upset, but not at you." Brandon sat next to her. "I understand what you're saying about each of us having a life purpose. But I can't see any sense in suffering the way Terry did."

"Terry's *physical* being suffered, not his soul."

"What about his wife and daughters, is there a purpose in them having to watch Terry die like that?" His doubting eyes roaming her face, he moved his head from side-to-side. "I'm sorry, Joycelynn, but some of what you say sounds like hogwash to me."

"Was Terry a good husband and father?" she asked, undeterred.

"He was a great husband and father. Even if he had to pull extra shifts, there was nothing his wife or kids wanted that they didn't get. Heck, the guy drove a rusty old van so his wife could have a decent car."

"Was he a good friend?"

"You know he was!" Fighting months of anguish begging release, he bitingly asked, "What are you getting at, Joycelynn?"

"I'm highlighting the many, many gifts Terry brought to this world. I didn't know him personally, only through his sister's stories. When I met Dee at a mini kindness rally, she told me about her brother's illness. She also said that he was the most honorable person on the planet. When she asked for my autograph, she opened the book to the chapter on *integrity* and had me sign next to the quote: '*My word is my contract; my handshake, my seal; and, my conscience, my witness.*'"

"Terry always kept his promises," Brandon offered, seesawing between enjoying warm memories of his friend and the miserable heartache doing so elicited.

Joycelynn reached out and gently touched his arm. "Terry was a tremendously giving and loving person with a beautiful soul." Smiling compassionately, she lowered her voice to a near whisper as she finished with, "It seems to me that he *did* fulfill his life purpose and was summoned home."

Brandon leapt up, flicked on the gas fireplace, and glared into the yellow and blue flames. Joycelynn's words loaded into his mind like bullets into a shotgun. Readying to shoot holes into her Pollyanna theories, he clenched his fists and breathed. *Summoned home. A life purpose that included god-awful agony.* Unable to stop himself, he spoke his mind, "You've obviously never witnessed someone you love recoiled in pain and pleading for another shot of morphine, or watched a grief-ridden wife wiping tears from her dying husband's eyes."

Vigorously shaking his head, he concluded his outburst with, "I'm glad Terry's suffering makes sense to you, because it sure as hell doesn't to me."

Joycelynn glanced down at her fidgeting hands and remained quiet.

Now he'd done it. He was angry at death, not Joycelynn. Dialing down his ire, he explained, "I appreciate that you're trying to help me come to grips with losing Terry. And as much as I want to discuss your spiritual theories, I simply can't fathom a divine purpose for the hideous ungodly suffering he and his family endured for nearly a year."

Joycelynn tilted her head upward, her pursed lips relaying her regret for making him angry.

Hating that he'd hurt her feelings, as a way of apologizing for his tirade, he said, "Please...finish what you were saying."

"We can talk some other time," she said, still nervously playing with her entwined fingers.

Not wanting their evening to end with Joycelynn thinking he was a verbose bully, he tried again, "If you don't finish what you were saying, I'll be up half the night wondering about what you wanted to share with me."

The corners of her mouth curled slightly as she considered him.

"I promise not to lose my cool again," he encouraged, relieved that she again seemed relaxed.

"The point I was making earlier, is that the sacrifices Terry made, and the love he gave on earth, will radiate forever. The people whose hearts he touched will continue his legacy of love—first here on earth, and then eternally."

"What do you mean by *his legacy of love?*" Brandon asked, being careful that his lingering frustration didn't reach his tone.

Her concerned blue eyes roaming his face, she explained, "The compassion people felt for Terry when he was ill, and the love he germinated throughout his life, are already echoing forward. His eldest daughter enrolled in nursing college. His youngest daughter is visiting schools dressed as an enormous orange garbage bag, and teaching kids about the importance of recycling, reusing and reducing packaging. Dee has plans to spearhead a grief group."

"If what you say is true—that Terry's soul chose a purpose-path which included an insidious illness, then he was an infinitely better man than I am." Glancing away, he finished with, "Personally, I'm hoping for a brain aneurism that takes me out in a flash."

"We dread suffering because of our physical nature. At Source our souls are motivated by concern for all on earth and beyond, not our temporary bodies."

Brandon looked back toward Joycelynn and their eyes locked. She was strikingly pretty, and he was raked raw. It would be wonderful to cart her off to his bedroom and fall asleep in her arms.

Lowering her gaze, Joycelynn began folding the dog's blanket. "I think we're both talked out," she murmured, sounding tired.

"Scruffy and I'll walk you to your car," Brandon offered, as they rose off the couch and made their way toward the kitchen.

After Joycelynn put on her boots, Brandon held her coat while she pushed her arms into the sleeves. Catching a whiff of her vanilla tinged perfume, his libido rocketed. When she turned around so that they were face-to-face, he contemplated kissing her.

Joycelynn took a step backward and began buttoning her coat. "When my best male friend and roommate, Eugene, suddenly died from a heart attack, I spent several weeks numbing at the casino. When my dog died, I went to bed for days." She smiled sympathetically. "Even though I believe in an eternal loving Source, I still have difficulty processing loss."

Brandon nodded, then called and leashed Scruffy.

"Maybe we can catch a movie sometime this week," he suggested on the way to her car.

"I'd like that," she answered in a sincere somber tone.

Watching her driving away, Brandon felt lost and lonely. Terry was gone and he'd miss him forever. Joycelynn's theories were interesting, but she had no more proof of a next life, or a meaning for life, than his God-fearing parents. Perhaps there was some truth in everyone's beliefs. At the moment, he didn't care. He just wanted to stop hurting.

FORGIVENESS

> "You are loved, not for anything you did or didn't do;
> but because at Source, there is only love."
> Anonymous

Their latest *Heartmind Wisdom* anthology scheduled for printing with Balboa Press in a few weeks, Joycelynn spent the weekend editing. Most of their coauthors were sharing their life-gained wisdom and healing messages with a readership for the first time. All of their submissions were profound and inspirational, with some triggering tears and others laughter. From Dennis's account about the little boy who was shunned for being different, to Sudipta's story of widowhood and her subsequent immigration to Vancouver from India, to Larry's shedding of two hundred and thirty pounds—Joycelynn was awed by one incredible life journey after another. It was after three a.m. Sunday when she crawled into bed elated and exhausted. When the alarm rang at nine, she hit the snooze button, and contemplated skipping the Sunday chapel service. She didn't, though, because her friend, author and psychotherapist Ted Kuntz, was the guest speaker.

Two hours later while listening to Ted, Joycelynn thought about how much she admired the fiftyish soft-spoken man whose chosen path was to help others find peace within. She knew the story of how a routine childhood vaccine resulted in his young son, Josh, becoming plagued by frequent and violent seizures. Understandably angry at first, followed by many months of frustration, he'd slowly and wisely come to see his precious child as his spiritual guide and teacher. He honored his relationship with Josh by authoring the book *Peace Begins with Me,* and by sharing their treasured father-son experiences through his counseling practice and talks. Ted was an amazingly gifted speaker and a wonderful person, so it didn't surprise her that whenever he spoke, the congregation always welcomed him with respect and love.

As the service concluded and they stole a quiet moment to catch up, Ted's warm blue eyes held hers as he asked, "Are you and Elizabeth coming to the World Kindness Concert tomorrow night?"

"We'll be there," she assured him, truly looking forward to the annual concert. Taking a sip of her coffee, her thoughts changed to the business appointment she and Elizabeth had booked for later in the day. "This afternoon, we're meeting with Denise Hagan to discuss adding her music to our PowerPoint slideshow. "I'm so excited I have butterflies in my stomach." Self-conscious about her admission, she lightly laughed, then continued more seriously, "Denise's music is incredibly inspiring and healing. When we were designing our first *KiK* visual presentation, I listened to her every day, all day long, for about two months straight."

"She's as gracious and lovely as her music. I'm certain you'll like her." Grinning, Ted confessed, "You're not her only aficionado. When I first heard her CD *For Those Who Hear*, I played it over and over again. Denise's music absorbs you into a web of peace so serenely wondrous, you never want to stop listening."

"Thank you for introducing us to her music. If you hadn't played her song 'Perfect Replications' as part of your talk last year, we might never have known about her."

"You're welcome," Ted returned, his expression softening as he asked, "How are *you* doing? Have you had any relapses with your gambling addiction?"

"No relapses; although, I sometimes still get triggered. My gaming reform mission helps to keep me strong; the most difficult part is completely forgiving myself. Even though I'm aware of the many gifts overcoming my addiction unfolded, the times I misled friends and family haunts me now and again." She sighed. "Guilt is a powerful foe."

"That it is," Ted sympathized. "For an addict, casinos are an equally powerful foe because they have both intrinsic and extrinsic motivators. It's a double whammy. Intrinsically, the attraction for you was the social aspect of gaming—the fun and the people. Extrinsically, there was the thrill of winning. I read an Ipsos Reid Public Affairs report that said, although only about five percent of the general population is at risk of becoming compulsive gamblers, this statistic doubles for casino gamblers." Dropping the two fingers he'd held up for emphasis, he finished with, "You told me that your gaming addiction coincided with the death of a close friend and a divorce, so don't be too hard on yourself."

"I know you're right, and I don't admonish myself too often, but every now and then...," she said with a weak smile. "My family and friends have been very forgiving, and for that I'm truly grateful."

"I'm glad you have support. And it doesn't surprise me that you're the only one still in the forgiveness process. Healing from addiction takes time and work." His blue eyes narrowing thoughtfully, he advised, "When one of my counseling clients is suffering from guilt, I often recite a quote from your Kindness is Key visual presentation: '*You are loved, not for anything you did or didn't do; but because at Source, there is only love.*' If you remember that your friends, family and God forgive you, it might help you to completely forgive yourself."

Joycelynn nodded, thinking of how often she referred to the same quote. There was another *KiK* lesson she also needed to improve upon, which was finding more balance between work and play. She generally sidestepped the issue by rationalizing that her work felt like play; however, since spending time with Brandon, she was beginning to recognize the difference. "Apparently, I'm a living example of the saying *the teacher teaches what he or she needs to learn.*"

"Life is a process and we're all continually learning." His empathy apparent, he smiled his understanding, before saying, "I wish I could visit longer, but I have another speaking engagement this afternoon." He glanced about the room before leaning forward and quickly hugging her. "I don't see them, so would you say goodbye to Elizabeth and Barbara for me?"

"I think they're in the backroom going over next month's chapel activity calendar. I'll let them know you said goodbye."

Briefcase in hand, as he headed for the door, Ted remarked, "I'm looking forward to hearing about your visit with Denise."

"I'll tell you all about it at the World Kindness Concert," Joycelynn returned, eternally grateful for his friendship and generous introductions to everyone he believed would help further hers and Elizabeth's goal to seed kindness, one heart at a time.

Glad to have a few minutes alone while she waited for Elizabeth, Joycelynn sat on the long bench at the back of the chapel. Sipping the dregs of her coffee, she wondered how Brandon was doing. She hadn't heard from him for a few days and was amazed by how often he came to mind. When her cell phone rang a few seconds later, instinctively knowing it was him, she smiled. Checking the caller ID and getting confirmation, she wondered if she were manifesting her heart's wishes, or was more psychic than she gave herself credit for being. She answered with, "I knew it was you."

"I knew it was you, too." He laughed heartily.

"Ha-ha," she flipped, pleasantly aware of how happy he sounded.

"Are you up to going to a movie tonight?"

"I'm exhausted from working late the past few nights," she said, inwardly groaning as she realized how pitiful her answer sounded. When she was younger, she'd been grateful for her answering machine because she could screen calls from guys phoning for a last-minute date. For a teenager, admitting you had nothing to do a Friday or Saturday night was social suicide. Telling Brandon that she'd done nothing but work all weekend was an equivalent dating faux pas.

"Come on," he coaxed, "Matt Damon's starring in *Hereafter*. I'll pick you up."

"You don't even believe in an afterlife. Why would you choose a movie about eternity, psychic phenomena and love?"

"Because it has your name all over it," he answered, smug pride lighting his voice.

Eyes closed, Joycelynn debated whether she could muster enough energy to watch a movie without falling asleep. She considered suggesting that they get together on another evening. Mentally going over her schedule, she decided against Monday because that was the World Kindness Concert. Tuesday, she and Elizabeth were hosting an author call info session for their next *Heartmind Wisdom* collection. Wednesday, was Writers Café. Friday, she was teaching. Her only next free evening was on Thursday.

"You're too tired, I understand," Brandon said, misinterpreting her lengthy silence and sounding disheartened.

Knowing he assumed she was blowing him off, Joycelynn quickly said, "I have a meeting in Steveston this afternoon, but if you make it an early show, I'll go." Perhaps she needed a break from work more than she needed rest.

"I'll pick you up at six."

"I'll be the one with the black bags under my eyes," she quipped before hanging up. It was the third time Brandon had asked her out at the last minute, which seemed unromantic and smacked of commitment phobia. Not that she was one to talk. It had been a long time since she'd even considered the possibility of a romantic relationship.

Watching the sun skipping across the wrinkling blue waters of the Fraser River as it rushed to meet up with the Pacific Ocean, Joycelynn thought about how much she always enjoyed visiting the picturesque village of Steveston. Once the world's busiest fishing port, and still home to Canada's largest fishing fleet, the town was also a trendy tourist area with dozens of restaurants lining the boardwalk. As you ventured from the water's edge, additional eateries were intermingled with an eclectic array of stores selling everything from clothing to fishing tackle. Her favorite store was *Serendipity's Backyard* with its incredible selection of inspirational and spiritual books, music, candles, and jewelry.

"We have an hour before we're scheduled to meet with Denise Hagan," Elizabeth said as she parked her jeep. "What do you want to do?"

"Let's get an ice cream cone," Joycelynn chirped, feeling fresh and alive. She'd expected to feel dragged out and tired, but felt the exact opposite. She gave the credit for her elevated mood to the glorious day and how much she was looking forward to finally meeting Denise.

"Ice cream! You'll freeze to death eating something that cold in this temperature," Elizabeth cried out. "More importantly, I want to get back into my skinny clothes before our next *Heartmind Wisdom* live-streamed book signing."

"I've come to love my prosperity ring," Joycelynn teased, pinching her waist. "It's proof of life's riches and gifts."

"You don't have a prosperity ring," Elizabeth countered. "Besides you were too thin before."

"I'm certainly not thin anymore," Joycelynn guffawed. "I might hide it with clothing, but I definitely have a middle-age muffin top." When she first hit fifty, she'd been horrified with the way her body succumbed to the forces of gravity, pulling everything downward, and rearranging her frame so that a couple of extra pounds on her hips became the least of her worries. Menopause had come along shortly afterward, bringing her the gift of freedom from what her mother's generation had called the *curse,* and her generation referred to as a *friend*. Surprisingly, being in her fifties afforded her other freedoms and gifts, too. She was less concerned about her physical appearance, and more concerned about who she was on the inside. This was one of the reasons her active gambling addiction had horrified her. Depleting her nest egg had initially scared her half to death, too. But over time, she'd discovered that being nearly broke provided her with a tremendous opportunity to grow and learn. As she had stated during her chapel talk, another realization that had helped her recover was recognizing that the personality traits that had led her away from her divine pathway, employed more positively, became the very traits that led her back to her life purpose.

"I still think we should get ice cream," she said, beaming when Elizabeth acquiesced with a nod. "We should also incorporate an exercise on spinning adjectives into our *KiK* self-kindness seminars."

"Is that your version of exercise? You want to *spin* adjectives instead of taking a *spin* class?" Elizabeth retorted with a light laugh.

Her concentration on the course content idea developing in her mind, Joycelynn playfully rolled her eyes before saying, "As I told everyone this morning, examining my addiction caused me to realize that the personality traits that led me to gamble are the exact ones that make me successful in business. I'm *social, self-motivated* and *determined*, which are great attributes for business and a gambling addiction. From the door staff, to the dealers and fellow gamers, casinos are a very *social* and friendly place. Twenty-four-seven, it's a continuous party den. When I won, thinking that I was on a winning streak, I was easily *motivated* to capitalize on my luck. When I lost, I went back *determined* to regain my losses."

"But how does that lead you to spinning adjectives? I don't get it."

"*Determined* is my word for describing myself. My mother called me *stubborn*, which hurt me when I was younger. But as I got older, I realized that I wasn't stubborn, I was determined. Same attribute, but when applied positively, it becomes a strength. I was also labeled as being *too emotional*, which I now chose to view as being *heart-motivated* and a compliment."

"Heart-motivated *is* a compliment," Elizabeth assured her, admiration entering her tone.

"During the Hay House I CAN DO IT conference last weekend, Gregg Braden said that the key to healing our world is *coherence*, which happens when the heart emits altruistic electrical signals to the brain. Heart-motivated feelings, and their accompanying positive thoughts, heal inward and outward into the community."

"I remember, because what Gregg said caused me to realize the correlation between *kindness* and *coherence*—both are *key* to healing ourselves, others and our planet." Her gaze turning quizzical, Elizabeth asked, "How would you spin being *shy*?"

"Do you think being shy is a desirable or undesirable trait?"

"I don't like being shy, yet I sometimes feel that way."

Joycelynn thought for a moment and then offered, "*Shy* could also mean that you let other people shine by giving them the spotlight, which is actually true about you. I never realized that you sometimes feel shy. I just thought you had a flare for bringing out the best in others."

"That's really how you see me? Thanks!" Elizabeth chirped. "I guess every personality trait has its gifts. What's important is how you apply your primary characteristics in your life."

"It's unfortunate that when other people don't like what you do or say, or want to control you, they spin who you are in negative ways. If it happens a lot, especially when you're young, you might buy into the labels," Joycelynn said. "Maybe teaching people how to spin their individual negative labels positively will help repair some of the residual damage."

"How would you spin *egocentric*?" Elizabeth asked.

"*Egocentric*, used productively and spun kindly, would be *self-assured*, *confident* or *centered*. An egocentric person pursuing what he or she believes is right, would be a powerful force."

"Powerful, but not necessarily desirable if that person cared only about self-gain," Elizabeth cautioned.

"I agree. If we include spinning adjectives in our seminar content, we'll have to be certain to examine the possible impact of each trait as it pertains to one's purpose-path. Being *determined* didn't work so well during my gaming days, but it serves me well when I'm trying to meet a project deadline."

"*Irresponsible* could be spun into *fun-loving*, *spontaneous* or *carefree*. *Stupid* could be *innocent*, *unaware* or *open-to-new-ideas*," Elizabeth said, obviously excited that spinning adjectives would help others to view themselves in a more positive light.

"Learning to put a kind spin on the labels that each of us owns or believes about ourselves, would also help people to be more kind to others, too," Joycelynn offered. "For instance, if someone seems to be a *know-it-all* or *extremely opinionated*, instead of viewing them in a negative context, we could encourage people to think of that person as being *well-read*, *confident* or *eloquent*."

"Or *insecure*, as is often the case when you scratch below the surface of someone who overcompensates by being a braggart." Elizabeth momentarily stopped walking and faced Joycelynn as she asked, "What would you say about that?"

"If I were talking to someone who was complaining about another person, I'd explain that boasting is often a mask for insecurity, and that the braggart was simply a sensitive person seeking approval. If I were talking with the boastful person, I'd explain that the best way to *get love* is to give *love* by reaching out and helping others."

"I like it," Elizabeth said as they arrived at the ice cream store and they each ordered their favorite flavor—chocolate. Let's start by incorporating a spinning adjectives exercise into our mini self-kindness seminars, and go from there."

"We should also start including Louise Hay's mirror affirmations," she said, recalling the founding mother of self-help magically retrieving a shiny compact mirror from her bra during the I CAN DO IT conference. In her mind's eye, she could still see Louise sitting on a bar-high stool, her long legs elegantly draped in zebra-striped silk pants, radiating the gleeful aura of a young child playing in a sandbox.

"We should!" Elizabeth agreed. "I so admire Louise Hay. She seemed so comfortable perched on stage, in front of three-thousand conference goers, pulling things from her underwear, and oozing cool charm as though she'd just happened upon a confidence sale and purchased the entire kit and caboodle."

"She's an amazing woman," Joycelynn agreed, before changing the subject. "Brandon called. We're going to a movie tonight."

"Good! He seems like a nice guy." Then, as easily as if they were talking about the weather, Elizabeth asked, "Has he kissed you yet?"

Scrunching her nose, Joycelynn studied her friend. "You sound fifteen, not fifty-something."

"The heart doesn't age. That which makes your pulse race when you're a teenager, still causes belly somersaults when you reach middle-age."

"Brandon seemed to want to kiss me a couple of times, but I didn't encourage him."

"Don't you want a relationship?"

"I don't know, so I'm being cautious."

"Cautious or scared?"

"Both," Joycelynn admitted. "I'm being cautious because I'm still getting to know him." From what Dee had said, Brandon was cut from the same cloth as both of her ex-husbands—good looking, charming, flirtatious guys always on the lookout for another skirt. Riding sidecar to a man's fantasies was a road she vowed never to again travel.

"And you're scared because...?"

What was holding her back was that her divorces had scarred her deeply, shaken her faith in her own judgment, and derailed her trust in men. "You know why I'm scared...I'm afraid of failing again."

"How come you're not afraid to fail at business?"

Joycelynn licked her ice cream cone. "Because I don't think I'll fail."

"So why do you think you might fail at love?"

"Because I've been divorced twice, remember?" She held up her bare ring finger.

"Oh, I get it. You don't mind being brave with your business goals, but you're a chicken when it comes to your heart."

"Not chicken, cautious."

Elizabeth's brow lifted. "Sorry, girlfriend. When it comes to romance, you're more afraid than cautious."

"I promised myself that I'd never compromise my love again," she voiced the mantra she'd adopted from one her dancers, who as a way of reassuring her that she'd made the right decision in divorcing her second husband, offered the advice that *to be true to oneself, you must never compromise your love.*

"If you don't open yourself up to the possibility of love because you're afraid, you're still *compromising* your love."

Kerpow! Elizabeth's wise words hit her with a mental punch. Protecting her heart was costing her one of life's sweetest gifts—romantic intimacy. "What if he turns out to be like my exes, or some of the guys I dated when I was younger?"

"You're strong, you'll survive," Elizabeth returned genially.

Joycelynn watched the seagulls gleefully floating above an old battered fishing boat as it docked. When it came to a relationship with a man, she felt a lot like that boat—withered and worn out. But when it came to business, she was more like the seagulls—alive and eagerly open to all possibilities. It seemed that her heart needed to have a talk with her head. Dumping the last half of her cone into a nearby garbage container, she promised, "I'll think about what you said. However, I'm still going to be cautious."

"I don't doubt it, girlfriend." Elizabeth laughed. "Just remember, you teach that failure is really experience. What applies in business also applies in love. You're more experienced now. You know that where romance is concerned, you should keep your eyes and ears open. Now you just have to remember how to reopen your heart."

As they walked toward the restaurant where they were to meet Denise, Joycelynn studied the couples walking by. Some were laughing, holding hands and obviously madly in love. Others walked side-by-side in comfortable silence. She wondered if she'd ever know love beyond the canopied dreams of infatuation. *Would the day come when she'd walk beside a man in a silent bond born of weathered love? Was it possible that Brandon Ashton was that man?*

Though today was the first time they'd meet Denise Hagan, Joycelynn already felt a kinship with the velvet-voiced singer. When she and Elizabeth had first teamed together in their Kindness Is Key mission, it was Denise's music that kept Joycelynn centered and inspired. Whenever frustrated hope tugged at her financially or emotionally, she'd play Denise's CD *For Those Who Hear,* while she worked on their *KiK* visual presentation. In the singer's lyrics, Joycelynn found a heartfelt message of peace and love that helped her to release the regrets of her addiction and move forward. She hoped Denise would grant them permission to incorporate her music into their PowerPoint slide show, so that more people could benefit from the soulful woman's music magic.

Recognizing Denise from her promo pictures, when she walked through the door Joycelynn leapt up to greet her. As Ted Kuntz had said, the thirtyish woman had a saintly, wholesome quality that made you immediately like her. After making their way to the table against the far wall where Elizabeth was waiting, the three women exchanged introductory hugs, then immediately began their business discussion. That evening, Denise was recording the last song on her latest album and then flying out of town the next day, so their meeting would be short.

Joycelynn opened with, "I hope you agree with us that our visual presentation and your music are a perfect match, because Elizabeth and I are totally inspired by your voice and the lyrics and melodies of your songs. We believe our goal of seeding kindness one heart at a time, fits perfectly with your message of peace and love."

Denise smiled, her young face glowing. "Everything you emailed, and what we talked about on the phone, feels right to me." She turned to face Elizabeth. "I know Joycelynn's story. I'm aware of her gaming reform goals, her kindness aha moment, and how she arrived at wanting to help others. But I don't know your inspiration for wanting to spread love around our beautiful earth."

Her brown eyes meeting Denise's caring gaze, Elizabeth began, "I suffered bouts of deep depression from my early twenties until a few years ago. I tried everything from prescription medication to counseling. Yet, periodically, and for long interludes, an emotional funk would take hold, making concentrating difficult and finding joy impossible. I thought in slow motion. I moved in slow motion. It didn't help that during my last bout of depression, the chronic pain in my upper leg was diagnosed as hip dysplasia, and I underwent a hip replacement."

"The catalyst for my last stint of clinical depression was a question the facilitator asked at a Stephen Covey leadership course put on by a large corporation where I headed the Human Resources Department: '*Is your ladder against the right wall?'* The implication of what he was asking crashed my world. Suddenly, it was no longer acceptable that I was working upward of eighty hours a week and had exchanged my dreams for a paycheck. That was the end of corporate America for me."

"After talking with my husband, Mark, I handed in my resignation, thinking I was finally free to find work that resonated with my heart and soul. But instead of feeling free, without a work title, an employment position to tell me who I was, I felt lost and rudderless. Minute after minute, for days on end, the nothingness that was my existence strung into an endless insipid fog. For weeks, I sat in my rocking chair just staring into the eyes of my beloved Polish Sheepdog Batza. I was on prescription medication, but it did nothing to lift the emptiness that amputated me from my higher self."

"Logically, I had no reason to be depressed or feel lost. My husband supported me in whatever I wanted to do. We lived in a nice house and didn't have any financial worries." She nodded and smiled as a young man approached their table and asked if he could take the spare chair.

"One day, I made a decision. No matter how awful I felt, I was going to figure out how to heal. Someway, somehow, I was going to find the help I needed. I had long given up on being happy. All I wanted was to stop feeling so sad. I started reading self-help books; and fortunately, came upon one called *The Artist's Way*, which advised journaling as a way to one's purpose-path. At first, I didn't know what to journal. Some days, all I wrote was, *I don't know what to write, I don't know what to write.* Then, little by little, I started to reconnect with myself, my spirit and my soul."

Elizabeth picked up a pen from the table and regarded it as one would a sacred artifact. "Through journaling I was taken back to my youthful dreams of teaching and helping others, so I educated myself in the healing arts. I learned how to make candles, and studied Reiki, massage therapy and essential oils. I flew all over the continent taking courses, became a certified vision coach, and was recently ordained as a minister. Inch by inch, I found me. Found purpose. Found happiness."

Smiling understandingly, Denise softly sang a few words from a song she'd written from a young heart wizened by pain and sweetened with universal love, "*The answer lies in the sweet Divine whisperings, rising up through my soul. It's the sweet Divine awakening, that'll be bringing us all back home.*"

"Thank you," Elizabeth mouthed, checked tears glistening in her bright eyes.

"Enough you two, or I'm going to start blubbering," Joycelynn tittered as she turned on her laptop and started their *KiK* PowerPoint presentation that was the reason for their meeting. Within minutes, Denise was singing along with the songs they had chosen from her CD, and an impromptu audience had gathered around their table to watch and listen.

When the presentation ended, everyone applauded before going back to their own tables.   "I'll email you my formal permission, and the details of what you need to include in the credits of your presentation. But, yes, you can incorporate my music with your lovely presentation." Reaching for and placing her coat on her lap, Denise slumped slightly forward. "I hate to cut our visit short, but I have an incredible amount of work to do before I leave tomorrow."

"Is it possible to buy a few dozen of each of your CDs?" Elizabeth asked, as they all stood and Denise put on her coat. "We'd like to sell them at our seminars. We'll need dozens more if our latest nonprofit partnership comes through, which I think it will." She smiled. "Of course, we'll link your website with ours so that people can also purchase your CDs directly through you."

"Just email me with a list of how many of each you'd like," Denise said, a hint of her Irish accent coming through. "I'm sorry that I have to leave. Both of you ladies are delightful." She glanced from Joycelynn to Elizabeth. "I'm pleased that our hearts share a common thread, and delighted that we were finally able to meet."

"We're equally *delighted* to finally meet you," Elizabeth said as she and Denise hugged goodbye. "Don't worry about having to rush off. Finding enough time for everything we want to do is always a challenge for us, too."

"Maybe we can all get together for lunch when you come back," Joycelynn suggested as she escorted Denise toward the exit.

"I'd like that," Denise replied, smiling as she rushed out the door.

"Wow!" Elizabeth exclaimed when Joycelynn returned to the table. "Denise is amazing."

"She is," Joycelynn agreed. "I almost cried when she looked into your eyes and sang 'Sweet Divine Awakenings.'" Flopping down in a chair, she sighed happily. "Our entire meeting was wonderfully surreal."

"On the horizon at sunset, there's a notable black line that separates the dark and light. That's where I existed during my twenties and when I quit my human resources job to embark on my mission to find my true purpose," Elizabeth said. "I think Denise relates to what I went through, and that her music is inspired from her own challenges and hurdles."

"You're probably right about Denise. And I like your horizon analogy," Joycelynn said, feeling a familiar swell of admiration for her good friend. "Depression paralyzes hundreds of thousands of people physically and emotionally, many suffering so greatly they literally give up on life. But you didn't cave in to the dark; you found a way to the light. From journaling and meditation, to taking every therapeutic course you thought might help you or someone else, to becoming a minister at our church, you kept going. Now, even though you'd rather just forget about those dark times, you instead share your healing path with the world. Helping everyone you can, every hour of every day. I'm proud of you. I hope you know that."

"Thanks and ditto," Elizabeth said, blushing lightly. "I'm proud of you and our *Heartmind Wisdom* coauthors. We're all sharing our life-gained wisdom, much of it born of pain, to help our global brothers and sisters suffering similar traumas and fates."

Glancing about at the restaurant patrons who had gone back to their newspapers and laptops, Joycelynn commented, "Your pathway through depression, and mine through addiction, is why it's crucial that we keep spreading the message that kindness is the key to healing ourselves and our world. Like the expression *you can't see the forest for the trees,* many people face adversity, illness, loss, depression, and addiction with limited vision. They can't see the gifts in their challenges and pain, only the trunks and stumps that block their view."

"We will definitely reach more people now," Elizabeth assured her. "Anyone who listens to Denise's heavenly music while watching our visual presentation will definitely get the message that being kind—to one's self, others, animals, and our planet—is the key to world happiness and peace."

Packing up her laptop, Joycelynn suggested, "We should ask Denise to sing at our 'Largest Human Peace Sign' Concert."

"That's a great idea." Elizabeth secured her red wool poncho about her shoulders before turning to face Joycelynn. "Thank you for over a quarter of a century of friendship and for being my mission partner."

"Thank you for never giving up on me," she said, thinking of how Mark and Elizabeth had taken her in whenever her life went awry. She knew it was a rare husband who would be receptive to his wife's best friend living in their home, and that only an extraordinary friend would extend the offer in the first place.

"You're welcome." Elizabeth grinned. "You can repay me by seriously thinking about dating Brandon. He's a nice man."

"Maybe, I will. Maybe, I won't," Joycelynn retorted, ignoring an excited stewing of fear and anticipation. Wanting to change the subject, she cheekily chirped, "Let's get another ice cream cone."

Elizabeth rolled her eyes. "You're such a problem child. Why did I ever get mixed up with you?"

As they made their way out the door and into the bright fall sunshine, Joycelynn looped her arm through Elizabeth's and quipped, "Pure luck, my friend...just pure luck."

ACCEPTANCE

"My truth is but mine alone; as yours is yours.
For this reason I hear and see you free of
judgment, fear, anger, and resentment.
This is my promise to you. This is my gift to me."
E. Patricia Connor

Brandon arrived at Joycelynn's door a half hour early, carrying a bouquet of red carnations he'd grabbed when he stopped at a corner store for a chocolate bar. He realized she might not be ready, but wasn't prepared for her to greet him in well-worn purple pyjamas and with the phone tucked under her ear.

Smiling her hello while motioning him inside, she continued with her conversation, "The woman seemed fine when she left. Is she going to be all right?" Joycelynn paced as the other person responded. "Let me know if there's anything I can do. He's here, I have to go."

As she hung up the phone and walked over to him, Brandon handed her the bouquet.

Standing on bare toes and kissing his cheek, she thanked him and apologized in one long breath, "Flowers, what a lovely gesture. I'm sorry that I'm not ready."

Noting her sadness as he followed her to the kitchen and watched her arrange the carnations into a vase she retrieved from under the sink counter, he waited to see if she would share the news she'd just received. Whatever she'd learned had her worried.

"That was Elizabeth on the phone. Earlier this week, we were invited to be guest speakers at a psychic fair. One of the psychics gave too much information to her client."

"Too much information?" Brandon's brow furrowed curiously. "Isn't that what people pay for?"

"It's what they pay for, but can't always handle." Joycelynn stopped fidgeting with the carnations and met his gaze. "A young client wanted to know if her husband was having an affair."

"Ouch!" Brandon covered his heart with his hand.

"The psychic, who should have known better than to reveal something so potentially life altering, confirmed the woman's suspicions. Her client became hysterical. Distraught and crying herself, the psychic came running to me for help with consoling the poor woman."

"What did you do?"

"I told the client that it was possible the psychic had misinterpreted the cards, and suggested that she needed more proof regarding her husband's infidelity. She seemed relatively calm when she left." Pursing her lips, Joycelynn's eyes misted. "Elizabeth called to tell me that the young woman found proof her husband was cheating, and took an overdose of pills."

"Oh, my God! I didn't realize people took tarot cards that seriously. Is she going to be okay?" Brandon asked, immediately thinking of his aunt.

"It looks like she'll be okay physically. Emotionally, no one knows."

"Are you feeling responsible for telling the woman to find her own proof? If she was already suspicious, it's likely she was determined to keep looking until she found something that either proved or alleviated her fears."

In a quavering voice that gave ache to his heart, Joycelynn admitted what was obviously torturing her, "I wish that I'd offered to spend more time with her."

"Are you still up to going to the movie?" Brandon asked, leaning forward and tucking a stray hair behind Joycelynn's ear. "Would you rather stay home and talk?" Even without makeup, she looked adorably cute with her bright blue eyes trained on his.

"I think the movie will help to clear my head," she softly murmured.

"Movie it is." Bending forward, he brushed his lips against hers. When she didn't resist, he pulled her into him. She smelled shower fresh, and as the curves of her flannelette covered body melted into him, he deepened his kiss.

Joycelynn stiffened, jolting Brandon back to reality and giving him a bellyful of guilt. He'd kissed her on impulse, taking advantage of the fact that she was hurting, vulnerable and too dog-tired to resist being comforted. He was well aware of how attractive physical comfort seemed when you were suffering. After his divorce, he'd slept with more than one woman in a fruitless attempt to assuage the incessant sadness that followed.

Releasing his kiss, he laid his forehead against hers and whispered, "We should get going or we'll miss the movie trailers."

Seemingly relieved that he hadn't tried to pressure her into something more, Joycelynn barely nodded as she gazed up at him. "I should get dressed first." Inching out of his arms, she smirked before turning and hurrying down the hallway. "How come you didn't bring me a chocolate bar?" she hollered before disappearing into what he assumed was her bedroom.

Chuckling, Brandon made his way to the living-room and glanced around. Joycelynn's place was an eclectic array of traditional and contemporary. Her desk was an antique roll top, and what was likely the forthcoming *Heartmind Wisdom* manuscript was neatly piled to one side. Her sofa was modern and baby blue. A picture on one wall displayed angels dancing amongst butterflies. In another, two children held hands beneath a double rainbow. On the fireplace mantle, there were two framed pictures of her golden retriever, who she said had died a short time ago, but he couldn't remember what the dog's name had been. Everywhere there were piles of books. He picked up one entitled *Peace Begins with Me.*

"You can borrow that book if you like," Joycelynn offered as she came back into the room. It was written by a friend of mine, Ted Kuntz."

Looking fresh and youthful in her blue jeans and a soft pink cable-knit pullover, Brandon found it hard to believe that she was in her mid-fifties. Not that her age mattered to him. He'd dated older and younger women. In the end, he'd found a reason to leave each of them. Divorce took its toll, and for him that price seemed to be perpetual bachelorhood. He'd once adored his wife and didn't know if he could ever love like that again—trust like that again. He'd learned the hard way that everything your spouse does can profoundly affect your life; especially, when your wife decides she no longer loves you.

Thinking he might later use retrieving it as an excuse to get back inside Joycelynn's house and hopefully score a goodnight kiss, Brandon put the book down. He might never again marry, but he hadn't totally abandoned the idea of a committed relationship.

Hoping Joycelynn would mollify rather than magnify his fears, once they were in the car and headed for the theater, Brandon asked her, "Do you believe in psychics?" It bothered him that his Aunt Katharine might see something in a teacup that would induce someone to end his or her life.

"I discount no one's gifts, just as I discount no one's spiritual or religious beliefs," Joycelynn said, her expression caring, as if she sensed what was bothering him. "I don't view myself as a psychic, but I've received what I believe are messages from my spiritual guides."

"You hear voices?"

"Not voices…just a sudden, unexpected *knowing.*"

"If you don't actually hear anything, then why do you think that you're receiving messages and not just tuning into your own thoughts?"

"It's different; and sometimes the messages I receive are about events or circumstances that I couldn't possibly have known about."

"Like what? Give me an example."

"When I was younger, I fell in love with a man who claimed he loved me. After we were dating for about three months, we had a huge argument and broke up for a few weeks. When we got back together, one night when he was working late, I fell asleep on the couch waiting for him. While I was sleeping, I received three messages: One was that while we were apart, he'd slept with another woman. The second was that he owed thirty-two thousand dollars. The third message was something personal about him that I hadn't known."

"What did you do?" Brandon asked, thinking how dangerous it would have been if some of the women he'd dated had received messages about him.

"I confronted him. Told him I knew he'd slept with someone else and that he might as well admit it." She laughed. "He was horrified. The poor guy's jaw dropped to about his bellybutton."

"Did he admit it?" Brandon asked, deciding that the guy was a damn fool if he had. Especially considering that Joycelynn didn't have *concrete* proof.

"After a bit of hymning and hawing, he confessed that while we were apart he'd slept with his ex-girlfriend. So I asked him how much money he owed. He told me that he had a thirty-two thousand dollar mortgage on the house he owned jointly with his ex-wife."

"Did the third thing turn out to be true, too?"

"It did," she answered, without elaborating. "I've had other intuitive messages, which I believe are designed to protect or guide me. Because they're for me, not others, I don't view myself as a *psychic* or *medium*." She smiled wistfully. "I think psychic phenomenon is much like the color spectrum."

"*The color spectrum?*"

"The human eye can only detect certain colors: red, orange, yellow, green, blue, indigo, and violet—the visible wavelengths in our electromagnetic spectrum, which we call light."

Pulling into the theater lot and spotting a free space, as he parked his car, Brandon interjected, "I'm assuming that your argument is that there are other frequencies such as radio waves, gamma and x-rays that can't be seen, but can be measured."

"Exactly." Joycelynn nodded excitedly. "Maybe psychic energy operates on a scientifically immeasurable frequency—one that connects with our heartminds, rather than our brains. Are you familiar with the *Maharishi Effect*?"

"Not entirely, but I do recall reading something about it." He unfastened his seatbelt and turned to face her. "Refresh my memory."

Staring out the windshield, Joycelynn reached up and held onto the small silver cross hanging from her necklace. "Studies conducted in the Middle East during the early eighties proved that peace meditation radiates into the immediate community, affecting an increase in goodwill and a decrease in crime and accidents. Maharishi was the transcendental-meditation yogi who came up with the idea."

Brandon nodded. "And this is why you believe there's an immeasurable frequency connecting people's heartminds?"

"Yes, it is. The Maharishi Effect is also why we continually hold mini kindness rallies and annually attempt the Guinness World Record for the 'Largest Human Peace Sign.' According to the study, all you need to start a change in consciousness is the square root of one percent."

"That's ten people to affect one hundred thousand. Pretty powerful stuff," he retorted with a doubting guffaw. "I guess if people believe in God and angels, why not the Maharishi Effect."

"You're making fun of me?"

"Not at all," Brandon said as she faced him, one hand fisted on her hip, the other still clasping her cross. She looked peeved. "I'm not totally ignorant on the subject. I read Gregg

Braden's book *The Divine Matrix*. His premise that invisible energy connects all things, isn't far from your heartmind communication theory. So, no, I wasn't making fun of you."

"What possessed you to read Gregg's book?" Joycelynn asked, sounding surprised.

Brandon shrugged. "It was a Christmas gift from my Aunt Katharine."

"What did you think about Gregg's account of the *Double Slit Experiment*?"

Brandon wondered if Joycelynn was digging to uncover whether he'd read the book, or had just glanced through it. "I think it's interesting that light can behave either as a wave or a particle, and how observing a photon seems to affect its behavior."

"Me, too," Joycelynn said, delight dancing in her blue eyes. "It makes me wonder if light is intelligent. Why else would it vacillate between being a wave or particle, depending on whether the experiment is done with one slit or two?" She shook her head in disbelief. "Everything about quantum physics is fascinating."

"It is fascinating," Brandon agreed, getting out of the car and heading for her side. He wasn't surprised when Joycelynn hopped out before he could open her door. Meeting her at the rear of the car, he asked, "How come you never let me open your door?"

Appearing somewhat puzzled, she answered, "I never thought about it."

Taking her hand, Brandon admitted, "I'm a bit old fashioned."

"You're full of surprises tonight," she said, sounding teasingly sassy as she squeezed his hand. "What else should I know about you?"

"Now *you're* making fun of *me*."

"Sorry," Joycelynn simpered. "I'll be certain to add *sensitive* to my list of Brandon traits."

"You do that," Brandon curtly retorted, his head and shoulders jerking proudly straight. "And I'll add *cheeky little brat* to my list of Joycelynn traits."

Donning a bemused smirk, as Brandon opened the theater door, Joycelynn stood fashion-model erect and with her hands clasped behind her back. When he pulled out his wallet to pay for their tickets, she smiled demurely. Enjoying that she was having fun mocking him, walking toward the concession stand he laughed before asking, "Hotdog or popcorn?"

"I'll have both and a large coke!"

"I'm glad you're coming around to my staple diet." Feeling happier than he had in months, Brandon wrapped his arm about her shoulders and pulled her close. He understood Joycelynn wanting to take things slowly was why she'd stiffened when he kissed her earlier, which he thought was wise of her. But he couldn't deny that bedding her was on his mind more than not.

"I guess your way of thinking is more prevalent than I realized," Brandon commented as they headed home. "Maybe they'll make one of your inspirational novels into a movie."

"I'll keep my fingers crossed on that one," Joycelynn said with a hopeful chuckle. "I was impressed with the movie's exploration of the psychic realm and *near* death experiences. I'd have been even more impressed if they'd explored life *after* death in more detail, which is what I thought they were going to do because of the title, *Hereafter.* But then, it's hard to cover everything in one movie."

"It was deep enough for me," Brandon quipped. "If it weren't for you, I'd be happy to forget about all things supernatural and spiritual."

"My spiritual journey actually started out as a joke," Joycelynn confessed. "I used to wonder if our Creator had a great sense of humor. If she or he deliberately made our world just beautiful enough that we would want to stay, when the real joke is that we can go back to our utopic origins anytime we choose."

Brandon smiled. "A friend of mine, Bob Cochrane, is a pilot. He claims that when he flies his plane he knows there's a God. When he first told me this, I assumed what he meant was that he felt closer to Creation in the calm and silence of the bright blue skies. That he found peace above the clouds, where his busy day-to-day life didn't distract him."

"Sounds nice," Joycelynn replied dreamily.

"It does sound nice, but that's not why he believes in God." Brandon quickly glanced her way, then back at the road. "After a few beers one night, he told me a story about seeing a fiery green ball coming directly at his aircraft. He said he was scared witless and braced himself for the hit. But it never came. The green ball either went through or around them, then miraculously appeared on the other side of the plane. Bob said that at first he thought he might have imagined it, and wasn't going to tell anyone for fear that they'd think he was crazy." Brandon chuckled. "After about thirty seconds, his copilot said, "I'm going to church on Sunday!"

"Your friend isn't alone. When I was doing research for one of our *Heartmind Wisdom* books, I came across a report about similar occurrences around New Mexico. If I remember correctly, it was during the early fifties when there were numerous pilot sightings of fiery green balls. Of course, officials discredited the possibility that they were UFOs, proclaiming they were meteorites."

"Bob mentioned those reports, too. He also said, if what he saw was a meteorite, it must have been *intelligent* or it would have smashed into their craft."

"I guess anything is possible. I just keep an open mind," Joycelynn said reflectively. "I watched a documentary hosted by Stephen Hawking, the famous theoretical physicist and cosmologist. He says that life on other planets is more probable than questionable. Albeit, maybe not in the life shapes and forms we are accustomed to seeing on earth."

"So there isn't much that you *do* discount," Brandon teased. "You have your own theories on the purpose of life, and find no reason to discount flying saucers or psychic phenomena."

"I truly believe that we each choose our purpose before we come to earth. It's what makes the most sense to me. I just hope that my theories build on, rather than distract from, what other people believe." She sighed, thinking of his extremely religious parents and what they might make of her spiritual beliefs. "There is a great quote in one of our books: '*My truth is but mine alone; as yours is yours. For this reason I hear and see you free of judgment, fear, anger, and resentment. This is my promise to you. This is my gift to me.*'"

As Brandon pulled into her driveway and turned off the car, perching her hand on the door handle, she asked, "Would you like to come in for a glass of wine?"

"Wine sounds good," he answered, lifting his brow and staring at her hand on the door handle.

"Sorry, I forgot." She retracted her hand and placed it on her lap. "I'm not used to anyone wanting to open the door me."

"Well, get used to it," Brandon said as he exited the car.

"Do you prefer red or white wine?" she asked as she handed him her keys so he could unlock the front door.

"Red." Brandon grinned as they entered the house and he helped her off with her coat, and then hung it in the hall closet along with his own. "Thanks for doing that."

"Thanks for doing what?" Joycelynn asked, pretending to be clueless.

"For allowing me to be a gentleman."

"If it makes you happy, you can open the wine, too," she playfully snapped as she led the way to her kitchen. "I never did understand everything about women's liberation. As far as I'm concerned, men and women should both be courteous to one another."

"So you weren't part of Gloria Steinem's burn-the-bra brigade?" Brandon asked as Joycelynn handed him a corkscrew and a bottle of wine.

"I believe in equal rights, and equal pay for equal work, if that's what you're asking?" Joycelynn retrieved two glasses, placed them on the kitchen island, then sat down on a stool while Brandon opened and poured the wine. "When I was in my early teens, I was intrigued by the hippy movement; especially, their peace initiatives. In my later teens, I was very much dedicated to the women's movement. The ideologies of both groups greatly influenced my now championing people and kindness." She opened her eyes wide. "I guess I've always been an idealist."

Brandon sat on the stool across from Joycelynn. "Which brings us back to your theory about why souls would need a school."

"Cheers!" Joycelynn held her glass up and clanked it with Brandon's. After taking a small sip of wine, she asked, "Are you sure that you want to listen to me babbling? It seems that whenever we get together, I talk too much."

"I wouldn't ask, if I didn't want to know," he assured her. "Don't worry. If I get bored, I'll yawn a few times or just drop my head on the counter like this." Flopping forward, he draped his torso over the kitchen island, closed his eyes and feigned snoring.

Joycelynn laughed. "That should do it." She took another sip of her wine as he straightened in his chair. "The way I see it, our Source existence, by whatever name one chooses to treasure it, is a place of pure love where the enlightening emotions hold no place. Fear, hate, anger, jealousy, anxiety, greed, etcetera, don't exist. Because our Source world is perfect and void of conflict, suffering and pain…souls don't have the opportunity to experience the entire realm of feeling-motivators. Earth provides the opportunity for us to *choose love* over all other emotions. A few of the lyrics from Denise Hagan's song 'Perfect Replications' express it best: '*I carved you from a diamond and polished you with love. Then I sent you out beyond the veil so you might choose the love.*'"

"Your reasoning is that earth and its mixed bag of emotions exists because at Source souls don't have the opportunity to actually choose love, since they exist in absolute love." He thought for a moment. "Why would our Creator even care? What's the motivating factor?"

"I'd imagine that because our Creator is omnipotent and omnipresent, and thereby aware of all emotions, his or her motivating factor is wanting for all souls to *choose*, *appreciate* and *celebrate* love."

"The other day, you said something about wiser souls choosing to come to earth as sacrificial teachers, so that the rest of us have an opportunity 'to *learn* and *be* and *do* what we are intended to learn, be and do.' You must believe that there is some hierarchy of souls."

Joycelynn hid her surprise that Brandon was quoting her word-for-word. "I believe that earthly souls who choose pure love over all other emotions become angels—Creation's direct link between Source and earth."

"Angels! I should have guessed that's what you'd say." He lightly laughed. "You pretty much have an answer for everything."

"Thanks…I think." Wondering if she were coming across as a know-it-all, she smiled self-consciously.

"It was meant as a compliment," Brandon assured her.

"Good, because I've told you before, you can knock me off of my soapbox anytime you want."

"I like listening to you. Keep talking."

Joycelynn studied him intently, deciding he was genuinely interested. "Have you ever read anything on the Tao Te Ching?"

"Nope. I half listened to a discussion about the Tao in my university days, but it went in one ear and out the other."

"The Tao Te Ching, which in English loosely translates as the *Way to Virtue Book*, was written by an ancient Chinese philosopher, Lao-tzu, believed to be a God-realized being who lived about twenty-five hundred years ago.

"That much I remember," Brandon interjected. "Lao-tzu and Taoism predate Jesus and Christianity by about a half a century."

Once again impressed by his memory and intelligence, Joycelynn smiled before saying, "My theory about life being a school for souls is somewhat based in the Tao teachings that to know one thing, we must know the other. The challenge is being able to recognize each without interpreting, labeling or judging."

"You're saying that the Tao espouses being an impartial observer of life, rather than a self-appointed judge and jury."

"Exactly. Just as *far* is a reference for *near*, and *up* a reference for *down*...*good* is merely a reference for *bad*, *ugly* for *pretty*, *old* for *young*, etcetera."

"I can see how the Tao ties in with your beliefs about sacrificial teachers and your theory that we all emanate from love." Grinning mischievously, he added, "What really impresses me, though, is that you read an ancient text!"

"Don't get too excited." She laughed at how his brow arched upward. "I didn't read the actual Tao Te Ching. I read Dr. Wayne Dyer's book, *Change Your Thoughts—Change Your Life: Living the Wisdom of the Tao.*"

"I've actually read a couple of his books and watched him on public television," Brandon said, as he stood and made his way around the kitchen island. "Wayne Dyer is a smart man." Standing behind Joycelynn, he wrapped his arms around her waist and nibbled on her neck.

Chills scattered along her spine as she craned her neck forward and distractedly whispered, "Is this your way of knocking me off my soapbox?"

Swiveling her chair so that they were facing, Brandon looked deep into her eyes as he bent forward and touched his lips to hers.

Despite how great it felt to be touched like a woman—to want and be wanted—just as they had earlier when he kissed her, alarms rang for Joycelynn, so she turned her head. "I can't do this," she murmured. "I have to do the friendship thing first."

Brandon's shoulders dropped forward as he groaned, "You're tough." Kissing her forehead, he throatily asked, "How long do you imagine that this friend courtship of yours is going to last?"

"Long enough for me to make certain that you aren't going to morph into someone resembling one of my exes." Jutting her chin forward, she added, "Besides, if you can be old fashioned, so can I."

"Uh-huh." Brandon chuckled as he went back to the opposite side of the island and sat down. "I thought there was no eye-for-an-eye in your philosophy."

Relieved that he was teasing, not angry or insulted, she laughed. Then, wanting to ensure that he didn't see her reluctance to kiss him as anything more than her need to take things slowly, she said, "Elizabeth and I are going to the World Kindness Concert tomorrow night. A friend of ours was supposed to go with us, but she came down with the flu. Which means we now have an extra ticket, if you'd like to go with us?"

"What's a *kindness concert*?" he asked, obviously wanting to make certain what he was getting into before agreeing to go.

"It's a musical celebration of kindness! The concert founder and master of ceremonies is Brock Tully, who is a personal friend and a coauthor in our first *Heartmind Wisdom* anthology. You can watch previous annual World Kindness Concerts on YouTube. I'm not certain who is in the lineup this year, but performers generally include local greats such as: Denise Hagan, whose music accompanies most of our *KiK* videos; Susan Jacks; Shari Ulrich; Bill Henderson from the Chilliwack band; Jane Mortifee; and, Michael Vincent. Hopefully, Ranj Singh and his band the Discriminators will be playing their wonderfully unique and upbeat blend of Indian and western music. Brock's quite a character, so the concert is always incredibly fun and inspirational."

"It does sound like fun. Chilliwack's one of my all-time favorite bands. And I remember Susan Jacks from the seventies, when she and her husband, Terry Jacks, were the Poppy Family." He smiled. "I'm beginning to think that *kindness* has become a major movement in Vancouver."

"It has!" Joycelynn agreed. "I'm contemplating approaching the mayor about changing Vancouver's tourist slogan to 'the *kindest* city in the world.'"

"With Kindness is Key and the World Kindness Concert both stemming from Greater Vancouver, your slogan seems fitting," Brandon said, with a slight bob of his head.

"It *is* fitting since *Kindness Rocks* is also a Greater Vancouver based organization."

"What's Kindness Rocks?"

"It's an organization that Brock Tully and two inspirational performers, Jeanette O'Keeffe and Jonas Falle, started to stop violence and bullying in schools. Through education and music, they teach kids how to take charge of their lives without hurting themselves or anyone else. It's a very creative initiative." She smiled. "Jeanette and Jonas will likely be singing at the concert, too. They have an Abba tribute band called ABRA Cadabra."

"You can *definitely* count me in for tomorrow night," he said as his incredible green eyes locked with hers. "As much as I hate to, I should be going home. Judges are never impressed when a prosecutor sleeps through court."

Noting his amorous wanting and feeling her own urges resurfacing, Joycelynn was tempted to forfeit her resolve to keep their relationship platonic. But dating decisions born of desire and made in haste had never served her well before, so she glanced away. Clearing her throat, she said, "The concert starts at seven."

Seemingly amused by their shared sensual dance of catch and release, Brandon chortled as he rose from his stool and retrieved his coat from the hall closet. "Shall I pick you up or meet you there?"

"You're our guest, so why don't Elizabeth and I pick you up around six?" Joycelynn suggested as she walked him to the door.

"You paying for gas and parking works for me!" A cocky confident grin glided across his face as he trained his eyes on hers and backed out the door. "I'll see you tomorrow night." He winked at her as though he was thinking *it wouldn't take much to convince you to kiss me goodnight.* Then he turned and swaggered down her walkway with his head held high.

Putting away the wine and their glasses, Joycelynn mused that much like the hero in her latest inspirational novel, Brandon was a major flirt! Smiling, she thought of other traits they had in common: both were tall, handsome and charming; as well as, intelligent, kind and accomplished. Perhaps, she'd unwittingly manifested Brandon into her life. Laughing to herself, she switched off the lights and headed for bed. If we each create our own reality through consciousness, as Gregg Braden and others suggested, then the possibility was there. From here forward, she'd be careful what she wrote.

E G O

> "As a sense of self, ego is a great protector.
> As a sense of being separate from others,
> the universe and Creation,
> ego enhances the illusion that you are alone."
> E. Patricia Connor

During intermission at the World Kindness Concert, Brandon volunteered to get everyone coffee or tea while the women waited in the lobby. Joycelynn offered to go with him, but he refused, saying he had it under control. Waiting in line, he pulled out the small *Reflections* book he'd been given as part of the admission fee. It was one of several books authored by the master of ceremonies, Brock Tully. From what he'd seen so far, the guy was quite a character—juggling apples, moonwalking like Michael Jackson, telling silly jokes, and pretending to be shy when he was obviously a stage ham.

He'd glanced at Brock's website the night before, and discovered that his career included time as: a college football and basketball coach; a drug rehabilitation counselor; a recreation therapist; and, an inspirational speaker. In the early seventies, at age twenty-three, he hit what he referred to as 'Brock-bottom'. In his mission to help himself and encourage others to be kind, he'd cycled ten thousand miles throughout

Canada, the United States and Mexico—an enlightening yet grueling feat, he'd since repeated twice. His *Reflections* books were an accumulation of his insights on the human condition and life. He'd also written a couple of children's books. The upshot was that Brandon liked and admired the guy.

Catching up with Elizabeth and Joycelynn, Brandon noticed that someone new had joined their group. Joycelynn quickly introduced the mild-mannered man as Ted Kuntz, who Brandon remembered was a psychotherapist and the author of *Peace Begins With Me.*

"I'm so glad that we came," Elizabeth said, exhilaration lighting her pretty face. "Brock's hilariously entertaining. The energy in the room is incredible, and the beautiful music carries you off to the place in your heart where the angels live."

"You have angels living in your heart?" Ted teased. "I'm guessing you'll never need the services of a counselor; you seem to have all the guidance you need."

Joycelynn tipped her head as she accepted the coffee Brandon held out to her. "Elizabeth does have all the guidance she needs; especially, after her morning *positive affirmations* shower ritual. I don't know what happens in there, but when she hits the breakfast table, she's the most loving, spiritual person I know."

Elizabeth laughed. "What Joycelynn's *not* telling you, is that until the shower helps to ease my hip pain, I find it best to keep to myself."

Joycelynn affectionately glanced at her best friend, before explaining, "During my initial après gambling days, when money was tight and I lived in Elizabeth and Mark's basement suite, I quickly discovered that even earth angels have their rhythms."

"I want to hear about this magic shower ritual," Ted interjected.

"It's how I start my day," Elizabeth volunteered, smiling at Brandon as he handed her a cup of tea. "It involves being grateful, and asking for protection from my spiritual guides."

"Protection *from what*?" Brandon asked, feeling a little like he'd happened upon a clandestine society with a covert dialect. No one he associated with personally or professionally talked about spiritual practices or rituals.

"I ask to be protected from people or events that might hurt me, or my family and friends," Elizabeth explained. "I also seek protection from anything or anyone that might lead me away from my purpose-path. Afterward, I express my gratitude for life's many gifts, and for how I know my day will unfold."

"I noticed you used the word *know*, not *hope*, for how your day will unfold," Brandon said. "Does that work?" Just in case Joycelynn had more questions, he'd put Gregg Braden's *The Divine Matrix* in his briefcase, and was rereading it during his bus ride to work. He'd just finished the section on the "Lost of Mode Prayer" and found it interesting that some ancient philosophers advised praying as if one's hopes and dreams had already happened. It seemed like wise advice, and flowed with the law of attraction in Ronda Byrne's *The Secret*, which he hadn't read, but at the insistence of an ex-girlfriend had watched the video.

"Absolutely! *Knowing* equates with believing and is much more powerful than *hoping*," Elizabeth explained. "Intention, conviction and trust in the universe keep me anchored and centered. I used to suffer from depression, and found that traditional treatments weren't very helpful, but that positive affirmations were exceedingly healing. It's how I stay physically and emotionally healthy." She smiled. "Joycelynn does much the same, but her ritual is at night before she goes to bed. You should take her thirty-day challenge."

"What thirty-day challenge?" Brandon asked, as all eyes shifted toward Joycelynn.

"After I quit gambling, my life seemed to be more filled with challenges than rewards. Broke and consumed by worry, it seemed as though my life would never be right again. One night, deciding to count my blessings instead of my regrets and losses, while sitting on the edge of my bed with my palms turned upward, I expressed my gratitude for my hands and all they allow me to do."

Exchanging knowing glances with Elizabeth, she continued, "Surprised by how many of life's gifts I simply took for granted, expressing gratitude for my hands became my nightly ritual. Within weeks, I was back on track, feeling good about myself and moving forward, instead of looking back. So much so, that we've incorporated both Elizabeth's and my gratitude practices into our *KiK* seminars. Mine's called The Thirty-Day Grateful Hands Challenge."

Knowing that if he were broke and living in his friends' basement, he'd have a devil of a time finding anything for which to be grateful, Brandon asked, "Could you give me an example?"

Passing her coffee to Elizabeth, Joycelynn positioned her palms facing upward and next to each other. "I am grateful for my hands because today they allowed me to drive my car to the store for groceries to nourish my body. I am grateful for my hands because they held the phone that allowed me to communicate with those I love. I'm grateful for these hands: that allowed me to pet the gorgeous golden retriever that befriended me in the park; for giving me the tools to wash my hair; and, that made it possible for me to applaud my appreciation for the wonderful performers we've heard tonight." She reached for her drink, before finishing with, "I'm grateful for my hands because they allow me to hold this delicious coffee that was a gift from a friend."

Brandon's heart warmed as he pictured Joycelynn sitting on the side of the bed, wearing purple pyjamas and with her palms turned up in gratitude. "Listening to you, I have a whole new appreciation for my hands and the amazing daily gifts life offers." The woman had been to hell and back; yet, she still had the aura of wide-eyed wonder. Elizabeth was just as impressive. She had battled and overcome depression, and exuded grace even though she suffered with incessant hip pain. "You two are remarkable."

Grinning, Ted asked, "Are you going to enroll in one of their *KiK* seminars?"

"I just might," Brandon answered, then recognizing the one voice he didn't want to hear, he froze.

"Brandon Ashton, you're such a traitor."

Obviously recognizing Diane's syrupy voice from their encounter at Starbucks, Joycelynn's head jerked around. Resisting rolling his eyes, he introduced the intruder, "Everyone, this is Diane." It hadn't occurred to him that she'd be there, but it should have. She'd left a message in his voicemail inviting him to a fundraiser, which he hadn't returned, never imagining that her invite was to the World Kindness Concert. Diane's style was more art gallery or opera.

"We could have come together if you'd returned my call," Diane whined, while looking past the group and waving at someone she recognized. When Brandon didn't respond, she glanced accusingly at Joycelynn, "I guess you're the reason he never calls."

Joycelynn opened her mouth to speak, before folding her lips inward and pinching them shut.

"Don't forget, you promised Daddy that you'd come this Friday," Diane said, coyly gazing up at Brandon from beneath thick black lashes. "See you then." She strode away, her body-hugging red silk dress accentuating her wiggle, as the faux fox scarf tossed across her shoulder swayed back and forth like a tail.

"Who was *that?*" Elizabeth asked, her eyes dancing amusedly as she looked squarely at Joycelynn. "And why does she have her claws out for you?"

"Diane is Brandon's favorite harem girl," Joycelynn quipped. "We met at Starbucks. The woman seems to have a knack for popping out of nowhere."

"She's pretty," Elizabeth said.

"She's *pretty* scary and apparently bent on stalking me," Brandon grumbled, looking directly at Joycelynn. "Please tell me that you're free this Friday. Her father, Judge Harry Rogers, turns seventy-five this week."

All eyes focused on Joycelynn as she struggled with his invitation. "I'm not comfortable attending a party where the hostess believes I've commandeered her man," she finally answered. "It doesn't seem very kind; especially, considering that she's already feeling rejected by you. Isn't there someone else you can ask?"

"If I show up with *you*, she'll get the hint," Brandon blurted before catching and chastising himself for his selfish disregard of both women's feelings.

Winking at Joycelynn, Ted asked, "How could you possibly refuse such an eloquent invitation?" Chuckling as he faced Brandon, he quipped, "Not much of a ladies' man, are you?"

Hearing Terry's favorite expression sent another wave of heat to Brandon's already hot cheeks. "Guess not," he stammered, feeling glum and dumb. "Sorry, Joycelynn, that's not what I meant...well, it is...and it isn't."

Appearing sorry for him, Joycelynn acquiesced, "I'll go with you if you promise to call Diane beforehand and explain that you and I are just friends." Waving an admonishing finger, she half-kiddingly added the covenant, "Don't you dare leave my side during the party. If Diane doesn't believe you and I are just friends, and clobbers me, I might need you to call an ambulance."

"This is probably none of my business," Elizabeth intervened, "but why don't you just tell Diane that you're not interested?" She glanced from her best friend to Brandon, sympathy in her eyes as she noted Joycelynn's apprehension and his embarrassment.

"Oh, I tried to tell her," Brandon defended himself, while realizing he hadn't been sufficiently direct. Hoping to discourage her, he'd been slow to, or hadn't bothered returning her calls. But he hadn't outright told her that he wasn't interested. Diane liked living life on the edge, and pretty much did what she wanted when she wanted. Rumor around the courthouse was that she'd started dating a lawyer from one of Vancouver's largest firms, which Brandon hoped was true. Diane might be feeling jilted, but he doubted that past her bruised ego, *he* mattered at all. "I think she enjoys taunting me because she thinks that I'm trapped," was what he offered the curious group waiting for his explanation.

"Trapped?" Elizabeth screeched, as all eyes widened.

Frustrated and embarrassed, Brandon barked, "Her father's a judge and I'm a prosecutor in his court. Do the math."

"Career suicide," Ted offered. "Are you sure taking Joycelynn to the party is a good idea? Diane might make a scene. Or tell her father that you're dumping her without warning. If she does, he'll likely sympathize with her and resent you."

"Good point." Brandon raked his fingers through his hair. The dating scene was beginning to wear him thin. "I better talk to Judge Rogers beforehand." He'd simply find an excuse to meet with him in his chambers, and as an aside, ask if it would be okay if he brought a friend to the party.

"Dating is a complicated business," Ted commiserated.

"In my case, marriage was also complicated," Brandon rebutted, recalling the night that his ex-wife confessed her affair and asked for a divorce. Not that he blamed her. The demise of their marriage was textbook typical—husband neglects wife for work; wife finds solace in the arms of another. They had managed to remain friends and occasionally spoke on the phone. But he was still suffering from the sting of her betrayal and his failure as a husband. Feeling like a dumb ass for having asked her in the first place, Brandon directly faced Joycelynn as he said, "I'll understand if you don't want to go to the party." Wishing it were beer, he drained his coffee.

"It might be fun," Joycelynn said, gently patting his arm as the lobby lights flickered. "We should return to our seats. If you like, we can talk more about it later."

Since being divorced, Joycelynn was the first woman Brandon truly enjoyed and admired. She was what his mother would call *marriage material;* however, the crash and burn of one til-death-do-us-part was enough for him. Never again would he risk that depth of pain or loss. Losing Terry wasn't within his control—setting himself up for another failed marriage was. Frustrated and confused, he followed the group back into the theater and took his seat.

Whispering near his ear, Joycelynn asked, "You okay?"

"I will be." Forcing a smile, he wrapped his arm around her shoulders. Her hair felt soft against his skin and smelled like a sweet mix of vanilla and flowers. Kissing the top of her head, he silently mouthed, "*I think I'm falling in love with you, sweet angel. Don't break my heart.*"

The following day, talking with Elizabeth with the phone on speaker mode and sitting on the dresser next to her closet, Joycelynn groaned as she rejected one outfit after the other. "What the heck am I going to wear Friday night?"

"Did Brandon say where the party was being held?" Elizabeth asked.

"At Judge Roger's place in the British Properties."

"Swanky or casual?"

"Semiformal, so I'd say somewhat swanky. According to Brandon, we're having cocktails at seven, dinner at eight, and live music at ten." Joycelynn considered the plum colored crepe dress she'd worn to their first *Kindness Rally*. Recalling her teenage experience with a pair of crepe pants that had shrunk two inches while she walked home one drizzly evening, she absentmindedly asked, "Do you think it will rain?"

"Of course, it will rain. It's November and this is Vancouver. Your hair holds up well in damp weather, so don't worry, just remember to take your portable sunshine."

"Can I borrow some of your jewelry?" Joycelynn asked as she recalled the glittering diamond necklace hanging in Diane's ample cleavage. Not one for jewelry, her own accessories were mostly made of crystal or glass.

"Yes, you can." Softening her tone, she added, "You're falling in love with Brandon."

"I am not!" Joycelynn shrieked, as she moved a bright green jacket and spotted the dress she'd worn to a friend's wedding. "I think I'll wear that sapphire silk shift with the wrap around shawl." She pulled her sweatshirt over her head. "I'd better try it on and make sure it still fits."

"How come you won't admit that you're falling for Brandon?" Elizabeth pried. "You're certainly going to great lengths to impress him. I don't think I've ever known you to be this nervous about a date, not even when you met your last husband."

"My last husband is the reason I'm going to take my sweet time. Before Brandon gets a piece of my heart, I want to be absolutely certain that he isn't going to morph." Joycelynn studied herself in the full-length mirror, thankful that her dress still fit. A little frustrated, she asked, "Didn't we just have this conversation the day before yesterday?"

"Apparently, you're a slow learner," Elizabeth kidded. "What do you mean by *morph*?"

"You know exactly what I mean. Guys pretend to be one way, and then when the chase is over and they have their prey, their true colors come to light."

"Mark didn't morph. He's still the sweet guy I married."

Searching the bottom of her closet for her sapphire shoes, Joycelynn pleaded, "Can we *not* talk about this?"

"The last thing I'll say is, don't forfeit your future happiness because your exes proved that they weren't deserving of your love. Like I said the other day, it's time to start operating from a place of love and let go of your fear."

"I don't know how to stop being afraid!" Joycelynn fought back tears, surprised that she was still emotionally raw. *She'd been divorced for half a dozen years, for goodness sakes!*

"I'm sorry if I'm upsetting you. But until you allow yourself to love with all of your heart, even at the risk of getting hurt, you're *compromising* your love. Which you said, you were never going to do again, remember?"

Joycelynn flopped down on the bed and reached for a tissue from her nightstand. "I know you're right. But I'm not just scared, I'm terrified. Brandon's a great guy and I really like him," she said, lowering her voice to a whisper, "but what if he changes?"

"I don't think he will," Elizabeth reassured her. "He's more stable. You met both of your ex-husbands when they were in transition. The first one had just moved to Vancouver, hated his career and ended up going back to school. The second needed help rebuilding his crumbled business. I think each of them saw you as their damsel in shiny armor."

What Elizabeth said made sense. There were warning signs that she was more committed than either of her ex-husbands had been—big bright red flags that she'd whitewashed with excuse after excuse.

"Joycelynn, you wear your heart on your sleeve. Brandon's the same way. If it helps, I think he's falling in love with you, too."

"Brandon's falling in love with me?!" Jolting upward, Joycelynn paced in excited terror, while arguing against the possibility. "I don't think so! You're just imagining what you *wish* was true."

"He looks at you with loving eyes, and listens to everything you say as though you were testifying in court. You told me that he's an atheist. Yet, he came to the chapel; albeit, to ask you to his aunt's barbecue. He encourages you to talk about your theories and our kindness mission. He invites you out on a date every chance he gets. Just how much proof do you need?"

"Brandon wants me to save him from Diane," Joycelynn said. "How do I know he's not just another guy in constant need of rescuing?"

"The guy wants an ex-girlfriend, a.k.a. current stalker, to get the message that he's not interested. He doesn't need *life* rescuing. He owns a condo on West Beach. He has a stable relationship with his family, even though he disagrees with them on many issues. He was a loyal friend to Terry until the very end. He loves his job as a prosecutor, and women drool when they look at him!" Elizabeth sighed, sounding slightly impatient. "Brandon Ashton respects you as a woman and his equal. You'd be a crazy fool *not* to fall in love with him."

"Does Mark know you feel this way?" Joycelynn teased.

"I admit to being in love with Brandon, but for you, not me. I'm happy with my husband." She lowered her voice, "It's you that I worry about. All you do is work. You haven't even bothered to get yourself another dog, and I know it's because losing Robin broke your heart."

What Elizabeth said was true. Where Brandon was concerned, she was pushing away *joy* to avoid *pain*. Not only by semi-rebuking his advances, but in espousing her theories about the purpose of life and sacrificial teachers, without encouraging him to fully grieve losing Terry. She hadn't recovered from losing her dog; yet, she was suggesting Brandon somehow accept the loss of his best friend because she believed it was

Terry's purpose-path. "I'm such a fool," she whispered into the phone.

"You're anything, but a fool," Elizabeth assured her. "But you've been in self-protection mode long enough. It's time to risk opening your heart again. Go get yourself a cute little mutt from the pound. Tell Brandon how you feel. Or at the very least, admit it to yourself."

"If I promise to think about it, will you promise to get off my back?" Joycelynn lightly chided.

"It's time, girlfriend," Elizabeth continued, undeterred. "You have to let go of your past relationship experiences, just as you did with your gaming experience. You can't teach what you don't practice." She paused before adding, "It was you who said, *'As a sense of self, ego is a great protector. As a sense of being separate from others, the universe and Creation, ego enhances the illusion that you are alone.'*"

"That's your quote, not mine. And exactly how do you think that bit of wisdom applies to me?"

"It applies because you've shut yourself off from love. You aren't alone. You have me, your family and the love of Source to guide you. It's the self-protecting emotions of your ego that are keeping you stuck and afraid, not reality. You teach that animals, people and souls are all interconnected through the universal web of love-energy, or our heartminds. You know that although you can't be with Robin on earth, your love connects you to him through all time and space. Your marriages didn't work out, but the love you once shared can't be erased. Just as the love you feel for Brandon can't be erased, even though you're doing your best to ignore and deny your feelings."

"I know you're right. I've been hiding behind my work and writing long enough. It's time to be brave again."

"Brandon's the perfect guy for you."

"You're sure that he's not going to morph, and start demanding his dinner on the table, or some other macho thing that'll make me crazy?"

"You might want to check out his favorite sports. He could be a couch jock," Elizabeth teased, before saying she had to go and hanging up.

Perhaps it was time to make some changes, Joycelynn mused as she rehung her party dress and put on a pair of jeans. Shored by Elizabeth's wise words, she decided that she'd once again risk her heart to a male, provided he came with four legs, not two.

Within an hour, she drove into the yard of her friend Maggie's local animal shelter. She felt lighter, happier, and a little like the Pied Piper as she climbed out of the car and a trail of dogs followed her up to the house. Knocking on the door, she laughed aloud as a pintsized poodle crossbreed excitedly jumped at her legs. When her girlfriend didn't immediately answer, she knocked again and hollered, "Maggie, I need a dog! Open up!"

"When did you become so impatient?" Maggie asked as she opened the door and hugged Joycelynn hello. "I was on the phone."

"Sorry, but I'm excited." Joycelynn composed herself. "How are you?"

"I could be better," Maggie answered, sounding downtrodden.

"What's wrong?" Joycelynn asked, following her friend through the tiny house and into the kitchen.

"I was counting on a financial contribution from one of our supporters, but he can't do it this year," she said, motioning for Joycelynn to take a seat at the table.

Sitting down, Joycelynn asked, "How much do you need? I could write you a check."

"You and Elizabeth have already helped out enough." Maggie shook her head. "I won't take more money from either one of you this year, so don't even go there."

"What will you do?" Knowing that Maggie meant what she said, Joycelynn's heart sunk. "The animals have to be fed and I'm sure you have veterinarian bills."

"I'll make it. I have some money in reserve, and a couple of other people to call." A sly grin lighting her blue eyes with mischief, she cheekily added, "If you take one of the bigger dogs, you'll help with the food bill."

"How big?" Joycelynn asked, laughing at Maggie's cunningness. The woman was a marvel, the way she recruited volunteers and secured free services so that the meager donations she received stretched as far as possible. "You do remember that my yard is small and not fenced?"

"Spoil sport." Maggie poured water in the coffeemaker. "I guess a horse is out of the question."

"Ha-ha," Joycelynn quipped. "What about this cute little guy?" she asked, referring to the poodle crossbreed that had settled on her lap.

"He has an owner. I'm dog-sitting for an elderly lady who's visiting her sister in Florida."

"Florida sounds nice." Joycelynn drifted to the last vacation she'd taken. It was when she went to Cancun with her ex-husband, and it seemed like a million years ago. Elizabeth was right, it was time for her to come out of hibernation and start living again. She wondered if Brandon might be interested in a tropical vacation, which brought home the realization that if she took home a dog, her freedom would again be limited. But love came with responsibilities, and scheduling around a pet's needs wasn't so much a sacrifice, as it was a privilege. For her, kindness was love in action. Animals, however, were *unconditional* love in action.

"How do you feel about adopting a husky-collie mix?" Maggie asked. "He's under a year old. A couple of days ago, I found him tied to my doorstep with a note attached to his collar saying that his owner couldn't take him to the homeless shelter. He looks a bit scruffy and undernourished, but the vet says he's healthy."

Joycelynn's heart ached for the homeless person who had to choose between shelter for himself and keeping his dog. Living on the streets was a tough go in the warmer months. In the winter it could be fatal. It seemed unbearably cruel than anyone should have to give up their pet so that it didn't freeze to death. "Maybe I can house him for the winter and try to find his rightful guardian in the spring. Did the note mention the dog's name, or how to contact the owner?"

"This isn't the first time a homeless person, or a family in financial distress, has dropped off an animal," Maggie said somberly. "Occasionally, an owner does come back for the dog." She poured the coffee, adding cream to Joycelynn's before placing the cups on the table. "Girlfriend, it's up to you. But if you take this dog, I don't think you're going to want to part with him later."

"You're probably right," Joycelynn mused as she thought about what Maggie had said, and then asked, "Can I meet this dog? Where is he?" She glanced about at the array of animals lounging everywhere.

"He's with Robert in the trailer. I kept him in here last night, but the poor thing barked and paced for hours. I think he misses his owner." She picked up the phone and dialed her sole employee, who worked for board and cigarette money. Within minutes, the man and the dog came bounding through the door.

"It's nice to see you." Joycelynn returned Robert's extended hug. "How've you been?"

"Great!" he chirped, then shoved his hands in his pockets. "You taking Hobo with you?"

"Is that what you're calling him?" Maggie asked and then lightly laughed.

Robert appeared mortified as his glance dropped toward the floor.

Seemingly sensing that she'd hurt his feelings, Maggie quickly asked, "Did you name him after *The Littlest Hobo* television show?"

"It's a great name," Joycelynn interjected. "I might have to change it just a bit. Some people refer to homeless people as *hobos*. I wouldn't want anyone to think that I'm being insensitive if they hear me calling out Hobo's current name."

Robert nodded that he understood.

Joycelynn walked over to pat the stray dog standing as close as physically possible to the worker.

"I think his owner must have been male," Maggie supplied. "He seems happiest with Robert.

"Maybe, I shouldn't take him," Joycelynn said.

"You gotta take him!" Robert bellowed, sounding desperate. "My cat, Scamp, won't come out from under the bed."

"Your cat's afraid of the dog, that makes sense," Joycelynn offered, smiling at Robert. He was such a gentle soul. Maggie had befriended him a few winters back, when he had knocked at her door asking if she had any work. He'd been far skinner then and a bit of a drinker. She'd made him a deal that if he helped around the shelter, he could stay in the trailer at the back of the property. She'd supply him with food and money for smokes, but if he wanted alcohol, he'd have to find the funds elsewhere and agree to never bring it onto the property. Robert had eagerly accepted her terms, and had apparently quit drinking.

Maggie handed her a treat, which Joycelynn held out, noticing how cautious the dog was about taking it. "He's a bit timid. If it doesn't work out, can I bring him back?" It wasn't her intention to sound cold-hearted, but if the poor animal only felt comfortable around men, it didn't seem fair to make him live with a female owner.

"You know you can," Maggie answered as the dog nudged Joycelynn's hand so she'd pat him again. "But I don't think it's going to be a problem."

Joycelynn scrunched down, sitting on the back of her haunches as she took the dog's head into her hands, and face-to-face with him asked, "Hey, boy, would you like to come and live with me?" The dog responded with a large woof, playfully pounced on her, knocking her flat on the floor before he began licking her face.

"I think that's a *yes*," Robert cheered. "He's never done that with me."

"I'll give you some dog food for tonight," Maggie thoughtfully offered. You can start him on whatever you wish tomorrow."

"He eats anything," Robert excitedly supplied, "especially cat food!"

"I'll bet he does." Joycelynn gently nudged the dog aside, sitting up as she asked, "Do you have a leash I can borrow?" Though she still had Robin's leash, she hadn't thought to bring it along.

Maggie nodded as Robert fetched a red leash from the entrance way, where dozens more were hanging.

Looping the lead around the dog's head, Joycelynn apologized, "I want to get this guy home and settled. Do you mind if I don't stay and finish my coffee?"

"You were just distracting me, anyway," Maggie jested, walking Joycelynn to the door. "Call me if you need anything."

Loading her new companion into her car, Joycelynn's mind whirled with a cocktail of excitement, fear and guilt. She was excited to be a pet guardian again, afraid of how incredibly much she was going to love her new companion, and feeling guilty that she was somehow betraying the poor homeless person who had given up his beloved pet. She hadn't offered to pay Maggie anything because her girlfriend would likely refuse the money. Instead, she'd drop off an anonymous cash donation the next day. She also planned to find a way to reunite the dog with his rightful owner, which would undoubtedly rip her heart in two. But as Elizabeth had so wisely said, once felt, love connects souls through all time and can never be erased.

LIVE

❧

"Sing like no one's listening.
Love like you've never been hurt.
Dance like nobody's watching.
And live like it's Heaven on earth.
Mark Twain
American Author and Humorist

When Brandon arrived to pick Joycelynn up for Judge Roger's dinner party, he was surprised to be greeted by Elizabeth, her husband and two dogs.

After giving Brandon a quick hug, Elizabeth introduced everyone. "This is my husband, Mark." She waited as they shook hands. "The Golden Lab sniffing your pockets for treats is Charlie. He's our dog. The husky-collie mix sulking in the corner is Joycelynn's. She calls him Rescue because he's from an animal shelter." Tilting her head toward the droopy-eyed dog, she explained, "Apparently, since she brought him home, Rescue won't eat unless he's handfed. We're here to ensure that he doesn't starve to death while you two are out. He's also afraid of other dogs, so he's a bit of a challenge."

"He looks healthy enough. What was he doing in a shelter?" Brandon asked, glancing around for his date. Unable to see Joycelynn, he presumed she was still getting ready.

"He was dropped off by a homeless person. Unfortunately, the dog isn't welcome wherever his owner is staying for the winter." She smiled warmly. "You know Joycelynn. She's now on a mission to reunite the two of them. I'm sure she'll tell you all about it."

"Tell him about what?" Joycelynn asked as she joined them, her head tilted sideways as she fumbled with putting on the second of the diamond and sapphire earrings she'd borrowed from Elizabeth.

"Rescue's story," Elizabeth supplied as she stepped forward and finished hooking the earring for her friend. "About what a bleeding heart you truly are," she said loud enough for everyone to hear before whispering, "Brandon's eyes almost popped out of his head when he saw you."

Joycelynn wrinkled her nose at Elizabeth, then made her way to Brandon and hugged him. "You're looking very *Gentlemen's Quarterly* in your suit and overcoat." She beamed up at him. "Your haircut looks great."

Helping her on with her coat, Brandon resisted an urge to kiss the nape of her neck, as he softly murmured, "You look absolutely stunning." The familiarity of her sweet vanilla tinged perfume warmed him deep inside. With Joycelynn on his arm, what had once threatened to be a boring affair, now promised to be the soirée of the year.

"Don't forget to feed him at eight," Joycelynn reminded her friends as Rescue came toward her, his sorrowful brown eyes seemingly pleading with her to take him along. Her expression worried, she stooped to pet him. "I'm sorry for deserting you when you're still getting accustomed to your new home. Standing, her faint smile flattened. "You be a good boy for Elizabeth and Mark."

"Rescue will survive a few hours without you," Elizabeth assured her, rolling her amused eyes as she glanced at Brandon. "New mothers are always such worrywarts."

"I'm his aunt," Joycelynn said as Elizabeth gently nudged her toward the door. "Rescue goes back to his owner in the spring. Sooner, if the angels are listening." Glancing over her shoulder for a final peek at the doleful dog, she sighed.

"When we talked this week, you didn't mention you had a new dog," Brandon commented as he backed his car out of her driveway.

"It was a spur of the moment decision," Joycelynn explained, while debating how much she wanted to divulge about what had inspired her to adopt Rescue.

"Adopting a pet is a major decision," Brandon said, sounding curious and hurt.

"I should have told you," Joycelynn admitted sheepishly, suddenly feeling as if she'd done something wrong. She hadn't told him about her sudden adoption of Rescue because she didn't care to explain her reasoning. Without sounding pathetically neurotic, how could she reveal that her fear of being hurt made her afraid to love a dog, never mind a man? Especially, after the way she'd bulldozed Brandon with her theories on the purpose of life before he had sufficient time to grieve the death of his best friend. Taking a bracing breath, she decided that the quicker she came clean, the better—even if her confession sent him running for the hills. "I was feeling guilty, I guess."

"For what?" Brandon's head twisted sideways. "I'm not upset. Rescue's your business."

Joycelynn raised her hand to forestall him saying more.

His brow furrowing, Brandon looked back at the road and hesitantly asked, "What's wrong?

"Nothing's *wrong*. I'm trying to apologize and I'm not sure where to begin.

"Apologize for what?" he asked, his creased brow buckling deeper as he shot her a quizzical glance.

"For babbling on about the purpose of life, when you were first trying to deal with Terry passing over. It was insensitive. What you needed was time to grieve and adjust. Instead of giving you a caring ear, I spent hours yakking about how he had fulfilled his mission and was summoned home." She lowered her gaze to her hands, her voice trailing away, "I'm sorry for not being there for you in the way I should've been."

"What are you talking about?" Brandon asked, sounding dumbfounded. "You did help me to deal with Terry dying."

"If I did help, then I'm glad. But I still think I should've been more supportive and sensitive. Not quite so…preachy."

"You weren't *preachy*," he argued. "The day we met, I was so angry and mixed up, I was dazed. Meeting you helped, and so did your theories." He gave her a caring smile. "Your beliefs about Source and life purpose may not have been able to bring Terry back, but they brought me back."

"But I wasn't totally honest," Joycelynn said in a shaky voice. "In fact, when you find out about all my fears, you're going to think I'm a hypocrite."

"Everyone has fears, Joycelynn," Brandon reasoned, blowing off her concerns with logic.

"I'm trying to tell you that even though I believe with all my heart that we all return to the lovingness of Source, and that our souls are eternally interconnected through love, I want my family and friends alive and well in this world. I can't even imagine how I'd cope with losing someone I cared for as much as you loved Terry." Every night she thanked Source for keeping her family safe and intact, and for sending her miracle friends Elizabeth and Mark. She might be solid in her faith, but she was no different than anyone else—she deeply feared losing the people she loved.

"That doesn't make you a hypocrite," Brandon countered. "Terry was my best friend and I miss him greatly. But he's gone. I can't change that and neither can you. What I can do is remember him. Recognize that *who I am* has a lot to do with *who he was*, and be grateful for having had such a generous and genuine buddy. You helped me to see that, so I don't understand why you feel the need to apologize, or think that by theorizing about life and death you were being hypocritical."

Either Brandon wasn't hearing her, or she wasn't being very clear. She had so much more to say, and his logical responses were driving her crazy. "Please don't tell me that I have nothing to apologize for," Joycelynn blurted as her emotions took rein of her head, and the rest of what she had to say came tumbling forth like a downhill boulder. "I can't even get over losing my dog! I have theories for life and theories for death. But I'm still human. You asked me if I regret being childless, and I gave you my pat answer about not missing what I never had. But that's not entirely true. I was pregnant once and I lost the baby. Twice, I married men that I thought loved me, which apparently they didn't, because they both treated me like crap! Rescue was supposed to help me to stop being afraid to open my heart again, and now I won't even be able to keep him because I'm going to give him back to his owner." Fighting a powerful urge to cry, she locked her arms across her chest and shut up.

Brandon did a quick shoulder check and switched on the car blinker.

He's stopping the car! Joycelynn clamped her crossed arms tighter and cringed. First, he blocked her apology with his legal-like retorts and logic. Now, he was going to make a mountain out of a molehill. She could just imagine his pending inquisition: *Why are you suddenly so emotional? Are you angry with me or life in general? Or are you simply certifiably nuts?*

The car parked, Brandon flicked on the flashers and unclipped his seatbelt.

Preparing her defense, Joycelynn's mind scrambled for rational snippets to explain her irrational tirade. She was exhausted from sleeping on the floor with Rescue, who had panted and paced for hours, and didn't settle down until she managed to coax him into curling up with her in his makeshift bed on the floor. She was also edgy about attending Judge Roger's party as a pseudo date, when their host's daughter had a wild crush on Brandon. Then there was the possibility that she was the victim of one of those rampant hormonal surges that women her age complain about. Root-cause aside, she was walking on the edge of insanity. Hoping Brandon was about to throw her a lifeline and not over the brink, she dabbed at a runaway tear and relocked her arms.

Placing his hand on her shoulder, Brandon gently said, "I didn't mean to upset you by asking why you didn't mention adopting Rescue. I was curious, that's all. And I don't think you're a hypocrite."

He was tossing her a lifeline, which doused Joycelynn's anger but fuelled her humiliation. Her cheeks flaring, she continued glaring downward.

"Why are you angry with me?"

"I'm not angry with you," she finally responded, a catch in her voice as she clung to her tarnished dignity. "But I'm not perfect one hundred percent of the time. So if you're looking for someone flawless, or if you're going to stop the train every time I have an emotional hiccup, then we're in trouble."

"Could you be perfect ninety-nine percent of the time?" he asked in a coaxing timbre.

"Could you?" she haughtily snapped, not quite ready to let go of the anger veiling her self-recrimination.

"You don't think that I'm perfect?" Brandon slapped his hand against his chest as he flopped back on the driver's door and his head hit the window with a thug. "I'm crushed."

"You're a bad actor." Biting back a grin, Joycelynn shifted so that she was sitting more upright and toward him. "How come you pulled the car over?"

"Because I thought you needed to talk?"

Though he hadn't repeated her rapidly fired concerns, knowing they were likely running through his mind, Joycelynn's cheeks soaked up another blood geyser. "Apparently, I need to talk about the things that bother me more than I realized," she confessed, wondering if there were a chance in heaven he'd forget everything she'd said during her mini-meltdown. "But you can't fly in like Mr. Fix-it and magically sweep away my troubles. You have to let me say what's on my mind. Otherwise, I'm just going to find different ways to express what I'm feeling."

"Is that what you think I was trying to do?" He slumped forward. "My ex-wife accused me of not caring about her feelings. She said that she left me because I was so tuned out, I might as well be living on Pluto." Lowering his gaze and his tone, he finished with, "I don't want to make the same mistake with you."

And there it was—his kneejerk reaction to his ex, meeting hers. Like her, Brandon was divorce-fragile. Dating was not for the weak-hearted. Not wanting to repeat their mistakes, they were both guilty of overcompensating, overstating and overreacting. Wow! No wonder, over the years so many of her dancers swore that they'd remain single until the day they died. They were trading the possibility of love for the sake of self-preservation. The seemingly hopelessness of it, welled her eyes with tears.

Reaching for her hand, Brandon cajoled, "If you cry you're going to ruin your makeup."

"The judge's stalker-daughter would love that!" Joycelynn's sniffled, then smirked. "Diane will definitely believe we're just friends if I show up looking like I thought the party theme was the *Rocky Horror Picture Show*."

Brandon chuckled before becoming serious. "Diane's no longer a problem. I took Elizabeth's advice and called her. I told her that I was seeing you now. She asked if I was in love with you, and I told her that I am *very much* in love with you." He tightly squeezed Joycelynn's hand. "I hope that doesn't scare you."

Joycelynn glanced everywhere but at Brandon. Had he just told her that he loved her, or was he merely relaying a fib he'd concocted to get Diane off his back? Was he expecting her to say that she loved him, too? Did she love him? Was Elizabeth right? Was she too emotionally guarded to see the obvious? Theorizing about love was one thing...throwing her hat into the ring again was an entirely different matter. She was happy living on her own. Writing when she felt like it. Coming and going as she pleased. Eating when she was hungry, not because some guy announced that it was dinner time. There was a lot of freedom in being single, and considering her emotional meltdown a few minutes earlier, was she even ready for a commitment?

"Tell me what you're thinking," Brandon murmured in a heavyhearted tone. "Because the horror flashing across your face, and the knot twisting the bejesus out of my gut, tell me that I may have spoken too soon."

Joycelynn lifted her head and stared into his searching green eyes. Was she just seeing what she wanted to see, or was Brandon truly as kind, sincere and loving as he seemed? Dee had said that he was a bit of a player, dating woman after woman since the day of his divorce. But that wasn't what she saw.

"You need to say something before my heart leaps into my throat and chokes me to death," Brandon urged, his expression vulnerable and worried.

Faintly smiling, Joycelynn tried to untangle the past from the present, and fiction from fact. Should she heed Dee's warning, or trust her own instincts? Many times she'd witnessed what might have been a heavenly match between two of her dance members, snuffed out by rumors. Gossip was a natural aftermath of bruised feelings, which was unfortunate because different people brought out varying traits in each other. What went wrong in one relationship wouldn't necessarily go wrong in the next. Still, there were always risks. Past the honeymoon whirlwind of romantic love, could she and Brandon go the distance? Would she bring out the best in Brandon, and vice versa? Were they a match made at Source?

"I get it," Brandon said, misinterpreting her lengthy silence. "It's too soon for you." He bobbed his head resignedly. "I do love you, Joycelynn Rose. And I'm willing to wait until you *trust me* and your *own feelings* before we move our relationship forward." He regarded her sorrowfully before glancing toward her hand locked in his. "But at least tell me whether you're interested in an *us*, or if I'm totally off base?"

As he lifted his gaze to again meet hers, the genuine tenderness she saw in his eyes unhinged yearnings she'd long ago declared taboo. Brandon's divorce had messed him up, too. It was unfortunate that a few females had since suffered the aftermath. However, having witnessed how gently he'd tried to finesse his way out of anything serious with Diane, she realized his intention wasn't to hurt any of them. She knew that she could trust that he wouldn't deliberately hurt her either.

"You're not totally off base," she said, smiling at him as the fog clouding her heart and judgment slowly lifted. She permitted the moment to be just what it was—peacefully loving. She thought of how nice it would be to curl up next to him when the frostiness of an imperfect world chilled her spirits. Imagined lying blissfully cocooned in his strong arms on lazy, promise-blessed days. Mark Twain, the famous American writer and humorist, was right when he suggested: *"Sing like no one's listening. Love like you've never been hurt. Dance like nobody's watching. And live like it's Heaven on earth."*

Flashes of the couples walking together in comfortable silence at Steveston intermingled with her analogy of the weathered fishing boat, and the free spirited seagulls eagerly seeking whatever gifts would be tossed their way. She had a choice to make. She could live beneath the shattering hurts that shadowed her hopes, or embrace her scars as part of what made her whole. As Mark Twain so aptly put it, *love like* she'd *never been hurt.* It was then that she softly whispered, "I choose you."

Brandon expelled a relieved sigh and beamed. "I choose you, too," he murmured, leaning across the console and taking her into his arms as they shared their first unguarded kiss.

His lips softly floating over hers, Joycelynn melted into the magic moment—savoring the taste of the tip of his tongue, the feel of his face touching hers and the smell of his musky aftershave. Imagining her fears floating away on dove wings, she released her past hurts to the sky, and opened the place in her heart that belonged to Brandon. Wave after wave of titillating desire tingled and teased her wanting. Like she'd never been hurt, she relished the innocent sweetness of pure unconditional love.

Slowly releasing his embrace, Brandon laid his head against hers. "We need to talk more about some of the things you told me earlier. However, I think our immediate priority is getting to the party before we are infinitely beyond being fashionably late." Lightly tapping the end of her nose with his finger, he said, "I know you're worried, but don't be."

If it were only that simple, Joycelynn mused. She believed and taught that the purpose of life on earth was to choose love over all of the self-protecting emotions—hate, greed, jealousy, anger, resentment, and *fear.* Yet, that wasn't how she lived. Since her second divorce, fearing more heartache she'd stopped dating. When Robin died, she opted out of getting another dog for the exact same reason. She wasn't choosing *love,* she was choosing *fear.*

Adopting Rescue was a good first step toward accepting that fear of losing what you love is part of the human condition.

Fear born of the ego's illusion of being separate from others and Source—when in reality, all souls are eternally interconnected through love. In the future, she'd remind herself to operate from her heartmind, and honor her soulful origin by loving and living as openly, passionately and powerfully as possible. She would remember to always choose love.

Diane and her new beau were the first to greet them as they walked into the buzzing crowd gathered to celebrate Judge Roger's seventy-fifth birthday. His daughter seemed surprisingly cheerful, not bitter or disappointed, commenting that she was happy to see Brandon had brought a date. Joycelynn didn't know the woman well, but she seemed less flighty, more peaceful. Was she seeing the world through rose colored glasses, or was Diane in love, too?

Joycelynn thoroughly enjoyed the party, including her heartfelt conversation with Judge Rogers about her work at the Youth Detention Center and his time on the Juvenile Court bench. Bantering with Brandon about treat-training his dog being different from true mastering, she laughed so hard she nearly cried. Wrapped in his arms during the last waltz, she felt young and carefree. Her guard down, her heart open, life seemed infinitely filled with promise and joy. Until her Blackberry rang and Elizabeth informed her that Rescue had run away.

After hurriedly saying goodbye to Diane and her father, they raced for home. When they arrived, Elizabeth was beside herself and Mark was still out searching for the dog. Joycelynn quickly changed into jeans and a heavy sweater before racing out the door with Brandon.

An hour later, having circled the neighborhood numerous times with her head out the passenger window hollering for

Rescue, Joycelynn closed her eyes and flopped against the seat. When she did, in her mind's eye she could see Rescue patiently waiting outside the nearest homeless shelter. She immediately knew that the dog hadn't run away—he'd run to where he knew his master would likely be. Jerking upright, she excitedly instructed Brandon, "Head for Covenant House on Drake Street."

"*Covenant House*, what's that?" he asked, outwardly bewildered by her abrupt mood change.

"It's where Rescue is waiting for his owner."

"Rescue would have had to cross the bridge to get to Drake Street. How can you be certain he's there?" Brandon asked, turning the car toward downtown Vancouver.

"Because I saw him with my mind's eye. I know he's there," she breathlessly babbled. "I've been to that shelter. It doesn't allow dogs, but I found one that does. Rescue's owner mustn't have known about it, because he left his dog at Maggie's." She called Elizabeth's cell, and when her friend didn't answer, left a message saying that Rescue was fine and not to worry.

Brandon didn't bother challenging Joycelynn's knowing. "I hope you're right," was all he said.

By the time they reached Covenant House it was raining heavily, and Rescue was nowhere to be seen. "He's nearby," Joycelynn hollered as Brandon parked the car. "I'm going to look for him. Wait here."

"I'm coming with you." Brandon snatched onto her arm. "You're not running around this neighborhood by yourself."

"But what if he comes back here?" She pulled her arm free and jumped out of the door.

"You don't even know for certain that he was here," Brandon shouted as he ran around the car.

Ignoring the freezing rain dripping down her face, Joycelynn fisted her hands on her hips and glared.

Brandon forfeited the argument. "Let's circle the block together. If we don't find him, we can take the car and check other shelters. Okay?"

Miffed that Brandon didn't believe her, and scared that she might be wrong, Joycelynn stormed around the corner of the building. Spotting Rescue, she dropped to her knees and called him. When he woofed and bounded toward her, she laughed and opened her arms wide. Just as he had before, Rescue playfully jumped on top of her, knocking her off balance and backward. There was a loud thump as her skull connected with the sidewalk, then searing pain. Too dizzy to move, she squished her eyes closed and groaned.

"Are you okay?" Brandon asked concernedly, pushing Rescue aside and feeling behind her head. "No blood, but you have the beginnings of a dandy goose egg."

"I'm fine," Joycelynn said as Brandon helped her sit up. "I'm just a little woozy."

"Rescue stay!" Brandon commanded, taking charge. "You, my dear, are going to St. Paul's Hospital." He helped her onto her feet and into the passenger seat before going back for the dog, who surprisingly was still sitting there.

Holding the back of her aching head, Joycelynn watched as Brandon untied his necktie, looped it around Rescue's neck and led him into the backseat.

Within minutes, they were sitting in the hospital's emergency room. Thankfully, the dizziness had subsided, but the goose egg on the back of Joycelynn's aching head had swollen so much that Brandon said she looked as though she had a second nose. For most of their long wait, she rested against his shoulder, except for when she insisted that he check on Rescue. Each time he did, he reported that the dog was sleeping. By the time the nurse called for her, she was falling asleep, too.

After examining her, the doctor said that she might have a concussion, and advised her to stay awake for the next twelve hours. This seemed like an impossible feat to Joycelynn, until Brandon sweetened the deal.

"It's almost five a.m. and only two hours until dawn. Let's go to McDonald's, get a hamburger for Rescue, and coffee for us. Afterward, we can sit in the car outside of Covenant House and see if his owner shows up."

Immediately feeling better, Joycelynn's head cleared and her stomach churned with excitement. "That's a great idea. Let's go!" Jumping off the examination table, the room looped around her and she staggered. Brandon caught her and held on. "What would I do without you?" Settling under his arm, she let him support her bodyweight as they made their way to the parking lot.

Once in the car, Rescue greeted her with a wagging tail and a sloppy kiss, making her grin. When Brandon took out his hanky and wiped off the dog slobber, she started to giggle. Less than a week ago, she'd been worried that she'd never feel safe enough to love another dog or man—now, she was suddenly feeling and receiving more love than she could handle.

"What's funny?" Brandon asked, seeming thrilled to see her coming back to herself.

"Us...tonight...Rescue running away," she said, beaming at him. "When the Gods are angry, they answer your prayers."

Frowning, he asked, "What do you mean by that?"

"Don't look so worried," she said, laughing. "Earlier today, I prayed that I'd be able to find Rescue's owner. Then the silly dog ran away. I bumped my head and ended up in emergency. Now, we're going to go to McDonald's, and at daylight we'll most likely find his owner." She smiled. "That's pretty amazing, don't you think?"

He pecked a kiss on her forehead before fastening his seatbelt and starting the car. "I think you're pretty amazing. Your mascara is smudged, your hair is a rat's nest, and you're still beautiful."

"Thanks…I think," Joycelynn said, as she flipped down the sun visor and glanced in the mirror. "I look like a scarecrow!" She rummaged through her purse for a tissue and went to work on the smudges beneath her eyes.

"I think you look sexy."

"I think we should have had your eyes examined along with my head."

"There's nothing wrong with my eyes." Brandon started the car. "It's a guy thing."

"A guy thing?"

"You know what I mean."

"No, I don't."

"If I tell you, you'll probably clobber me."

"Then you better tell me before we get too far away from the emergency room."

"You look like we just finished making love." He glanced at her sideways, a big smirk lighting his ridiculously handsome face.

"You wish…." She smiled. It was one thing to open her heart; however, sleeping with him wasn't a step she planned on taking anytime soon.

At McDonald's, Brandon handfed Rescue two hamburger patties and about a dozen fries, before Joycelynn put a break to the feeding frenzy by saying, "You'll make him sick."

"*Make him sick!*" Brandon retorted. "He was probably raised on burgers and fries. I'll bet that if I toss a fry into the back seat, he'll gobble it up without caring if he's being handfed."

"You're on." Joycelynn twisted so she could witness the experiment. "What's the wager?"

"If he gobbles it up, you both spend the weekend at my place." He smiled slyly. "If he doesn't, Scruffy and I'll spend the weekend at your place.

"What kind of a wager is that?" Joycelynn chided. "You're such a manipulator."

"Are we on?" Brandon's widened eyes danced expectantly.

"You're on," she chirped, "but with conditions."

"What conditions?"

"At my place, you sleep on the couch. At your place, you sleep on the couch."

"The couch," he groaned. "You won't sleep in the same bed with me?"

"Not yet," she confessed, "I need time." She assumed that Brandon had spent a night, or two, with a woman he barely knew. That like many men, for him, physical intimacy didn't equate with emotional commitment. But for her it did.

"We're getting old, you know. You don't want to wait too long. I wouldn't want our first night together to be a snoring fest."

"We're not getting old...we're getting closer to Source."

"*Closer to Source. Is that your version of we're not getting older, we're getting better?*" He tossed a few fries onto the backseat and Rescue gobbled them down. "I win the bet and I still lose!" Chuckling, he fired up the car and headed back to the shelter. "Let me get this straight, win or lose, whenever we bet, it's me who has to sleep on the couch?"

"Sounds fair to me," Joycelynn remarked with a grin, relieved that Brandon wasn't angry about her stand on them not immediately sharing a bed. She was far from emotionally ready to take that step, however, the idea of spending a weekend together with him and the dogs made her feel happy. She flipped on the radio, pleased when she heard the announcer say that the next two days would be cold, but clear. If they didn't find Rescue's owner this morning, she'd look for him all of Sunday, and whatever part of Monday she could spare. It dawned on her that she'd miss the chapel service, but she knew that the powers-that-be would understand.

As the sun came up, at his insistence, Brandon stood outside the car with the dog leashed to him. Joycelynn remained in the car, with the window cracked open so that they could talk. She was chilled, but refused his urging for her to put on the heater, explaining that letting the engine idle was environmentally irresponsible. Together, they watched dozens of homeless people file out of the building. Some of them appeared wide awake, others looked dazed.

It seemed as though it was the very last person, a longhaired teenager dressed in a black hoody and camouflage jeans, which the dog recognized. Barking frantically, Rescue leapt forward, almost pulling Brandon off of his feet.

The teen stopped and stared at the dog. She could tell that he wasn't certain as to whether his eyes were playing tricks.

But when Rescue began whimpering, the young man bolted toward him.

Joycelynn tried to jump out of the car, but Brandon was ahead of her. His full weight against the door, he cautioned in a stern voice, "You stay put until I make certain that's Rescue's owner and not just someone he recognizes. I don't need you getting dizzy, falling down and cracking your head again."

Feeling trapped and frustrated, she was about to give Brandon a piece of her mind, when the teen dropped to his knees and bear hugged Rescue.

"Lightning! How'd you get here?" For a moment, the teenager didn't seem to realize that his dog was attached to Brandon via a bright blue tie. The dog jumped on him, but the teenager seemed to be expecting it, and managed to keep his balance. After a few seconds, he noticed the improvised leash and followed it up to the person holding it. "How'd you get my dog?" he asked, sounding snarly.

"She's looking after him." Brandon moved away from the car as Joycelynn fully opened the window.

"I'm Joycelynn and this is Brandon." When the teen didn't respond by giving his own name, she continued, "My friend Maggie let me keep your dog until we found you. She's the lady who runs the shelter where you left him. I heard you call him *Lightning*. Is that your dog's name?"

"How'd you know where to find me?" the teenager demanded to know, glaring up at her, his arm protectively across his dog's back.

Guessing that explaining her intuition would be fruitless, Joycelynn said, "He ran away last night, and we found him sitting outside here waiting for you."

"Is that right, boy? Did you miss me?" The teenager seemed pleased, and then his face went sour and pale, as he stood and shoved his hands into his jean pockets. "You gotta take him back. I can't keep him."

"Why is that?" Brandon enquired calmly, obviously hoping that the petulant adolescent would supply a little about how he ended up homeless.

"Cause he doesn't like other dogs. So no matter where I go, unless I sleep on the streets, I can't keep him." Appearing defeated and beaten, the teen's head drooped toward his dog. "He'll freeze to death."

Joycelynn's eyes stung. When Robin died, she'd been miserable and broken hearted for months. Having to abandon his dog was likely equally traumatic for the teenager. "I could keep him for the winter and give him back to you in the spring."

"Why would you do that?" His accusing eyes slid the length of Brandon's car, before he snippily asked, "You got some rich lady do-gooder complex?"

"Yeah, I do," Joycelynn retorted in a stern voice. "Just like you've got some chip on your shoulder that you think belongs on mine."

Stuffing his hands deeper into his pockets and cocking his head sideways, the teen cheekily asked, "What's the catch?"

Joycelynn was about to answer, when Brandon stepped in. "The catch is that you're going to meet one or both of us here every Saturday morning at exactly this time. We're going to take you and Lightning for breakfast, then for a walk in the park. If you don't show up, we'll assume you want us to keep your dog."

Squinting one eye as a sly grin crept across his attractive young face, the teen flippantly asked, "So do I get breakfast starting today?"

All three of them laughed as Brandon opened the car backdoor, stepped aside, bowing as he swept his arm through the air chauffer style.

"Lightning likes McDonald's," the teenager announced, jumping into the backseat. "Been eating there since he was a puppy."

Brandon closed the back door, ducked his head into the passenger window, and stole a quick kiss from Joycelynn before quipping, "I told you so."

More interested in learning about Lightning's owner, than in playing tit-for-tat with Brandon, Joycelynn turned so that she was facing the teenager in the backseat. "In case you didn't hear it before, I'm Joycelynn and that's Brandon. What's your name?"

There was a long hesitation before he answered, "North Bay."

Starting the car, Brandon asked, "*North Bay*, isn't that a city in Ontario?"

"That's where I was born." Staring down at his dog's head, the teen mumbled, "My real name is Michael."

"Pleased to meet you, North Bay," Joycelynn said. "I wish I had a nickname."

"Where're you from?" the teen asked as he stroked Lightning.

"The same place as you, North Bay, Ontario," she answered honestly, delighted that she had something in common with the teen. "My parents moved our family to Victoria when I was seven."

"No shit," the kid retorted. "We could be related. What's your last name?"

"Rose, like the flower," she responded, reminded of how glad she was that she hadn't changed her maiden name when she married. Lots of women did, which made sense if you had children so that there was family identity; otherwise, it was the one thing you came into the world with, that you could leave the world with. Well, that and your soul.

"Guess you're not my long lost mother." North Bay shrugged. "How about you, Brandon, you my long lost father?"

"If I were, you'd be in school, not wandering the streets homeless and dogless," Brandon said and then immediately grimaced.

Joycelynn realized that what Brandon had meant to convey, was that if he had children, he'd make certain they were cared for and safe. Instead, he came off sounding like a judgmental power-freak.

Brandon opened his mouth to explain himself, but before he could, the kid went ballistic.

"You ain't got no right sticking your nose into my business!" North Bay punched the back of the Brandon's seat. "I do okay by me. I don't need no big shot telling me how to live my life. You got it?!"

Joycelynn flinched, but knew to stay silent. There was little sense in getting into the middle of their debate. Besides, she was curious as to how Brandon was going to handle the teen's emotional outburst.

Brandon's knuckles turned white as he squeezed the steering wheel. "Sorry, man. It came out wrong."

"I ain't hurtin' nobody," North Bay stormed, too agitated to accept Brandon's apology. "I just gotta get myself some money. Then I'm going back to school."

"Back to school, eh?" Brandon bobbed his head. "What are you going to study?"

The teen stared out the window, and then in a barely audible sarcastic voice said, "Maybe I'll become a hotshot like you."

"*Hotshot's* an interesting career," Brandon said, seemingly unflustered as he pulled into the drive-through lane at the McDonald's he and Joycelynn had left a few hours earlier. "What do you want for breakfast?"

"Two Big Mac hamburgers and fries," the boy spit out. Then as if suddenly remembering his manners, but still hanging onto his anger, he added, "Please, sir!"

Brandon ordered the food, then pulling ahead to the pickup window he nonchalantly asked North Bay, "If you had a place to stay and the money you needed, what would you study in school?"

There was complete silence from the backseat, followed by what sounded like mumbled cursing, then more silence. Neither Brandon nor Joycelynn said anything, both of them choosing to wait and see what the teen would finally answer.

As Brandon paid for and retrieved the burgers and fries, North Bay finally muttered, "I'd be a carpenter, like my dad."

"A *carpenter*! My father was a carpenter," Joycelynn gleefully supplied, excited to have more in common with the teen. North Bay was doing his best tough guy act, which was typical for an adolescent; especially, one living on the streets. Because of her work at the detention home, she was familiar with the code by which he survived—act tough, or die weak.

"Your dad dead or something?" North Bay asked Joycelynn as Brandon passed him his breakfast.

"He's very much alive and lives by a lake just outside of Victoria, in a house that he built himself," she elaborated as Brandon headed the car toward Stanley Park. "My dad has been retired for a long time, but he sometimes still builds furniture and picture frames for his friends and family. He worked at the Dockyard refurbishing ships for most of his career. He's a very talented man."

"I'd like to build my own house," North Bay commented before chomping into his burger. "My family had a house," he continued between chews, "but my stupid father gambled it away." His voice trailing off, he finished his story with, "Mom left him for good when that happened."

Brandon exchanged knowing glances with Joycelynn.

"I'm sorry to hear that," Joycelynn said sympathetically. "Losing your home must have been tough on your entire family." His father's story was one that she knew all too well. She hadn't lost her home to the bank, but she'd sold it to pay off the credit cards that she had charged to the max. A friend she met at the casino had spent her entire retirement savings, and then sold her rental house to feed her addiction. Another had gambled away his kids' inheritance. One fellow was close to losing his farm, maybe already had.

Seemingly no longer wanting to talk about his family, the teen went to work on his second burger before asking, "You two married?"

"Nope, not yet!" Brandon joyfully supplied.

"Not yet...and maybe never!" Joycelynn blurted, and then seeing the crushed expression on Brandon's face, she explained,

"I'm divorced and not ready to consider ever getting married again."

"I get it," North Bay said. "My parents splitting up was a good thing. All they did was fight, anyway. Mom cried a lot."

"Hold on!" Brandon hollered. "Everybody talks about the marriages that fail, but what about the ones that work!"

Joycelynn was about to debate his point, but when she noticed his dog-tired bloodshot eyes, she changed her mind. Raising her hands in surrender, she smiled before saying, "You're right." Turning her head toward the backseat, she added, "North Bay, I think we better let Brandon win this one, or he'll keep harping on and on."

Brandon chuckled to himself. "I'll bet you a weekend at my place that we'll go the distance."

"You're still sleeping on the couch." She smugly smirked.

"We'll see about that," Brandon retorted with arrogant confidence as they pulled into the park and he stopped the car. "I'll bet you a weekend at my place that you can't resist me for more than five minutes."

"Gee, you guys...get a room," North Bay groaned as he leapt out of the car and Lightning bolted after him.

Joycelynn and Brandon laughed, as he lifted his arm and she snuggled against him to watch North Bay and Lightning playing. About the third time the dog fetched a stick, she turned to Brandon and commented, "You see, that's true mastering. No treat. The dog fetches the stick, brings it back and drops it."

"Look again!" Brandon chortled.

Joycelynn turned in time to see the teen pull a piece of his hamburger from his pocket and give it to Lightning. Apparently, all three of them had gone to the same dog training school.

Smiling, she commented, "I like North Bay. He has a good soul."

"I thought you said that all humans have good souls because we emanate from Source."

"I did say that. I also said that each of us has a purpose and that earth is a school for souls," she said reflectively. "Perhaps North Bay is part of our life purpose. Maybe we're meant to help reunite him with his father." It distressed her that gambling had destroyed the teen's family. She also found it intriguing that her own addiction healing path had led her to Lighting and then the teenager.

"I think the universe sent that kid to test my patience," Brandon jokingly growled.

"Could be. Maybe as payback for something awful you did in a previous life." She grinned.

"People pay you to talk like that?" he chided.

"They do!" she cheeked before becoming serious. "All I really have are theories. My true mission is simply to encourage people to look for the good in everyone. To stop judging each other, and realize that no matter what we *do* or *don't do*, each one of us emanates from pure love."

Nodding, Brandon squeezed her closer.

"The root of my hope for humanity comes from working with teens like North Bay," she explained. "Kids came into the detention center on all sorts of charges. Most were in there for running away from home, theft or breaking and entering. Though it was rare, some were charged with armed robbery or murder. The staff I worked with didn't judge the kids. Neither did we concern ourselves with their alleged crimes. Because we were insulated from the general population, we weren't subject to normal societal pressures and values. All we cared about was helping the kids."

"There's a lot of public pressure to punish kids, when what they really need is a firm hand and love," Brandon interjected.

"It seems peculiar now," she continued, "but there was an unspoken hierarchy of wishes we held for each one of our charges. The ones who did hard drugs, we wished only smoked marijuana. The kids who were potheads, made us wish that they only smoked cigarettes. Our wish for those who smoked cigarettes, was that they'd quit. The ones who stole cars, we wished only stole bikes. The ones who stole bikes, we wished just stole chocolate bars, etcetera." Looking directly at Brandon, she asked, "Does that seem odd to you?"

"It doesn't seem odd, it seems wise. You didn't have a magic wand, realized that you couldn't heal them completely, so you encouraged them to be better people, one step at a time."

Joycelynn nodded. "When I quit working at the detention home, I missed those little buggers like I'd miss a limb. For years, I dreamt about them at night, and worried and wondered about them during the day." She watched North Bay sitting cross-legged with Lightning's head on his lap. There was a faraway gaze in the teen's eyes as he stared into his own blankness. It was a look she'd seen way too often, on all too many young faces, and it made her heart ache. "What I learned from working with troubled teens is that no matter what they've done, everyone is good at his or her core. No one wants to be bad, or do wrong. Life sometimes just knocks a person off course."

"I'm not able to forgive and forget as easily as you, but I mainly work with hardened criminals, not teens. Brandon smiled. "Perhaps there was a time when compassionate intervention might have helped, but by the time someone graduates from juvenile to adult court, they're pretty much lost to the system."

"Same bus, different stop," Joycelynn said, while thinking that no one was ever a total lost cause.

"Working with those kids...being able to see past their actions and into their core goodness was how you came up with your idea of *sacrificial teachers*, isn't it?"

"It is," she admitted, no longer surprised by Brandon's astuteness. "Because of fear or guilt, quite often one of the teens in our care wouldn't be able to sleep, so we'd sit and talk. It was during late night chats, when their defenses were down, that I could see their essential innocence and goodness. Ninety-nine percent of our charges came from families that were far less than ideal, so they never really had a fighting chance. It made me wonder why fate lands some children in situations that breed violence and crime, when their core beings are as pure and loving as yours and mine."

"What do think about North Bay?" Brandon asked.

"I see a nice young man who has no idea where to turn, so he's living on the streets. It appears that his father gambled away their family home and North Bay's life with it. He hasn't mentioned what happened to his mother, but I'd guess from the fact that he's alone, he doesn't view being with her as an option."

"You're going to help him repair his relationship with his father, aren't you?"

"If he'll let me," she replied with a soft sigh. "Unfortunately, beyond that he loves his dog and wants to be a carpenter, we don't know much about North Bay."

"Whatever I can do to help, just let me know." Brandon rolled down the window and waved at North Bay to come back to the car.

As the teen and his dog piled into the back seat, North Bay asked, "Why didn't you guys come out?"

"It's a long story," Joycelynn answered, not wanting to tell him that his dog had nearly knocked her senseless and that she might have a concussion.

"I'm beginning to think that you two have a lot of long stories," North Bay retorted. "Must be because you're old."

"You little bugger." Joycelynn chuckled as she glanced at Brandon and they said in unison, "We're not old, we're getting closer to Source."

"My mom died from a brain aneurism," North Bay blurted, supplying the missing piece as to why he was homeless. "Nobody knew she was even sick. She just didn't wake up one morning."

The car momentarily filled with silence, before Joycelynn softly said, "I'm sorry for your loss. It must be hard for you." When a few moments passed and North Bay didn't respond, she compassionately probed, "How long ago did your mother die?" She wasn't making the same mistake twice. Never again would she babble on about purpose and Source while someone was grieving.

"About a year ago," North Bay answered in a small voice as he stared out the window.

"Do you have any brothers or sisters?" Joycelynn asked, hoping that he did.

"Nope, just me." North Bay hugged Lightning to his chest. "My father took off for the Athabasca Oil Sands project in Alberta. Said he was going to make some money and get us another house. But he never came back. The stupid jerk is probably still gambling away his paychecks."

Joycelynn heard the contempt in his voice and she didn't blame him. Undoubtedly, the kid saw his father as being a selfish idiot. He was too young to understand the horrors and helplessness of addiction. Knowing that it would just aggravate him, she didn't bother explaining his father's robotic compulsion, but she would one day. In the meantime, she hoped to get the teenager to open up. "So you've been on the streets since you lost your mother?"

"I lived with my Aunt Connie for a few months. She's pretty cool. But her drunken boyfriend moved in, so I got lost." Pushing out his bottom lip, he finished with, "She tried to convince me to stay, but I could tell that *he* was glad I was going."

"That's it! You're coming home with me," Brandon declared in a definitive tone. "Whatever personal belongings you have at the shelter, we'll get tomorrow."

Joycelynn had been contemplating the same thing, so wasn't completely surprised by Brandon's offer. North Bay couldn't be more than sixteen or seventeen, an age when he should be thinking about how lucky he was to have his entire future ahead of him. Instead, the kid was more likely figuring his whole life was behind him, and gone. His mother was dead and his father might as well be. His aunt had traded him in for a bunk-buddy. The only family he could trust was a dog, which he had given to a shelter so the animal wouldn't freeze to death in the winter. This was *not* a kid on the wrong path—this was a kid who needed help.

"What makes you think I'd wanna live with you?" North Bay snarled as he shoved his dog off his knee.

His reaction not what she was expecting, Joycelynn stiffened in surprise.

"It's not like you have a lot of options," Brandon calmly responded, ignoring the kid's tantrum. "Lightning needs to be with you, or he's just going to keep running away. You can't keep him in a shelter, not even one that's pet friendly, because he hates other dogs. You want to be a carpenter, and I have a friend who'll give you a job to get you started."

Joycelynn noticed that Brandon negated mentioning that he also had a dog that might present problems for Lightning. Hopefully, Scruffy wasn't territorial.

"Is he always this bossy?" North Bay growled at Joycelynn.

"It's the first I've seen," she admitted, while debating whether Brandon's offer to house North Bay was saintly or insane. They'd known the teen for a few hours, and it wasn't farfetched to think that he might rob her boyfriend's apartment and then bolt. She realized that her thoughts weren't exactly kind, but the human condition wasn't one of perfection. She was pleased that Brandon wanted to help North Bay, but she didn't want either of them getting hurt in the process.

"I won't steal from you," North Bay said, seemingly reading her fears. "In case you're wondering, I'm not into drugs either."

"I wasn't wondering," Brandon answered, straight faced. "I was just going to knock your block off if you ever tried anything that stupid."

Joycelynn inwardly chuckled at how easily Brandon handled the teen. She was fairly certain that North Bay wasn't an addict, because he didn't show any signs of drug-induced paranoia. And the way that he'd wolfed down two hamburgers, said he wasn't suffering from the gut-wrenching pain that generally followed an *ecstasy* high. She also knew that the teenager wanting to be with his dog throughout the winter, was Brandon's hedge against North Bay taking off with a sack full of his belongings before spring.

Settling into her seat, she decided that the guys would get along fine. Hopefully the dogs would, too. Happy for all of them, but saddened that her aunt duties were no longer required, she wondered if she should pay another visit to Maggie's animal shelter.

When they arrived at Brandon's place, and he insisted that she and North Bay wait in the outside hallway while he introduced the dogs, Joycelynn's angst skyrocketed.

Certain that Lightning would try to kill Brandon's dog, the teen animatedly provided a gruesome account of what he imagined might happen.

Brandon assured them both that he was a dog whisperer, and ignoring their fears and protests, slipped into his condominium and closed the door.

When she heard a faint yelp, Joycelynn tried opening the door but it was locked. Neither she nor the teenager dared knock, so they paced and waited. To distract herself, she asked North Bay questions about himself. In between grunts and mumbles concerning Brandon's hotshot ways, she learned that the teen had dropped out of school in grade nine, stayed in sporadic contact with his Aunt Connie, and had given up caring whether he'd ever see his father again.

When they were finally granted entry, Lightning stayed put on a thick blanket by the fireplace, while Scruffy eagerly greeted them with a mountain of slobbery affection.

North Bay quickly made friends with Scruffy, before going to sit on the floor beside Lightning. Glancing from the ocean view to the gigantic flat screen television, he flippantly asked, "You a rich lawyer, or something?"

"Yeah," Brandon replied cheekily. "I'm a crown prosecutor, so don't bother running off with my stuff unless you plan to leave the country."

"I'm no thief," the teen griped, glaring as a smug grin slid across Brandon's face. "If I'm staying here, I'm gonna need a bed." As though he thought it might be a problem, he added, "Just so you know, Lightning sleeps with me."

Glancing sideways, Brandon winked at Joycelynn before retorting, "Any other demands I should know about?" When the teen's sole response was an exaggerated pouty sneer, their host chuckled to himself as he gestured for North Bay to follow him down the hall.

The defiant teen took his time getting to his feet, stuffed his hands in his pockets and sauntered after Brandon. Lightning and Scruffy followed their masters. Joycelynn flopped into the leather armchair and closed her eyes. Exhausted, she groggily calculated that she was supposed to stay awake for another six hours, and then drifted off.

"Nice try." Brandon gently shook her awake. "You can't go to sleep yet. Besides, Scruffy needs a walk."

Joycelynn groaned in protest.

"Come on sleepyhead," Brandon coaxed as he helped her out of the chair. "A walk will do you good."

"Aren't Lightning and North Bay coming?" she asked, glancing around as she put on her coat.

"North Bay needs his space. He's probably going to snoop around and see what he can find." Brandon chortled as he leashed his dog.

"You aren't worried about leaving him here alone?" she enquired, slightly uneasy about Brandon inviting the teenager to move in with him.

"Nope." Brandon wrapped his arm around her shoulders. "My important papers and valuables are in the safe in my office closet. The thing weighs a ton, so North Bay's not going to cart it off. Besides, he's curled up in the center of his bed with Lightning. They'll probably both fall asleep."

"Sleeeep...." Joycelynn leaned into him. "I want to go to sleep, too."

He squeezed her affectionately. "You will, my sweet angel. Just not right now."

Kindness Key # 9

DREAM

❧

"Dreams are the seeds still in the universal storehouse.
To become a reality they must be chosen,
planted, tended, and harvested."
Reverend Barbara Leonard
Author of *Don't Just Stand There Sucking Your Thumb.*

Although Brandon often teased Joycelynn about which of them was going to sleep on the couch should they eventually spend a night together, for the next several weeks their relationship took a backseat to ensuring that North Bay and Lightning felt welcome and comfortable in their new home. The teenager proved to be quite intelligent, and after much bartering and bantering, finally agreed to complete his grade twelve at night school. However, calming more than coaxing was required when he animatedly and eagerly jumped at a day job as a sweeper and gofer for housing development mogul Mike Brown.

Brandon and Mike were longtime friends, and were as excited as the teenager about their plan for North Bay to learn his way around a building site before starting his carpentry apprenticeship. According to them, sweeping the floor and learning the functions of various tools was an important first step to becoming a master craftsman.

During the payoff dinner for Mike having agreed to hire the teenager, Joycelynn howled as she listened to one story after another. North Bay wasn't the first kid her boyfriend had rescued from the streets, just the most recent from a series his friend referred to as *Brandon's loser-to-riches work crew.* Mike had been the first.

The most hilarious story of the evening was about the fisticuff that had brought the two men together. Apparently, when they were both young adults, Brandon caught Mike pickpocketing an elderly gentleman. Horrified, Brandon tackled and headlocked Mike, and then dragged him to the nearest phone booth, where he called the police. For the fifteen minutes that Brandon had Mike's head noosed in his arm, he kept reiterating, *"I'm Superman and today's your lucky day, man. You just gotta make the right choice."*

Mike assumed Brandon was a borderline-psychotic, and somewhere around the fiftieth time he claimed to be a superhero, Mike started praying for the cops to hurry up and arrest him. Brandon's father, who at the time was the local police chief, showed up, handcuffed Mike, tossed him into the cruiser and read him the riot act. Juvy-jail, a.k.a. the juvenile detention home, was gruesomely portrayed as brimming with demented delinquents and sadistic guards who didn't give a rat's ass who beat the daylight out of whom. In the end, Mike had to make a choice—juvy-hell or repent. Repenting included his going back to school, a part-time job, and church on Sundays.

Totally freaked out and figuring his quickest route back to the planet earth was to agree to their conditions, Mike promised he'd do what they asked. He went back to school, but dropped out a month later. He lasted a total of fifteen minutes in church. The job he kept; eventually, working it into a permanent position, then his current housing development business.

"Can I have a housing development business, too?" North Bay fervently implored when they arrived back home and were greeted by two excited dogs.

"Can't see why not," Brandon assured him. "If you're serious about having your own business, then you better finish your grade twelve and take a few business courses. You'll need startup capital, so save your paychecks."

Smiling at his youthful enthusiasm, Joycelynn touched North Bay's arm as she said, "Barbara, our minister at the Inner Garden Chapel, says that *'Dreams are the seeds still in the universal storehouse. To become a reality they must be chosen, planted, tended, and harvested.'*" Brushing the teen's bangs off his forehead, she added, "You can do anything you decide to do. Just listen to your heart, choose a career that brings you joy, and go for it."

North Bay knelt to hug his dog. "Thanks, you guys." He buried his face into Lightning's fur.

She couldn't tell for certain, but Joycelynn thought the teen was crying as he suddenly jumped to his feet, grabbed the dogs' leashes, and headed out the door with Scruffy and Lightning.

The two of them were sitting cross-legged, side-by-side in front of the fire enjoying a glass of wine, when Brandon asked Joycelynn, "Do you think that it's possible Terry had a hand in bringing us together so that we could help North Bay? That all of us meeting was fated?"

"It's possible," she answered, thinking that *fate* was as good a word as any for the meeting of souls with similar purpose-paths.

Brandon bobbed his head, seemingly satisfied with her answer, so Joycelynn asked what was on her mind. "How come you never told me any of the stories that Mike shared at dinner?" Learning that Brandon's dad had been a police chief, and that the two of them regularly helped young adults find their way, had shocked and impressed her. More than before, she now realized that his father's stern ways were definitely born of protective love. Throughout his career, he'd undoubtedly witnessed many horror stories involving the young and the elderly. It made perfect sense that he wanted Brandon's Aunt Katharine and her friend Georgina at home where they were safe from harm. No wonder Brandon's mother didn't argue. She likely believed that her husband's concern was justified. Yet, Brandon was right, too: life is short, precious and meant to be lived—not squandered in fear.

"What's to tell?" Brandon answered modestly, his eyes brightening as he switched back to his preferred topic. "I think North Bay coming into our lives is some divine plan to ensure that we don't consummate our relationship until we're married."

Never certain if Brandon was joking, Joycelynn ignored a mid-region fluttering as he wiggled his eyebrows and grinned. So far he hadn't pressed the issue of them sleeping together, but he would one day soon. She wasn't against premarital sex, but neither was she for jumping into bed with him when there was an impressionable teen in the house. Brandon was well aware of her views, but occasionally tested her resolve with teasing remarks and lascivious innuendos. This was the first time that he'd tossed *marriage* into the equation. Not wanting to egg him on if he was teasing, or hurt his feelings if he was serious, she stuck with her own train of thoughts. "Your father reminds me a lot of some of my Youth Detention Center coworkers."

Brandon's shoulders slumped exaggeratedly forward as he pretended to pout because she wasn't taking his marriage-talk seriously.

After rolling her eyes, Joycelynn continued, "A bleeding heart by nature, when I started working at juvy, it incensed me that some of the workers believed what the kids needed was *tough* love. It especially bothered me when someone imposed what I considered a harsh punishment, such as canceling a day pass. I almost lost it when a probation officer refused a teenager the therapeutic help he was requesting, saying it was just the teen's ploy to make himself look better in court."

"That is a smart ploy! Judges love to hear that an offender is willingly seeking help," Brandon offered.

"It wasn't a *ploy*...it was a distress call." Placing her hand over her heart, she explained, "The teen called me into his cell and begged me to help him get counseling, so I approached his probation officer. His answer to getting therapy for the teenager was a flat-out, *no*! Two days later, when the teen was released on a promise to appear in court at a later date, he committed crash-suicide."

"What's crash-suicide?"

"Teen steals car. Cops chase teen. Teen goes over an embankment, crashes and dies."

"Exiting the system via a coffin is a pretty drastic and desperate strategy." Brandon shook his head in disbelief.

"And sad," Joycelynn added. "He was a very kindhearted teen who always stepped in and gave me a hand when the other kids were being excessively rambunctious. When he died, incredibly angry with his probation officer, it was all I could do not to storm into his office and yell, *murderer.*" She stared into the flickering fire as the teenager's handsome young face floated before her mind's eye. "It took me a long, long time to come to grips with the teen's senseless death, and to stop blaming his probation officer. But eventually I realized that just as I thought that my soft approach was best, his probation officer and our tough-love juvy workers believed that their approach was best. And that although we all made mistakes, together, we were giving a well-balanced blend of love and firm guidance to the young offenders in our care."

"Whenever you talk about your work at the detention home, you always look wistful and a bit sad." Brandon narrowed his affectionate gaze. "It must have been difficult for you to quit working there."

"Very difficult," she admitted. "But it was time for me to move on. Half of me had become numb from heartbreak, the other half overly sentimental. I began to doubt my effectiveness." She recalled the moment that she realized she had to quit. It was during a dinner with her family, when her dad asked her how her day had gone, and she recounted an incident with one of her younger charges. More a behavior problem than a menace to society, the detention home psychologist had placed the thirteen-year-old on a *behavior modification program.* Whenever the boy acted out, the workers were to cut off all communication, and place him in his cell for a short period. She had started sobbing at the part of her story where the freckle-faced teen had pressed his cute little mug up against the screen and repeatedly called out to her, and as part of his program she was required to ignore him. The alarm on her father's face confirmed what she already knew. It was time to resign; which she did the very next day.

"You'd have been a great mother."

"It wasn't in the cards," Joycelynn said regretfully.

"Not for either of us," Brandon offered. "I guess our mutual life purpose is helping other people's children." He reached for her hand. "Can you talk about the baby you lost?"

Reminded of her mini-meltdown on the way to Judge Roger's birthday party, Joycelynn blushed. This was the first they'd talked about her rapidly fired list of regrets and fears, and though she wasn't crazy about reliving the past, particularly that embarrassing moment, Brandon had a right to an explanation. "I can talk about it."

"You sure?" he asked, trailing his finger along her hand. "If it's too upsetting, I'll understand."

"Losing my baby was heart wrenching. It was also poignantly enlightening." She returned Brandon's caring gaze. "It's when I knew for certain that our spiritual being lives eternally. As incredible as it may seem, I know the exact instant that my fetus's heart stopped. When its spirit left my body, my baby cried."

Searching Brandon's face for hints of skepticism, and detecting none, she continued, "It took a bit of time for me to fully comprehend the significance of what happened—even longer to realize the inherent blessings in having glimpsed such intense love, and to understand the miracle of death."

"I thought it was a *blessing* when Terry died because he was suffering," Brandon said, visibly sad. "I don't think I'm ready to see the *miracle* in his dying."

"The *love* that forever bonds and connects our souls is the *miracle*," Joycelynn explained. "I grieved for my unborn child, the same way that you are grieving for Terry. Even though I still sometimes wonder how different my life could have been,

I'm thankful for the divine experience of having carried pure love within me—for knowing that Source emanates through us in love-waves."

Needing to feel physically connected with him, Joycelynn moved closer so that her knees touched Brandon's leg. "In his book *The Divine Matrix*, which I know you read, Gregg Braden talks about the invisible energy field that interconnects us all. It's more than a just a web, though. It's unburdened and unsoiled love, emanating everywhere: In the solid things you can see, taste and touch. In the invisible things you hear, feel and know. If you look into a young child's, Scruffy's or Lightning's eyes, you'll see it—unconditional love in pure form."

"Kids and animals love you no matter what," Brandon agreed.

She smiled. "I believe they love unconditionally, because animals, babies and toddlers are closer to Source, and that ingrained in their innocence is the love we all seek and often miss."

"That's the depth of love you felt when you were pregnant, and why you're grateful even though you lost your baby?"

"It is," Joycelynn answered. "Being pregnant and glimpsing Source's eternal all-permeating love is a gift. When writing about Source's omnipotent, omnipresent love in my last book, I asked the universe for guidance." Still sitting cross-legged, she scooted around so that she was facing Brandon directly. "Would you like to try the meditation that came to me?"

"I would," Brandon said as he leaned forward and gently brushed his lips across hers. "I love you, you know?"

"I love you, too." Joycelynn returned, sitting straighter and with her upturned palms resting on her bent legs.

Brandon mirrored her position. "I've never meditated before. What's next?"

"It isn't mandatory, but it helps if you close your eyes. She waited until he did as she suggested. "Your breathing should be deep and relaxed."

"*Deep and relaxed*...what if I fall asleep?"

"You won't." Closing her eyes, too, in a slow and soft cadence, Joycelynn began, "Imagine that you're standing on a grassy mountain top, where the view stretches for miles and fades at the horizon." She inhaled a deep breath and slowly released it. "Now look up into the vivid blue sky and see it as being alive with love-waves. Picture these rolling, endless waves of love as being invisible, weightless and soundless. Though you can't see, hear, smell, taste, or touch them, you can detect them with your heart. Taking deep breaths, allow that love to come through you and into this world. See yourself as a beacon receiving and emitting the universe's endless abundant love. Allow your mind, heart and soul to fully connect with that love. You're one with this world and one with our infinite universe. You are love-waves, invisibly, weightlessly and soundlessly emanating everywhere, through everyone and everything. You are love. You are Source."

Eyes opened, leaning forward and cupping her knees with his hands, Brandon murmured, "I feel relaxed and light, and as though love was literally coming through me, and then radiating outward."

Pleased, Joycelynn said, "I believe that our heart-sense is our *seventh* sense, and how we communicate with the universe and Source. It's the link between our finite and infinite worlds. What emanates from our hearts in this world, reaches the hearts of souls in the infinite world."

"Our seventh sense connects us eternally through love," Brandon reiterated, gently massaging her kneecaps. "That's why you see the *miracle* in death and the *gift* in losing your unborn child?"

"Yes, there is abundant comfort in knowing we remain forever connected through love."

"You still haven't told me why you the lost baby. Did something happen?" Brandon probed, his expression lovingly concerned.

"Something did happen," Joycelynn said, turning so that her back was to Brandon and positioning her torso between his outstretched legs. Supported by his chest, she felt safe and loved. "Are you sure you want the gruesome details?"

"Are they *gruesome*?" he asked, his voice climbing.

Joycelynn laughed. "Not *gruesome*, but definitely detailed, and we both have to get up early tomorrow."

"I'll risk falling asleep at my desk." Nuzzling his way through her hair, Brandon planted kisses along her neck as he huskily murmured, "If I had my way, you'd be spending the night here."

Joycelynn arched her back as the desire she so fruitlessly tried to harness, broke free in a rush of wanton heat. Rapt with wanting, she moaned as Brandon slid his hand under her sweater and an array of tingles skittered across her abdomen and below.

"Are you trying to have your way with me?" she whispered throatily, twisting around, unbuttoning his shirt and planting teasing kisses across his chest.

"I am," Brandon confessed as they both heard a key turning the front door lock.

"North Bay's home!" Joycelynn screeched, bolting upward and smacking her head into Brandon's chin.

"Ouch!" Brandon ran his hand along his jaw as North Bay and the dogs came barreling through the door.

"Sorry," Joycelynn apologized to Brandon as she pulled her sweater into place and finger-combed her hair. "Are you okay?"

"Nothing my dentist can't fix," Brandon groaned. "You have a hard head."

"Hi, you guys," North Bay said as he hung the leashes in the hall closet and the dogs slurped water. "Don't let me interrupt. I'm going straight to bed."

"You're not interrupting," Joycelynn quickly assured him as Brandon continued rubbing his jaw. "Did you have a nice walk?"

Her words were wasted. With the dogs hot on his heels, North Bay made a beeline for his room and closed the door.

"Where were we?" Brandon asked as he bent forward and softly kissed her.

"We were talking," Joycelynn answered between tiny kisses. "I thought you said that your jaw was broken."

"I heal fast; especially, when the incentive is right."

"You're wasting your breath," Joycelynn retorted, and then turning so that her back was to Brandon, she inched between his legs and rested against him.

Brandon groaned, "Darn kid. Dumb dogs."

"Great kid. Wonderful dogs." Joycelynn laughed. "And you can stop pouting."

"Your back's to me, so how do you know whether I'm pouting?"

"Because I know you." She giggled. "You're pouting."

"I know you want me," Brandon teased. "Admit it!"

"Do you want to keep bantering about something that's not going to happen, or shall I finish telling you what caused me to miscarry?"

"I want to know what happened, so the latter," Brandon said cheekily, wrapping his arms around her. "We can banter afterward."

Nestling into him, Joycelynn became serious. "I was working as a sales representative for a cosmetic manufacturer, and a few times each year, called on clients in northern British Columbia. It was late October and I was four months pregnant. Afraid to drive in the snow, my girlfriend, Roswyn, volunteered to come along. The entire trip up North was a disaster. Our flight was delayed for hours. Thick fog caused our pilot to abort his landing attempt at treetop level on our first milk-run stop in Terrace, scaring the heck out of us. Then the bus that transports passengers from the airport on Digby Island onto the ferry that takes you to Prince Rupert broke down, so we were squished into another one. The door on our first rental car wouldn't close properly, and we had to wait for a replacement vehicle."

"Sounds as if your trip was doomed from the get-go," Brandon interjected.

"It was. Hours late for my first appointment, my client retaliated by refusing to see me until after her lunch break."

"I'd have blown a fuse," Brandon said, reaching for his wine and offering her a sip. "Especially, after what you'd already been through with the plane, bus and rental car."

Joycelynn shook her head to the wine. "I was miffed, all right. Roswyn grumbled enough for ten people." Recalling how her girlfriend had stomped about the store, she chuckled. "But I bribed her with lunch and she calmed down."

"You're far more patient than I'll ever be."

"You're *very* patient," Joycelynn said, thinking of how well he had handled North Bay and the dogs barging in a few minutes earlier.

"Maybe at home," he said with a guttural chuckle. "At work, I'm a grouchy bear."

"Oh, sure," she laughingly retorted, before saying, "Getting back to my story, the second day of our fateful journey wasn't much better than the first. We had a nine hour highway jaunt between Prince Rupert and Prince George. Exhausted and anxious to reach our hotel, we weren't thinking clearly. The radio announcer kept warning of black ice on the roads near Prince George, but because we didn't realize how close we were to the city, we kept clipping along at what we thought was a safe speed. All was fine, until we crested over a huge hill and spotted a chain of cars stopped at a traffic light. Roswyn hit the brakes and we started to spin. She managed to right the car forward with some fancy steering while frantically tapping the brakes. But we didn't slow down. For the next several seconds, as she wrestled to keep control of the vehicle, I kept saying, 'You can do it! You can do it!' She denies it, but Roswyn glanced toward the embankment at the side of the highway, and imagining us rolling over and over, my heart thundered like a war drum."

Shuddering at the memory, Brandon rubbed her arms as Joycelynn took a calming breath. "I thought we were goners. Either we were going to plough into the cars ahead, or careen off the road and flip over. Seconds before we would have crashed, Roswyn pulled into a yield way, and we gradually stopped. Shaken to the core, we slowly drove to a nearby McDonald's. In the washroom, running hot water over my hands didn't succeed in calming my jittery nerves or warm me. I was still freezing cold and shaking like a leaf."

Brandon kissed the top of her head. "You likely couldn't warm up because you were in shock and your blood pressure dropped."

"I likely was in shock," she agreed. "We left McDonald's and drove to our hotel, which was just a few blocks away. Still rattled and rattling when we reached our room, I poured a half glass of wine that I found in the mini-bar, hoping it would help calm my nerves. I was aware that drinking alcohol was a no-no for pregnant women, but also knew that being physically distressed was harmful for my baby. After one tiny sip, an eerie, electric-like current started buzzing throughout my entire body. From head-to-toe, it felt as though electricity, not blood, was streaming through my veins. The buzzing sensation only lasted a few seconds, but it did me in. Roswyn went out for dinner. I went to bed."

"Is that when you think your baby died?" Brandon asked in a soothing timbre.

"I *know* that's when my baby died," Joycelynn answered. "When I woke up a while later, I could hear *two* of me crying. I was sobbing, and inches in front of me, there was a *second me* sobbing. It was incredibly surreal. Dumbfounded, sitting up and blinking back my tears, for a few seconds, I just gaped at *me* looking at *me*. The vision slowly faded, and unable to make any sense of what happened, I dismissed the incident as a stress-induced hallucination." She rolled the stiffness from her shoulders. "When we flew back to Vancouver the next day, I went to a prescheduled ultrasound appointment. The technician couldn't find the baby's heartbeat."

Comforted by Brandon squeezing her closer, she waited to see if he was going to say something. When he didn't, she continued, "Unbelievably sad and mixed up, my doctor advised me to let my fetus abort naturally. That never happened. A few weeks later, I underwent a therapeutic abortion."

"Losing your baby must have been incredibly rough," Brandon said, gently rocking her.

"It was," Joycelynn admitted, thinking of how sad she still sometimes felt; especially, around mothers with newborns. "Knowing that when a sperm fertilizes an egg there is a detectable electric impulse, it makes sense that electricity is also involved when a fetus dies. The electric-like buzzing sensation was my baby's spirit leaving its physical body. When I woke up and there were two of me crying, one was my unborn child. My baby's soul had found a way to convey his or her sadness because we could no longer be together, in physical form, in this lifetime."

"No wonder you're so spiritual," Brandon commented, as he again offered her wine.

This time Joycelynn took a sip before handing the glass back to him. Perhaps, if another conception were part of my destiny, my fetus's soul and mine would have eventually reconnected in this world, not between worlds." She sighed resignedly. "Now in menopause, it would appear that my gift in this lifetime isn't giving birth—it's experiencing the pure, peaceful and potent love-connection of our present world with Source."

After a long moment, Brandon whispered, "Source, God or whoever oversees our universe, certainly knew what they were doing when they picked you to communicate with an unborn spiritual go-between." He hugged her close.

"*Picked* me, what do you mean?"

"Who else would have turned such a wrenching loss into a divine blessing?"

"Each and every one of us honors Source in our own way," Joycelynn said, rotating to face Brandon. "Unfortunately, it's often only the most visible and esteemed professionals who get credit and recognition. Look at you and your father, you both help everyone you can. Your dad's lifelong mission, on and off of the police force, is entirely about helping others. You're dedicated to fair justice. Your colorful aunt and her friend give guidance, love and counseling through reading cards. Maggie devotes her time and energy to stray animals. Barbara thrives on helping the people who come to her chapel. Terry was committed to keeping the streets clean. Without any one of us, priest or beggar, our world becomes less."

As her impassioned speech came to an end, Brandon teased, "I don't know if I should apologize for being proud of you, or applaud."

"I'm soapboxing, again." Joycelynn blushed, as she turned back around and slumped against his chest.

"Are you pouting?" He tickled her sides and she laughed. "I'm proud of you. If you don't like it, sue me!"

"I might do that," she sassed. "You're wasting your time, anyway. I'm not ticklish."

Pulling her to the floor and straddling her, Brandon taunted, "Are you ticklish when you're naked?"

"You'll never know," Joycelynn shot back through laughter.

Grin wiped away, Brandon brought his face to hers. "Marry me, Joycelynn Rose. Marry me tonight."

"Marry you?!" Joycelynn screeched. "You're kidding, right?" Squinting, she studied his expression. *Was he serious or teasing?* She loved Brandon, and was ninety-nine percent certain that he loved her. They were both financially stable, shared the same values, and had a ton of fun together—but. "It's too soon, you know that," she exclaimed, recalling that people could hide their true nature for up to three years. "You've never met my parents and I've only met yours once."

"Then introduce me to your parents. Let's go right now!"

"Dad lives in Victoria and the ferries don't run this late. Mom lives nearby, but is likely already in bed."

His caring gaze trained on hers, Brandon assured her, "I'm serious, and not just about meeting your parents."

"It's too soon," Joycelynn countered logically. "You haven't met my parents or siblings. I don't even know if you have any brothers or sisters."

"I have one sister, five nieces and no nephews," he answered triumphantly. "Now that you know the makeup of my family, will you marry me?"

She loved Brandon, and if it were a year down the road, she would have jumped at his proposal. "You know that it's too soon," she reiterated, slightly deflated. "But I would like to meet your sister and nieces."

"You had your chance to snag me," Brandon jibed, his hangdog look comical. "When you're old and grey and complaining that no one loves you, you're going to regret turning down my offer." Pecking a kiss on her forehead, he flopped next to her on the floor and reached for her hand. "We should introduce North Bay to our families."

"You can meet my entire family at Christmas," Joycelynn suggested. "The usual routine is dinner on the twenty-fifth with my mom, sister and brother-in-law at their place in New

Westminster…followed by dinner in Victoria the next day, with my dad and the rest of my family."

"What about my parents?" he asked, sounding frustrated.

"We can't see your parents on Christmas Eve, because that's when Elizabeth and Mark have their annual Polish Christmas dinner."

Brandon grumbled something under his breath, setting Joycelynn on high alert. Flashes of her ex-husband freaking out, and slamming his fists on the table while hollering obscenities, spiked her anxiety further. Wincing, she became quiet and still as a stick.

"You okay?" Brandon asked, positioning himself on his elbow and peering down at her. "You look as though you just came face-to-face with the devil." When she didn't respond, he probed, "Did I say something wrong?"

Joycelynn took a deep breath while shaking her head. "I'm just worried," she answered, then looked away.

"About what?" Brandon placed his finger under her chin and gently turned her face toward him. "The holidays are going to be a bit problematic, but we'll figure it out."

Sitting halfway up, Joycelynn smacked a kiss on his cheek, before saying, "Thanks for not getting angry." Brandon wasn't like either of her exes. In fact, he wasn't the problem at all—she was. She was looking backward again: living in the fears of the past, instead of the joys of the future. It would take time, but she was going to work on her trust issue.

"Why would I get angry?" Brandon asked, before slowly connecting the dots and probing further, "Did one of your exes have an anger problem?"

"Uh-huh," she admitted.

Brandon laid his forehead against hers. "I might sometimes raise my voice when I get worked up about something. But I have a very long fuse. I think things through, and I don't go off half-cocked."

Relieved, Joycelynn smiled.

"We're good, then?"

"We're good."

Brandon quickly kissed her before asking, "What time is dinner on Christmas day?"

"Around five, I guess. Why?"

"I can ask my mom to have dinner earlier." He grinned mischievously. "We can take both dogs, and when no one is looking we can give them half of each meal. That way, we won't hurt anyone's feelings or explode from eating too much."

"And you think that everyone will be happy to have both of us, North Bay and the dogs all showing up for dinner." Draping an arm over her eyes, she groaned, "This is complicated."

"It is," he agreed, "and we still haven't tossed North Bay's family into the mix. He probably wants to see his Aunt Connie on Christmas day. I don't think we have to worry about incorporating his father into the schedule, because the kid doesn't seem to know whether the guy is even alive." Huffing out an exasperated breath as he flopped back, Brandon teased, "You're the inspirational speaker, so you figure it out."

Joycelynn laughed. "You're the lawyer, you figure it out." Feeling safe and happy, she rolled over and he lifted his arm so she could curl against him. "I love you."

"I love you, too," Brandon said as he held her. "Don't ever give up on us."

"I won't, I promise." She snuggled in closer. "Don't morph."

"I won't, I promise." He chuckled. "Whatever *morph* means."

"Don't mutate into someone I won't like," she said, smiling to herself.

"What you see is what you get," Brandon assured her.

Crazy schedules and family commitments included, Brandon was the perfect mate for her. Content to her core, Joycelynn's thoughts turned to Terry and how his death was the reason she met Brandon. In a roundabout way, Terry was her sacrificial teacher. Closing her eyes, she thanked him for helping her reopen and trust her heart. Nodding off for a moment, she heard him say, *"He's a great guy and you're welcome. Don't take any wooden nickels."*

BELIEVE

"Belief in your dreams, yourself, others,
and the guiding love of Source—
chart the walkway to true meaning, the highway to greatness,
and the flight path to the Life You Are Meant to Love."
Joyce M. Ross

After about a zillion phone calls and conferences, Joycelynn and Brandon had a holiday plan in place. His mother was thrilled that everyone was coming for Christmas breakfast and had made her own arrangements to go to her sister's for dinner. North Bay's aunt was happy to be included, and agreed to meet them for lunch. Joycelynn's friends and family were excited about sharing the holiday with the dogs, the two of them and North Bay.

"What would you like to get your Aunt Connie for Christmas?" Brandon asked North Bay over breakfast.

"Seeing *me* is her present," North Bay cheekily replied as he piled peanut butter onto his toast. When Brandon didn't respond, he softened his tune. "She likes that perfume, Oscar something."

"*Oscar de la Renta*," Brandon supplied. "It's my mom's favorite, too."

"Maybe we can get a deal if we buy a couple of bottles," the teen suggested, splitting a piece of toast in two and giving half to each of the dogs.

"What would you like for Christmas?" Brandon asked, expecting him to say a tool belt. Reports from Mike were that the kid could hammer a nail straight, wasn't afraid of the power tools, and could measure within a sixteenth of an inch. As a result, North Bay had been promoted from sweeper to apprentice carpenter.

"Could you go halfers for a computer?" North Bay sheepishly enquired. "Mike said that if I could come up with half, he'd pay for the rest."

"He said that, did he?" It was the first Brandon had heard about the deal, even though he continually checked with Mike as to the kid's progress. "Do you think Mike might have meant that you should save for your own half?"

"It's not my fault he didn't consider Christmas presents. Besides, if I have to save up at minimum wage, plus keep paying for Lightning's food, I'll be ancient before I get a computer."

"Ancient, you say." Brandon chuckled. "What's the second thing on your wish list?"

"I don't know. Surprise me." The kid stuffed the rest of his toast into his mouth and grabbed his jacket. "I gotta go. Mike will kill me if I'm not downstairs on time." He patted both dogs, then dashed out the door, letting it slam behind him.

Brandon quickly called Mike's cell. When his friend answered, he asked, "What's the deal with North Bay and the computer?"

"If he saves half, I'll give him the rest. Why?"

"He's trying to get me to spring for his half as a Christmas present!"

Mike roared. "That kid has an angle for everything. What are you going to do?"

"Your deal, your call," Brandon replied in his lawyer voice. "What's he want it for?"

"For school, of course. Most kids have computers these days."

Brandon sank back in his chair. He hadn't even considered that North Bay would need a computer for his studies. "I'm out of touch, I guess," he mumbled as the buzzer rang, indicating that someone was at the lobby door. "Gotta go. Let me know what you decide."

Checking the monitor, he saw Joycelynn smiling up at the camera, and she was loaded with presents. Brandon groaned. He didn't have a clue what to get for her, and her gifts were ready to be placed under the pathetic tree that he and North Bay had decorated. Kissing her cheek as he greeted her at the elevator, he teased, "You buy out the store?"

"Don't worry, they're not for you. I don't exchange Christmas gifts, in case you're racking your brain about what to get me."

"Thank God." He kissed her full on the lips. "So what are these?"

"They're birthday presents for North Bay."

Wondering why the kid hadn't asked for a computer as a combination Christmas and birthday gift, Brandon shrieked, "Today's his birthday?! How could I not know such an important date?"

"His birthday isn't until July. He needs clothes, so we're celebrating all the ones that we missed."

"You got him sixteen presents! Are you crazy?"

"If you consider socks, shoes and underwear as being gifts, then, yes. If you only count the jeans and shirts, then, no, I didn't."

"You got him clothes. How'd you know his size?"

"I went through the laundry hamper one evening last week when you two were walking the dogs. I found out his size, figured out his tastes, and went shopping."

"I could have taken him shopping," Brandon said, embarrassed that he hadn't thought to buy the kid some decent clothes. North Bay pretty much lived in his hoody, various T-shirts and jeans. He'd just thought that they were the kid's favorites, not that he needed clothes.

"I want him to feel comfortable when we make our Christmas rounds," she explained. "I just hope he likes what I picked out."

"If he doesn't, he'll probably sell them on the street so he can buy a computer," Brandon grumbled as he helped her stack the gifts on North Bay's bedroom dresser.

"Doesn't he use yours?"

"He wants his own. And he doesn't use mine because I keep it locked." He again mentally kicked his own butt. "I never thought to offer him the use of my computer, and he never asked."

"I think he tries to shrink around here," Joycelynn offered.

"*Shrink?*" Brandon shook his head bewilderedly.

"I mean that he does his best not to be noticed. He doesn't want to impose because he's afraid that you might start to regret his living here."

"I'm an idiot." Brandon spiked his fingers through his hair and plunked down on the teen's bed. "I'm not very in tune with him, am I?" He looked to her for reassurance, not certain that he deserved any.

"You're in tune, just not always aware." She bent to kiss Brandon's forehead, then headed for the door, wagging her index finger as she walked. "One way or the other, he needs access to a computer."

Brandon leapt up, grabbed her arm and spun her around for a real kiss. Afterward, he laid his head on her forehead as he said, "I love that you're so thoughtful, but you're spoiling the kid."

"You can't spoil kids with love. I don't know who came up with that dumb idea, but you'll never get me to buy into it." She fisted her hands on her hips. "If you want North Bay to succeed, he needs the tools to make it happen. Life has changed a great deal since we were in school."

Brandon nodded. "I suppose he needs a cell phone, too."

"Yes, he does. That can be your special birthday present." Joycelynn winked before heading for the elevator. "See you tonight. You're cooking, remember?"

Brandon smiled as he closed the door. Joycelynn was one smart lady. He would never have picked up on North Bay tiptoeing around the joint so that his presence wouldn't be an imposition. Neither would he have thought to get him a cell phone, or considered getting him a respectable Christmas outfit. He still wasn't sure the phone or the computer should be gifts. If the kid didn't save for them himself, how was he going to learn the value of money?

Having spent the day scouting parks and meeting with various city officials regarding suitable places to stage *KiK's* annual 'Largest Human Peace Sign' Concert, when Joycelynn arrived back at Brandon's that evening, she was totally exhausted. However, her energy quickly picked up when North Bay came bounding out of his room wearing his new black jeans, chocolate brown hoody and sneakers.

"Thank you! Thank you! Thank you!" The two dogs barking their heads off behind them, the teen gave her a lengthy bear hug that had her gasping for breath. When he finally released his embrace, she fell back against the hall wall, catching Brandon's countrywide grin as she barely uttered, "You're welcome."

"I don't know why you did it, but it's the nicest thing anyone has ever done for me." North Bay hung his head as he mumbled, "I love you guys," before bolting toward to his room.

"Where are you going?" Brandon hollered after him.

North Bay stopped in his tracks, shrugging as he stuffed his hands into the pockets of his new jeans. "I'm going to my room, like I always do."

"You spend far too much time in your room," Brandon said as he helped Joycelynn with her coat and hung it in the closet. "I picked up a movie that I thought we could all watch after dinner."

"Sounds good." North Bay turned to leave.

"Don't go running off. I need your help with dinner." Brandon tossed a conspiratorial glance at Joycelynn.

"You need help calling for pizza?" North Bay smirked.

"You cheeky bugger." Brandon dashed across the room and playfully noosed the kid's head in his arm. "Just for that, you're doing dishes, too."

"Don't we just chuck the paper plates in the garbage with the cardboard box?" North Bay bantered as he wrestled to get free, totally ignoring the dogs, which were barking excitedly.

"If you two don't settle down, you're going to have the neighbors at the door," Joycelynn scolded on her way to the kitchen. Spotting what was to be dinner, she chuckled. It wasn't pizza. It was brown paper bags filled with takeout Chinese food. Folding her arms across her stomach and leaning against the refrigerator, she waited for the show.

After fighting to be first through the door, the two guys took turns punching each other's arms. When North Bay spotted the takeout food, he doubled over with laughter.

"What? We're using real plates." Feigning self-satisfaction, Brandon puffed out his chest.

"It's almost like you cooked," North Bay jibed.

"Sometimes almost is good enough," Brandon countered with a minimum of conviction. "Now do me a favor and put out the food."

Leaning against the fridge next to Joycelynn, they watched as the teen plunked three plates and the bags of food on the table.

"We've got a guest for dinner." Brandon's eyes twinkled devilishly as he glanced at Joycelynn. "Don't you think we should at least put the food in serving bowls?"

North Bay grumbled something about what a waste of time and effort it was, then set about rummaging through the cupboards for big bowls. In protest, each door he opened, he slammed closed.

Knowing that her boyfriend was up to something, Joycelynn kept her eyes on Brandon.

"You happy now?" North Bay asked as he dumped chow mein, deep fried pork, and rice into the mismatched bowls.

"Almost," Brandon retorted. "We need serving spoons and cutlery."

"Who was your maid last year?" North Bay griped, as the dogs sniffed at the food on the table.

"Never mind last year. It's today that matters."

North Bay opened the cutlery drawer, his usual slouch jerking royal guardsman straight. "What's this?" he asked, slowing turning around, seemingly dumbfounded as he held up a cell phone with a bow stuck to it.

Joycelynn's heart melted. Brandon had taken her advice.

"That phone is how I'm going to track you down if you run off with my stuff," Brandon joked. "It has a kid-finder in it."

"*A kid-finder*," North Bay played along. "You planning on having it embedded in my ear?" He bolted across the room to shake Brandon's hand.

"Could do." Brandon snatched onto the teen's hand, pulled him in for a back slapping hug, overtly surprised when North Bay hung on for dear life. "Don't go getting all mushy on me now."

"Wouldn't think of it." North Bay hugged him harder, deliberately squeezing the breath out of him.

"Don't be going all macho, either." As North Bay released his hold, Brandon staggered backward and doubled over. "You trying to kill an old guy?"

"I think you might be cooking, after all." Joycelynn pointed at the table and laughed so hard her sides hurt. The dogs had not only finished the food in the bowls, they had ripped apart the bag with the fortune cookies and eaten those, too.

"Pizza!" Brandon and North Bay said in unison as they high-fived each other and roared.

Polish Christmas Eve dinner at Elizabeth and Mark's proved to be a culinary pig-out for Brandon and North Bay.

The teenager consumed three cups of borscht, and two full plates of various fish dishes, mushroom perogies and potato salad. Brandon paced himself with only one cup of the beet soup and two plates of food. Joycelynn limited herself to one small helping of each.

Aware of how he felt about organized religion, she wasn't certain as to how her beau would handle her best friends' Catholic tradition of breaking and sharing host wafers, while wishing each other a prosperous future. She needn't have worried, though, because Brandon seemed to thoroughly enjoy the experience. During breakfast at his parents' place the next day, he announced that he and Joycelynn would likely make it their family tradition, too. She didn't bother to point out the odds against there ever being room in their complicated holiday schedule to hold their own celebratory feast.

North Bay thought breaking bread was truly cool, and when they met his Aunt Connie for Christmas lunch at the Four Seasons Hotel, he excitedly described the ritual as being symbolic of the last supper Jesus got to eat with his disciples.

His aunt seemed nice enough and was very happy to see her nephew. The only sour point was that she insisted on calling him by his birth name. More than once, she reminded him that *Michael* was his grandfather's name, and that he should be proud to be called by it. Aside from that, their visit was pleasant.

In the car on the way to their next engagement, North Bay became quietly pensive. This was his first Christmas since his mother's passing, and considering his father's continued absence, Joycelynn assumed he had the Christmas blues. Wanting to give the teen the space he needed, Joycelynn flipped the radio on low and settled in for the drive.

Brandon apparently had a different idea and decided to cheer up the kid by suggesting, "How about when Joycelynn and I get married, we adopt you at the same time?"

"You can't do that," North Bay snapped gruffly. Then, in an innocent voice, he asked, "Can you?"

"We can do anything we like." Brandon reached for Joycelynn's hand. "Maybe not legally, but we could have some kind of ceremony."

"We can." Joycelynn smiled in spite of the sudden nervous twitching in her gut. Brandon was slowly but surely setting the stage for them to be married. Half of her liked the idea, the other half was petrified. She was done with gambling with her life. But which was the bigger gamble, not marrying Brandon, or marrying him?

"You should get married on Valentine's Day," North Bay piped up from the backseat. "That way you only have to get one present for two occasions."

"Good thinking." Brandon chuckled as they arrived at Joycelynn's sister's home. "Plus, I'll never forget our anniversary."

"You two are quite the pair, aren't you?" Joycelynn teased, though she wasn't really kidding. North Bay and Brandon had developed a relationship, which to an outsider would look like father and son. She chose to picture herself more as North Bay's older sister and Brandon's girlfriend. It made her feel younger. But the truth was, although they lived in separate places, since the teen had come into their lives, they'd become a family. It was then that she decided—should Brandon propose sincerely, she'd say, yes. Whether she'd agree to a Valentine's Day wedding, she wasn't quite certain. It seemed a bit too cliché and way too soon.

As she expected, her family in New Westminster and in Victoria loved both men and both dogs. Though they were all stuffed full and dead tired when they arrived back at his place late Boxing Day, Brandon insisted that she come in for a glass of eggnog before he drove her home. The minute they got in the door, North Bay dragged himself and the dogs off to his room. Knowing he was tired, not shrinking out of the way, neither of them encouraged him to stay and visit.

"That was a great Christmas." Joycelynn snuggled up with Brandon on the couch, her head on his shoulder.

"It's not quite over." Brandon leaned sideways, reached in his pocket and pulled out a small red velvet box. "This can be whatever you want it to be," he said, staring at her lovingly. "I can't imagine not having you in my life forever; however, I don't want to pressure you." Handing her the box, he finished by saying, "It can be either a promise ring or an engagement ring. The choice is yours."

Her heart beating faster than a hummingbird's wings, Joycelynn slowly opened the box. "It's beautiful," was all she managed as she stared at the heart-shaped solitaire diamond. She knew that he meant for it to be an engagement ring, for it was far too impressive to be a promise ring. Brandon was officially asking her to marry him.

Surprised by the tremendous sense of blissful harmony that engulfed her entire being, she realized that there would be many times they would walk together in tranquility. Many days that would be filled with laughter. There would be challenges, too. But they would get through them, just as they had their crazy, complicated and exhausting holiday schedule. Her eyes filled with happy tears as she took the ring from the box and handed it to him. "I'd like it to be an engagement ring."

Brandon slipped the ring on her finger, then after softly brushing his lips against hers, he used the corner of Scruffy's blanket to dab away her tears. When she laughed, he pulled her close to him, and tucking her under his arm, whispered, "I love you."

"I love you, too," Joycelynn said, silently thanking Source for sending her Brandon, North Bay and the dogs. Just in case their meeting was part of Terry's life purpose, she thanked him, too.

Closing her eyes, she nodded off in her fiancé's arms and dreamt that they were floating hand-in-hand amongst beautiful billowing pastel colored clouds in soft pinks, blues, greens, and purples. After a while, Terry came into her vision. Apparently, he was again visiting her because Brandon couldn't hear him. When she asked Terry whether he had any messages for his best friend, the sweetest smile slid across the departed man's face. "Tell him it's nice here and way to go, Bud." His voice and form slowly faded, so she wasn't positive, but she thought he also repeated what he'd said the last time he appeared to her: *"Don't take any wooden nickels."*

When she awoke it was morning, and Brandon was nowhere in sight. Still tired and too sore to move, lazily staring at the ring that was the symbol of their love, she thought about a quote from her book: *Belief in your dreams, yourself, others, and the guiding love of Source—chart the walkway to true meaning, the highway to greatness, and the flight path to the Life You Are Meant to Love.*

She would never have guessed that a life filled with the guilt, regret and shame of addiction, would be the first step in the pathway to so many gifts. Believing in herself had given her the courage to become an advocate for gaming reform.

Believing in others, gave her the courage to ask Elizabeth and Mark for the help she desperately needed emotionally and financially. Belief in her dreams had taken her back to writing. Believing in and asking for guidance from Source, had steered her toward becoming a kindness ambassador, which led her to Dee and then Brandon.

Living *the life you are meant to love* isn't rooted in circumstance, good fortune or miracles—it's rooted in belief.

Brandon came into the room carrying two cups of coffee and smiling as though he'd just won the lottery. "If you tell me that you've already had a shower, fed the dogs and gone for a run, I'm going to need to know what vitamins you're taking," she grumbled good-naturedly. "My butt's sore, my back aches, and I feel as though I haven't slept a wink."

"Good morning to you, too!" Brandon's smile widened as he handed her coffee. "It was your idea to sleep on the couch if you ever stayed the night, so don't complain to me." He kissed her forehead.

"You're right. It's my own fault." She smiled sleepily as she sat up straight and inhaled the sweet smell of vanilla. "Thank you." It crossed her mind to tease him about being overly confident that she'd eventually spend a night with him, just to see if he concocted an elaborate story for why he was now stocking her favorite coffee flavor. Instead she said, "I dreamt about Terry last night."

"I sometimes dream about him, too," Brandon responded contemplatively as he sat next to her on the couch. "It's weird, but whenever I dream about Terry, we're always sitting or walking together, but neither of us ever says anything. I always get the feeling that he's trying to tell me something, but he can't speak."

"I think it's you who can't hear," Joycelynn offered gently, then asked, "Does the expression *don't take any wooden nickels* mean anything to you?"

The hair on Brandon's arms sprang straight. "It was our secret code when we were kids; kinda like a pinky swear. No one knows our code, not even his sister," he said, his shock and disbelief visibly apparent. "Did he say anything else?"

"He said to tell you, *'It's nice here and way to go, Bud.'*" Taking a sip of her coffee, she noticed that Brandon had added just the right amount of cream.

Brandon rocked his head in disbelief. "Terry always said 'Way to go, Bud' when he was proud of, or happy for me." Tears dampened his eyes, as though the magnitude of how much he missed his best friend had just hit him like a flying baseball to the nose.

Joycelynn reached for and squeezed his hand.

After a few moments, Brandon's brow arched and his eyes opened exaggeratedly wide. "You must be right. There must be a reason for people and earth. We must all be souls on some kind of journey or mission." He cleared his throat and smiled. "I guess we better start taking our adopted son to church on Sundays."

"You didn't make that a part of the deal for him staying here?" she chided. Though she sometimes teased them about it, she never pressured Brandon or North Bay to go with her on Sunday mornings. She loved honoring Source at the Inner Garden Chapel and spending time with Barbara Leonard, Elizabeth, the various guest speakers, and their fellow worshippers. The guys, however, were free to *believe in* and *do* whatever they pleased.

"Can your minister marry us?" Brandon asked, sounding hopeful.

"We're a relatively new chapel, so not yet. Barbara's waiting for her marrying privileges to come through, which I think will be sometime in January, or early February."

A wide grin leapt across his face. "I told you that North Bay was right when he suggested we get married on Valentine's Day!"

"You're not going to turn out to be one of those *I told you so* husbands, are you?" she asked, pretending to be worried.

"I might." He pulled her close. "But only when I'm right."

"Being a typical guy, I'm guessing that you're predicting that'll be most of the time." She snuggled into him, feeling happily relaxed; although, she realized their quiet time together wouldn't last long. North Bay would likely come charging out of his room any minute. When he heard the good news, his animated congratulatory response would likely involve him whooping and the dogs barking.

Brandon kissed the top of her head. "I was right about you."

"I was right about you, too. I guess we were both right."

"You should've been a lawyer. I was right about that, too."

"Is having the last word going to be another one of your annoying traits?" She poked him in the ribs, knowing she had him in conversational checkmate: if he answered he'd be doing exactly what she was accusing him of doing.

Brandon held up his cup and winked.

ACTION

> "Once I have mastered peace within,
> only then will I experience peace
> in my family, my community, my
> country, and finally, the world."
> Ted Kuntz
> Psychotherapist, Speaker & Author of *Peace Begins with Me.*

Elizabeth was the first person Joycelynn called with the good news, followed by her family, then Barbara Leonard to ask if she'd marry them in the small chapel. Talking with each of them, Joycelynn had the feeling that everyone had been holding their breath hoping she'd find the man of her dreams. After having met him, apparently they were all hoping that man was Brandon.

"Thank Source!" was her best friend's initial response, followed by an excited frenzy of wedding ideas, encouragement and marriage advice. Her younger sister commented that Brandon was not only a nice man, he was gorgeous. Her older sister offered to make the wedding cake, which Joycelynn gleefully accepted. Both sisters enthusiastically agreed to be her bridesmaids. Her brother teased her about saddling herself with another ball and chain. Her father seemed very pleased when she asked him to walk her down the aisle. Always protective, her mother questioned whether she was certain Brandon was right for her. When Joycelynn assured her that he was, she said she was happy for both of them. Barbara was the most animate of all, gaily going on about how honored she was that Brandon and Joycelynn would be the first couple she married at the chapel. She was equally elated that they were going to unofficially adopt North Bay at the same time.

After the last call, blissfully content, Joycelynn flopped back on her bed. Not one person had said that they thought she and Brandon were getting married too soon, or implied anything other than sheer happiness for both of them. Elizabeth's encouraging comment that this marriage would be the one that lasted forever, was the closest she heard to anything remotely negative. Knowing her best friend was speaking from a place of love, not animosity, Joycelynn ignored the kick to her gut that always accompanied any reference to her previous marriages.

Lying on the bed staring up at the ceiling while she waited for Brandon to report in with the results of his announcement calls, Joycelynn contemplated how she wanted to decorate the dance hall for their reception. They were getting married on Valentine's Day, which was a Monday, and had decided to hold their reception the following Saturday at a special singles dance reunion, so that everyone she loved could be part of their big day. After a half hour of waiting for Brandon's call, too excited to wait any longer, Joycelynn hit the speed button to his landline. When he answered he sounded distraught.

"What's wrong?" she asked, her heart thumping as she jumped to worst possible scenarios. Had his parents told him that he was stupid for marrying a recovering gambling addict? Did they think she and Brandon were getting married too soon? Were they insisting that the wedding be in their church?

"It's North Bay," Brandon whispered. "I'll have to call you back."

"Is he hurt?" she shrieked, her stomach churning.

"Not physically, but he's pretty upset," Brandon answered. "His father's in town and wants to see him."

"I'm on my way," Joycelynn's said, not bothering to ask Brandon if he thought she should come over. North Bay was her adopted-son-to-be, and she intended to be there for him—always.

Within a half hour, she walked through Brandon's door to find the teen sitting on the couch hugging his dog. After a concerned glance at her fiancé, she went to sit next to North Bay. "You okay?" she asked as she stroked Lightning's fur.

North Bay's emotionless eyes stared through her. After a few moments, in a voice marred by frustrated hurt, he numbly mumbled, "My father's back in town and wants me to go live with him."

"What do you want?" Joycelynn asked, worriedly glancing at Brandon. North Bay was sixteen, which meant that legally he was still a minor. If he was dead set against living with his father, he could go the family court route. Having abandoned his son, his father would have a tough time convincing a judge that the teen should be returned to his care. She hoped it didn't come to a court battle because it would further harm their father-son relationship; perhaps, beyond repair.

"I want to stay here!" North Bay bellowed defiantly. "It's not fair if Lightning has to leave Scruffy."

The idea of not living with North Bay and his dog saddened her, as did the prospect of the teenager being further distanced from his biological father. Forcing a smile, she calmly said, "We'll work this out together. You're not alone anymore. You have Brandon, me and the dogs. Who knows, maybe having your father back in your life will be a good thing."

"If he tries to make me live with him, I'm just gonna run away," North Bay threatened.

"That's it!" Brandon shouted, his hands clenched as he paced. "I'm calling my dad. He'll get one of his buddies to run a criminal record check, and we'll soon know exactly what North Bay's father has been up to. Maybe he's…," he started to speculate, getting carried away by his emotions and likely about to suppose something such as *wanted in Alberta and has come running back to escape the law*. But when Joycelynn shot him a warning glare, he shut up.

Drawing her eyes away from her zealous fiancé, Joycelynn calmly suggested, "Why don't we meet with your father and see what he has to say? We could invite him to come here for dinner so he can see how happy you and Lightning are living with us. Once he knows that you're being well cared for, maybe he won't insist that you live with him."

North Bay's snarly frown softened as he considered Joycelynn's suggestion.

Brandon stopped pacing and went to join them on the couch. With North Bay sandwiched between them, he playfully shoulder-checked North Bay and boasted, "I'll even put him in a headlock and tell him that I'm Superman, if that's what it takes to make him see reason."

Picturing that scene, both Joycelynn and North Bay chuckled. Curious, Joycelynn asked the teenager, "How'd your father find you?"

"Aunt Connie gave him my cell phone number," North Bay answered, sounding a bit peeved that she had.

Remembering their conversation about whether giving the teen a cell phone was a good idea, Joycelynn leaned forward and faced Brandon, her warning gaze wide beneath raised eyebrows as she relayed the message, *don't you dare say I told you so.*

Catching her drift, Brandon chortled before asking, "What's it going to be, Joycelynn's suggestion to have dinner with your father, or my Superman idea? Because I'm thinking that if you choose my idea, I should rent a costume."

"Dinner *and* you wear your Superman costume," North Bay shot back, sounding more like his good-natured self.

"Dinner it is." Brandon jumped up and retrieved the teen's cell phone off of the floor where he'd thrown it after speaking with his father. Holding it up to his ear, he grinned as he said, "Still ticking, so I guess it's still working."

Groaning, Joycelynn rolled her eyes at her fiancé's dumb joke.

North Bay reached for the phone and checked to see that his cell was indeed still working. "Sorry, man. I shouldn't have thrown it." He grimaced repentantly before saying, "I'm gonna call him from my bedroom."

Joycelynn moved her legs out of his way as North Bay nudged his dog off of his lap and stood up. "Try not to get too upset by anything he might say," she cautioned. "Remember, we're right out here, if you need us."

North Bay nodded as he slinked toward his room and Lightning followed him.

"Yeah, and don't give him your Hotmail address. I don't want you chucking your new computer across the room if he emails you," Brandon teased as the kid disappeared, and he slid across the couch so that he was sitting right next to Joycelynn.

Relaxing a little, Joycelynn lifted Brandon's arm and snuggled up to him. Dying to tell him about the positive responses to her wedding announcement calls, she asked, "Did you get a chance to talk with your family?"

"Why would I talk with my family?" Brandon asked, doubling forward as she jabbed his ribs with a good poke. "Mom was ecstatic. Dad was reserved at first, then happy. He thinks that Aunt Katharine will have to cut her hippy shenanigans short and come home by Valentine's Day."

"Doesn't your dad like me?"

"He likes you a lot," Brandon quickly reassured her. "He just doesn't like it that we're not getting married in *his* church."

"We can get married in your parents' church if it keeps peace in the family," she offered, slightly disappointed by the idea.

"No, we can't! It's our marriage, not his." He smacked a quick kiss on Joycelynn's cheek. "But thanks for offering."

"Do you think that your aunt will come home early? The idea of her shortening her trip because we're getting married doesn't feel right."

Pulling Joycelynn with him, Brandon puffed out his chest as he sat further back on the couch. Planting his long legs on the coffee table, he boasted, "I've already taken care of that little problem. I phoned Aunt Katharine on her cell and she *is* coming to our wedding." A mile-wide grin spread across his face. "I've already booked her and Georgina two roundtrip airline tickets so that they can fly in for the wedding, then go straight back to California the next day."

"Your father's going to kill you." Her fiancé was both smart and conniving. "Don't you dare use trickery tactics like that when you're dealing with me." Narrowing her gaze, she kiddingly warned, "I know where you sleep."

"No, you don't," Brandon played along. "You've never been in my bedroom! You haven't even met Fat Cat."

"You have a cat!" Joycelynn exclaimed, bolting upright. "I want to meet him...or her."

"Fat Cat's *male*," Brandon supplied, seemingly amused.

Joycelynn jumped off of the couch and headed for the hallway. Brandon always kept his bedroom door closed, which she assumed was because he was too lazy to make his bed, and likely had clothes tossed everywhere. She never considered that he might have a cat hiding in there away from the dogs.

Laughing, Brandon followed her down the hall and into his room. Fat Cat was curled up in the middle of the bed, and barely acknowledged them as he nonchalantly lifted his head.

Sitting on the paisley patterned brocade bedspread, Joycelynn gently stroked the cat's fur. The room smelled fresh. His closet doors were ajar and she could see that his pants, shirts and suits were organized by color, as were his shoes, which were perfectly aligned beneath his clothes. The en-suite door was open, and she could see that his toiletries were also neatly aligned. "You're a sneak and neat freak," she teased him, feeling somewhat inadequate about her own housekeeping regiment. Always on the run, she generally tossed her clothes on her bedroom floor, where they remained until she did the laundry.

"I'm not a sneak. I told you I had a cat the first day we met," he said truthfully, not mentioning his fear that when she finally met him, Joycelynn might want to put his cat on a diet. "The neat freak part might be true."

"How are we going to live together?" she groaned, flopping back on the bed. "Compared to you, I'm a complete slob."

"We'll get a housekeeper," he said, straddling himself over top of Joycelynn. "I told you I'd get you into my bed one day." Bending his head, he nibbled her ear.

"We're back to *I told you so,*" Joycelynn complained, wrapping her arms around his neck and ignoring the goose pimples his nibbling aroused.

Brandon responded by licking her face like a puppy would.

"You're such a pain," she giddily protested as she yanked her arms down and tickled him, delighted when he wriggled wildly. Inching her fingers into his sides, she taunted, "If you want me to stop, you have to say *uncle.*"

Brandon grabbed her arms, pinned them above her head and grinned.

Fearing he'd lick her face again, Joycelynn whipped her head to the side, laughing when Fat Cat sauntered across the bed and put his nose to hers.

"You two should remember to close the door tightly," North Bay quipped from the doorway as both dogs barged past him and into the room. Fat Cat immediately bounded off and then under the bed. Lightning went straight for the cat food, and Scruffy leapt up beside them.

Joycelynn and Brandon exchanged *oh-oh* glances, then both jumped up.

North Bay hooked onto Lightning's collar and dragged him out the door, then stood just inside the room as Brandon did the same with Scruffy. When both dogs were locked out, Joycelynn knelt down and tried to convince the cat to come out from under the bed.

Once the commotion settled, Brandon sat on the bed and asked North Bay, "How did your conversation with your father go?"

North Bay shrugged. "He said he'd come to dinner."

"Did you set up a time?" Brandon asked, as Joycelynn scooped up Fat Cat and gently rocked him.

His shoulders slumped, North Bay plopped down on the opposite side of the bed. "Tonight," he supplied, wincing as though wondering if he'd done the right thing.

"Works for me," Joycelynn chirped, as Fat Cat jumped out of her arms and onto the bed. "Who's cooking?"

"You are," Brandon quipped, "unless you want Pizza or Chinese."

"I haven't cooked for anyone but myself for a long, long time," Joycelynn teased, her arms raised in surrender. "But if you two are brave enough to trust my culinary skills, then I'll do my best *not* to give you food poisoning."

"I'm feeling brave," Brandon said cheekily. "How about you North Bay, are you feeling brave?" He tackled the kid from behind, pulling him backward and putting him a headlock. "Show me how brave you are, North Bay," he taunted, as the teen fought his way free and jumped on Brandon.

Thinking *boys will be boys*, Joycelynn headed for the kitchen. She'd find out which, if any, spices Brandon stocked, and then go shopping. Just before she closed the bedroom door behind her, she hollered over her shoulder, "Brandon's ticklish."

Contrary to the picture that North Bay had painted of his father, Brandon was pleasantly surprised when the fiftyish man arrived exactly on time, and wearing a smart sportcoat, dress pants and a crisply ironed shirt. He introduced himself as Dylan Brown, and politely refused Brandon's offer of a beer, saying he'd prefer a cup of coffee.

Joycelynn headed for the kitchen and returned a few minutes later carrying a tray with three coffees and a coke for North Bay. She'd obviously already figured out that in addition to having a gambling addiction, Dylan might also have a drinking problem.

The first few moments were awkward and strained as they all settled in the living-room, until Dylan asked his son about his schooling plans.

North Bay was reluctant to answer at first, but became increasingly excited as he told his father that he was working toward his grade-twelve equivalency, and would be a journeyman carpenter within a few years.

Dylan seemed pleased that his son was following in his career footsteps. On the way to the dinner table, he put out his hand to shake Brandon's as he said, "It's nice, what you've done for my boy."

Deciding he liked him, Brandon shook the man's hand and nodded. Although his heart and head were at odds, he inwardly acknowledged that living together would likely give Dylan and North Bay the best shot at repairing their relationship.

"We usually eat pizza or Chinese takeout," North Bay volunteered, digging into his mashed potatoes, "but Joycelynn and Brandon are getting married soon, so we're hoping that she cooks for us sometimes." The teen smirked conspiratorially at Brandon, who winked back.

"If they're getting married, I guess it's a good thing that I came back to town so you can move in with me and give the newlyweds some privacy," Dylan said, obviously hoping to persuade his son with commonsense tinged with guilt.

"We're perfectly happy with the idea of all of us living together," Joycelynn interceded, tapping her nails on the table. "North Bay's a lovely boy, and the two dogs get along well."

"Surely, it's going to get a bit crowded once you're living here fulltime," Dylan countered. "Spending a few nights a week with these two might be fun. But I don't know if the same would be true if they were both always underfoot."

"Where's your place?" Brandon asked, hoping to avert Joycelynn and Dylan turning their friendly debate into an all-out war.

"Coquitlam," Dylan answered as he glanced toward his son. "Might be a bit of a bus ride for you getting to and from school and work, but as soon as I find job, I'll buy a car and maybe drive you."

"I'm not moving to Coquitlam!" North Bay bellowed. "I'm staying here. Mike picks me up in the morning, and my school's fifteen minutes from here." Sneering, he continued ranting, "Give me a good reason why I should move twenty or thirty miles away. And don't say it's because you're my father, because you ain't been around for two whole years. You didn't even come for Mom's funeral." His fists locked around his eating utensils, his eyes glaringly defiant, he threatened, "I'll just run away. Go back to living on the streets where you can't find me."

A long silence followed as Joycelynn and Brandon exchanged distressed glances.

"I get it," Dylan eventually said, and the hangdog look on his face said that he did. "I don't blame you for not wanting to live with me. Everything you've said is the truth...except for your complaint that I wasn't at your mother's funeral. I was there. I drove all night long to make it on time. Damn near didn't, because the junker I rented crapped out in the mountains, and I had to hitch a ride the rest of the way. I saw you crying by your mom's coffin. I saw you shrug off your Aunt Connie when she tried to comfort you. And I watched you standing by your mother's grave for hours after everyone else had left."

"Why didn't you tell me you were there?" North Bay asked, appearing puzzled and hurt.

Dylan put down his fork and leaned his elbows on the table. "You'd just lost your mother, and I could see you were hurtin' badly. I figured you didn't need me adding to your grief."

North Bay glanced down at Lightning, gave him a piece of chicken, and then began stroking the dog's head.

All of them too upset to eat, the three adults exchanged silent glances.

After a few minutes, the teenager mumbled, "Provided I can bring Lightning, I might *think* about coming to your place on weekends. If I leave without him, he'll run away." Seemingly worried that his father wouldn't believe him, he added, "Just ask Brandon."

"It's the truth," Joycelynn volunteered, when Brandon didn't immediately jump in to backup North Bay. "Your son loves his dog so much, that when the weather turned cold this fall, he gave him to an animal shelter so Lightning wouldn't freeze to death. I adopted him and named him Rescue. The poor animal missed his rightful guardian so much, the first chance he got, he traveled dozen of miles and across a bridge to find North Bay."

Getting up from the table, Joycelynn walked over to North Bay and placed her hands on his shoulders. "Dylan, we love your son. As you know, Brandon and I are getting married. The wedding is on Valentine's Day, which is a Monday. I realize that it might entail taking a few hours off of work should you find a job, but we'd like it if you came. Because with your permission, we'd like to informally adopt North Bay at the same time."

Surprised that Joycelynn was springing their adoption plans on the guy so soon, and fairly certain that North Bay's father wasn't going to like the idea, Brandon waited for the explosion.

All heads turned toward Dylan as he glanced from one pair of inquisitive eyes to another. "I can see that I'm outnumbered and outwitted." Squinting, he cocked his head and twisted his mouth sideways. "I didn't know what to expect when I agreed to having dinner with the three of you. On the phone, and a few minutes ago, North Bay made it pretty clear that he wants to live here, not with me. I'll be honest and say I'm disappointed about that, but not for the reasons you might think."

After a few seconds, he explained, "When North Bay's mother threw me out, I swore to myself that I'd quit gambling, and headed for Alberta's Athabasca Oil Sands to make as much money as I possibly could. My goal was to save enough for a down payment on another house. My credit was destroyed, but hers was good. I figured she might take me back if she had a nice house to live in again."

Clearing his throat, he glanced downward. "She died before I could make that happened. Her dying hit me hard; so after her funeral, I went back to gambling and started drinking pretty heavily. For the next six months, I poured myself into a bottle and wrapped myself up in self-pity. I spent every dime I had saved, and then some."

Taking a deep breath, he looked squarely at his son. "Your Aunt Connie called me when her boyfriend moved in and you moved out." Dylan chewed on the inside of his cheek for a moment. "That did it! I knew that you needed me. So I dried out, went back to working double shifts, and saved up enough to come back here and start again. That's when I called you."

North Bay glared at his father. "You were gone for two whole years and didn't even bother to call or write. Why should I believe that you give a crap now?"

"When she was alive, I called your mom every month. She made it pretty clear that she didn't want me near you. She said that I wasn't setting a very good example, and that her leaving me wasn't just about the money. Claimed she didn't love me anymore. I kept calling just the same. Every time I asked to speak with you, she said you were out. After she died and you went to live with your Aunt Connie, I called *her* every month. She told me to leave you alone until I dried out and quit gambling for good. She was right to keep you away from me then, Son, because I was pretty messed up." He sucked in a long breath, leaned way back in his chair, and cupped his knees with his hands. "I know how hard these past few years have been for you. It may be a lot to ask, but perhaps one day you'll be able to forgive me."

For what seemed an eternity, North Bay said nothing. When he couldn't stand the silence any longer, Brandon decided to say what he was thinking. "Dylan, you appear to be a decent guy, and I don't hold your gambling or drinking against you. Everyone's life-path is different." Pausing, he glanced at Joycelynn, hoping that she wouldn't kill him for what he was about to say. "My fiancée, here, was an addicted gambler. You may have read about her, or seen her on the news."

When Joycelynn smiled, Brandon continued, "She quit gambling and is now a gaming reformist, as she calls it. She thinks, and I agree with her, that casinos are predatory hellholes; mere breeding grounds for addiction and all the social ails that it causes." Leaning to his right, he placed his huge hand on North Bay's slight shoulder. "This kid of yours will likely be as surprised as you to learn that it was Joycelynn's gambling addiction that led her to become a kindness ambassador. She's very successful and now teaches others to be kind to themselves, as a way of encouraging them to be kind to others."

Looking directly at Dylan, he said, "My point is, bad things happen to good people...don't be too hard on yourself." Squaring off with North Bay, he added, "And don't *you* be too hard on your father." Sitting way back in his chair, he crossed his arms over his chest. "You've both lost a woman you loved dearly and two years of loving each other. Don't waste any more time looking backward. It's today forward that counts." His voice trailing off, he finished with, "Life is short."

Pride shining in her eyes, Joycelynn reached under the table and squeezed Brandon's leg.

"Are you sayin' that I should go and live with my father?" North Bay asked, his worried tone matching his expression.

"I'm not telling you what to do," Brandon responded as he put his hands up, surrendering any further involvement in the decision. "All I'm saying is that when you get back to loving each other, the rest will work itself out."

Dylan remained quiet, seeming to want to leave the decision of where he wanted to live in his son's ballpark. After a few more minutes, North Bay resumed eating his dinner as though nothing had happened. Not knowing what else to do, the rest of them picked at their meals.

When he had completely cleaned his plate, the teenager claimed he was tired, and without bothering to say goodnight, headed for his room.

"Well, I guess that's that," Dylan relented when the three adults were alone. "North Bay has made it pretty clear that he wants to live here, and I get it. I haven't been much of a father for the past half a dozen years, not just the last two. I was living with his mother when I first started gambling heavily. Sometimes I'd get caught up in a poker game and stay away for days on end. I lost our home, which split up our family, and eventually landed my kid on the streets. I'd hate me, too."

"He doesn't hate you, he's afraid. He thinks that if he moves in with you, something might happen to send you back to drinking and gambling," Joycelynn offered empathetically. "I know that look he gives you. It's the same doubtful expression I saw on my loved ones' faces for the first few years after I quit gambling. He doesn't trust your word, and you can't blame him. He wants to believe in you, but he's hurt and scared."

Dylan nodded. "God, I wish none of this had happened." He peeked in his coffee cup, and seeing it was empty, picked up a napkin and twisted it in his hands. "You know, North Bay's mother and I fought a lot, but until I started gambling heavily, it was never about anything serious. She'd rag on me about taking out the garbage or mowing the lawn before it turned to hay. But we loved each other. We had a good life."

His reminiscent smile fell flat as his eyes locked with Joycelynn's. "Then one Saturday night, we decided to go gambling at the new casino that had just opened in our area. She won big that night…about a couple of thousand dollars. That was a ton of money for us, so she talked me into going back the next weekend. I won big that time. We were hooked. Thinking that we'd finally found our gravy train, we both decided to run our luck to the end. Well, we did that, all right." He shook his head. "We both lost the money we'd won and a lot more. After a few more weekends, she gave up; said gambling was a poor man's stupidity tax. But I kept going." Sighing, he finished with, "What I wouldn't give to turn back the clock."

Sitting straighter in her chair, Joycelynn reached out and placed her hand next to Dylan's. "My story is similar. I lost everything, too. Except I wasn't married, I was recently divorced."

"Did you get divorced because of your excessive gambling?" Dylan asked.

"No, there were other reasons for my divorce. The catalyst for my addiction was winning a large jackpot; although, getting divorced a short time later didn't help. Neither did losing a good friend, who died shortly before my addiction kicked into gear."

"There are a lot of hurtin' and lonely people in the casino," Dylan offered. "I can't believe how many elderly people, most of them probably on meager pensions, are in there for half the night trying to chase away their emptiness...many likely losing his or her kids' inheritances along with their own dignity. I feel sorry for each and every one of them."

"Do you attend Gamblers Anonymous meetings?" Joycelynn asked.

"Every day and twice on Sunday," Dylan responded proudly. "The first thing I did when I came back to town was find a local meeting. How about you?"

"I didn't go that route," Joycelynn answered. "I read a lot of self-help books, regularly attended chapel services, and solicited the support of friends and family. Two good friends,

Elizabeth and Mark, helped me out financially by letting me stay at their place. At my request, they kept a pretty close watch on me, so I couldn't sneak off to the casino. Eventually, I found my way back to me." Her expression caring, she added, "And you will, too."

Brandon noticed that Joycelynn didn't elaborate on her kindness aha moment, likely for fear the conversation would veer away from the intent of the evening—reconnecting North Bay with his father.

"It's finding my way back to my son that has me most worried," Dylan confessed, solemnly looking toward North Bay's bedroom. "I let him down big time, and he's just a kid."

"He's a resilient kid," Brandon offered encouragingly. "He's bright and has a big heart. Just give him time."

"I miss North Bay, and I'd like him around all the time. But I know that he's happy here," Dylan said, sounding hurt. Bobbing his head as if trying to accept that his son wasn't coming to live with him, he turned to face Joycelynn and half grinned. "I can see why he'd take to you. You're much like his mother. She was a good little woman…pretty, kind and a fine cook."

"Thank you." Joycelynn ignored Dylan's sexist depiction of what he obviously thought were the most important female qualities. "Coquitlam is a long way for North Bay to commute to work and school. I heard you say that you might chauffer him back and forth once you get a job and a car." Tilting her head sideways and smiling demurely, she said, "I can't see the logistics of that working out in the long run. Can you?"

"I guess not," Dylan agreed.

"I'm going to suggest something that I think will work for all of us," Joycelynn continued. "A few miles from here, I have a house that needs some work. I bought it earlier this year, with the idea of having my retired father help me fix it up. He's a carpenter, too." Shifting in her chair, she folded her hands in her lap. "I don't have a view of the ocean like Brandon does, but my house is in a cul-de-sac and overlooks a greenbelt. The area is very pretty and peaceful. Brandon and I have decided that after we're married, we'll live *here*. We haven't talked about it, but I don't think we should sell my house, because real estate in the immediate neighborhood is undervalued."

She quickly glanced Brandon's way, before looking back at Dylan and saying, "If you're willing to do the renovations, I'll pay for the materials. In exchange for your labor, you can live there, rent free, for the next two or three years. That should give you enough time to finish saving for a house of your own. Because it's not far from here, North Bay can split his time between both of our places without worrying about how he's going to commute to work and school." Crossing one leg over the other, she reasoned, "Maybe you can work on the renovations together, which I think North Bay would like. Your son is ambitious and wants to have his own housing development business one day."

Brandon affectionately squeezed Joycelynn's knee. He liked her idea. It took the pressure off of North Bay having to choose where to live, and ensured that their budding family stayed intact.

Dylan had listened intently to everything Joycelynn had said. Seemingly wanting to give him time to think about her offer, she began clearing the dishes off of the table.

When Dylan finally spoke, his narrowed glance trailed Joycelynn as she moved about the kitchen. "I'm grateful for your offer, and I'll think about it." His brow furrowed deeper.

"But I need to know…besides loving my son, why would you help me out? Take such a huge financial risk on a self-professed gambling addict who has been known to go on extended drinking binges?" Cocking his head sideways and grinning guy-to-guy at Brandon, he asked, "What's to say that I won't just freeload off of you for a few years, then skip town without doing any of the work you want done?"

His fiancée had started the ball rolling, so Brandon decided to let her keep it in play. He understood Dylan's guy-to-guy condescending grin, heard the flippant sarcasm in his tone, and realized the man thought Joycelynn was a fool for trusting a complete stranger. He waited for what was sure to be a fiery response from her.

Joycelynn rejoined them at the table. Sitting schoolmarm straight, she rested her clasped hands on the table and looked pointedly at Dylan. "Why would I think that because someone has an addiction, or two, that he or she isn't a good person?" Glowering, she inhaled a deliberately long breath before finishing with, "Because if you're implying that I shouldn't trust you because of your addictive nature; by association, you're also implying that I can't be trusted because I'm an addict and was once foolish enough to gamble away my life savings."

Dylan sheepishly glanced toward the floor. After a few minutes, he said, "North Bay was reluctant about spending some weekends with me in Coquitlam. How's he going to feel about me living so close by?"

"I'm going to discuss that with him later," Joycelynn answered, her shoulders and back relaxing. "There are a few other things I need to talk to him about, too." Her voice tender, she smiled before asking, "How do you feel about Brandon and me including our unofficial adoption of your son in our wedding ceremony?"

"To be completely honest, at first I thought it was weird… two people who've known my son for a few months wanting to unofficially adopt him. But I can see how much you care about him, and vice versa. I'm guessing that your plan came about because my boy felt he was all alone in this world, and you wanted to show him that he wasn't." Twisting his mouth, he glanced between Joycelynn and Brandon. "I still think it's a bit left field. And even though it seems a bit unnecessary now that I am back in his life, I'm not going to oppose your adoption idea. Like I said before, Joycelynn reminds me of his mother; although, my wife was never quite as opinionated or vocal." He smiled guiltily at Joycelynn, as though apologizing for his earlier remarks.

Joycelynn returned his smile and nodded.

"A teenage boy needs a loving mother who'll hold his hand when his heart gets broken and bring him chicken soup when he's sick." He turned to face Brandon. "He also needs a strong man in his corner; someone who'll kick his butt when he gets off track. That's why I moved back." He ran his hand along his grin adorned chin. "But I can't see any problem with my son having two men watching his back."

Brandon extended his hand and Dylan shook it. Joycelynn followed suit, shaking North Bay's father's hand before saying, "I hope you can come to our wedding-adoption ceremony. It would mean a lot to us and to your son."

"I'll do my best," Dylan said, pushing his chair back from the table and standing. "I should get going. It's a long bus ride back to Coquitlam."

"I'll drive you." Brandon jumped up and headed toward the hall closet.

Taking his coat from Brandon, Dylan argued, "That's way too much to ask. I'll just take the bus."

"I insist." Putting on his own coat, Brandon winked at Joycelynn. "That way she has to do the dishes." In keeping with Dylan's attitude toward females, he considered quipping something about her being a *good little woman,* but didn't. If he was ever foolish enough to say anything anywhere nearly that sexist, he wouldn't put it past Joycelynn to clobber him.

Standing tiptoe, Joycelynn kissed Brandon's cheek, then whispered in his ear, "I cooked. The dishes will be waiting for you when you get home."

After retrieving a book she wanted North Bay to read, Joycelynn checked the airflow crack at the bottom of his bedroom door. The light was still on, so she knocked. When he hollered "come in" she opened the door. A dog by each side, he was still dressed and lying on his bed with his arms crossed over his chest. "You okay?" she asked as she sat in the chair by his desk.

North Bay shrugged.

"Your father seems nice enough," she offered, uncertain of what reaction her comment might elicit from North Bay.

"Nice people don't abandon their wives," North Bay snarled, then rolled over so that his back was to her.

"I said he seems *nice*, not perfect," she calmly replied. "I thought the story was that your mother threw him out."

"She did, but it was his fault. He lost our house, not her!"

"I get it. You think he's a jerk," Joycelynn said, not wanting to debate his father's qualities. "What do you know about addiction?"

After a few seconds, North Bay slowly rolled over and faced her. "How come you didn't tell me you were a gambling addict?"

"It wasn't because it's a big secret, if that's what you're thinking. Before today, the only time you and I talked about your father's gambling problem was when we met. Back then, you had a pretty big chip on your shoulders, and I didn't want you tarnishing me with the same brush that you painted your father. I wanted you to get to know me first."

She gave him a second to respond, and when he didn't, she continued, "Addiction isn't a choice, it's an uncontrollable craving. For me, gambling started out as a fun activity that slowly developed into a robotic compulsion that I couldn't control. My husband and I used to go gambling once or twice a week, but we limited how much money we spent. When our marriage started to crumble, and he began spending most of his free time in the bar, I went to the casino. During the same period, our roommate and my closest male friend, Eugene, suddenly died from a heart attack. I got up one morning and found him dead in the backyard. Partially because I wanted to numb, and partially because Eugene and I had shared some good times gambling together, for the next several weeks, all I could think about was going to the casino. Those unfortunate circumstances, combined with a big win and one neighborhood casino opening after another, by the time I finally split with my ex, I was addicted."

"Do you still gamble?" North Bay asked, repositioning himself so that he was resting on his elbow.

Joycelynn shook her head. "It took me another year to realize that I needed help. When I finally accepted that I couldn't quit on my own, I signed myself out via the government's Voluntary Self-Exclusion Program. It turned out that the program was a bit of a farce. None of the casino staff cared when I went back gambling. The end result was that within a three year period, I gambled away what remained of my savings, and more. I'm now suing the government in hopes of encouraging them to put some teeth into their self-exclusion program, so that what happened to me won't happen to other people."

North Bay bolted upright, his young face naively impressed. "You're suing the government. Cool!"

"Not *cool.*" Joycelynn frowned. "Like your father, I wish none of this happened. I wish our provincial government had never opened casinos. I wish that I never started gambling, or had been able to quit when it first started becoming a problem for me. There's nothing *cool* about being involved in a lawsuit, or in anything that led up to it."

North Bay said nothing as he twisted his mouth from side-to-side, the way she'd noticed his father did when he was thinking. It was a peculiar facial expression, and one she hadn't noticed the teen doing before. It made her realize that although their relationship was currently on rocky ground, their bond was strong.

"Are you saying that my dad couldn't stop gambling because he was sick?"

Joycelynn nodded.

"How come my mom didn't know that? How come she kicked him out?"

"I never knew your mother, but I'm guessing that she tried to help your father stop gambling."

"She wouldn't have kicked him out if he had cancer, or something?"

"No, she probably wouldn't have. But it's not quite the same thing. Unless you've suffered from addiction, it's pretty difficult to understand the severity of the compulsion." Even though she'd lived through the nightmarish hell of addiction, Joycelynn could barely understand it herself. She still had trouble grasping the zombie-like compulsion that had her driving to the casino while her mind repeatedly screamed, *don't go!*

"Don't be angry with your mother, North Bay. I'm sure she did what she believed was best for *you*."

"Dad says he loved her. Why wouldn't her threatening to leave him make him quit gambling?"

"Because he couldn't quit. It's hard to understand, but the urge to gamble overrides everything—commonsense, financial security, self-respect, and love." Her heart aching for him, and all the other children and teens caught in the crossfire of a parent's addiction, she said, "I have a book for you to read. It's written by a friend of mine, Ted Kuntz, and it's titled *Peace Begins with Me*."

She handed North Bay the book, and he stared at the purple cover. "It's about Ted's little boy Josh who developed a violent seizure disorder. When Josh first became ill, his father spent much of his time resenting that he couldn't have the healthy child he once knew, and still wanted. It's not exactly the same as what you and your father are going through, but the principles are similar. I know you wish you still had the same father you had before his gaming addiction caused you and your mother so much pain and suffering. However, like my friend, you have a choice—you can keep resenting the loss of the father you once knew and continue being angry at him. Or you can forgive him, and learn how to love him for who he is now, which is a recovering addict who's doing his best to right his wrongs."

With his head down, North Bay asked, "What if he starts gambling again?"

"I don't believe he will," Joycelynn reassured him. "The first thing your father did when he came to town was find a Gamblers Anonymous meeting. I think he's far enough along in his recovery to make it this time. But there are no guarantees. With addiction, relapses are always possible. I'm asking you to read this book because just as Ted couldn't wish away his son's violent physical spasms, you can't wish away your dad's addiction. The best you can do is love him for *who he is*, not who you *wish he were*."

A sly, sheepish grin slid across North Bay's face, setting Joycelynn on alert. "What?" she asked.

"I was eavesdropping. I heard you tell him he could live at your place after you guys get married."

"What do you think of the idea?" she asked, making a mental note to explain to North Bay that eavesdropping was both an invasion of privacy and dangerous.

"I'm glad I get to keep living here." He shrugged. "It's not like he'll be right next door where he'd be on my back every day." Pushing the dogs off of the bed, he crawled under the covers.

Realizing that North Bay had been listening at the door for their entire discussion, Joycelynn didn't bother telling him that his father had also agreed to their informal adoption plans. "You have big ears, my friend; don't one day get yourself hurt by misinterpreting something you overhear," was as close as she came to chastising him for eavesdropping. Planting a kiss on his forehead, she whispered, "Goodnight. Don't let the bedbugs bite."

"Mom used to say that," North Bay said.

"It's one of my mother's favourite expressions, too." She smiled as she turned off the light, motioned the dogs out of his room, and then closed the door. She might not be doing the dishes; however, it appeared as if she was in charge of taking the dogs for their late evening walk.

Brandon came through the door as Joycelynn was putting on her coat. "You leaving?" he asked, appearing surprised and disappointed.

"No, just taking the dogs out. North Bay's gone to bed, and I wasn't certain when you'd be back."

"I'll take the dogs out…if you do the dishes."

"Nice try." She leashed Scruffy, while Brandon leashed Lightning. "I prefer fresh air to dishpan hands."

"I'll come with you," Brandon offered. "The dishes aren't going anywhere."

"Then, you can walk me to my car at the same time. I'm bushed and I want to get up early tomorrow." She was diligently trying to complete her current novel because there was another one in her head that was screaming to be written. As well, she still had three coauthors' stories to edit before sending their latest *Heartmind Wisdom* anthology to Balboa Press for publishing.

Brandon nodded, and though he appeared disappointed that she was going home, he didn't protest. "Thanks for cooking dinner tonight. I know North Bay and I pushed you into it."

"We might as well have ordered takeout." She laughed. "Except for North Bay, nobody ate much."

"What I did eat, tasted great," he said, then added, "You're *a good little woman...pretty, kind and a fine cook.*"

Not taking his bait, she looped her arm through his as they headed out the door with the dogs. "I love you, you know."

"I love you, too!" He lifted her gloved hand to his lips and kissed it.

As they walked along the seawall in front of Brandon's place, Joycelynn savored the crisp air filled with the scent of pending snow. She'd heard about other couples who'd married quickly and lived happily thereafter. Before meeting Brandon, she'd never imagined herself being that lucky. But here she was, arm-in-arm with her fiancé, strolling along in comfortable silence. Since she'd *released fear* and *chosen love*, many things had happened. Some of those happenings were rewarding, others challenging, and all of them wonderful. One of Ted Kuntz's quotes in the book she'd leant to North Bay came to mind and she smiled: "*Once I have mastered peace within, only then will I experience peace in my family, my community, my country, and finally, the world.*"

PROSPERITY

"There is no way to prosperity, prosperity is the way.
Dr. Wayne Dyer
Spiritual Teacher, Author and Speaker

Peeking through the cracked-open door of the counseling room where her father and she were waiting for the ceremony to begin, Joycelynn smiled. She'd expected to feel nervous, which she did a little, but mostly she felt blessed.

The chapel was tastefully decorated with tiny red hearts and miniature crimson roses. Dressed in her official minister's garb, Barbara Leonard was standing at the podium, and appeared very elegant with her silver hair swept up into a bouquet of curls. Cecilia was poised at the piano awaiting her cue to begin playing. Joycelynn's mother, brother, Dee's husband, Dylan, and North Bay's Aunt Connie were seated in the front row on one side. Seated on the opposite side, were Brandon's parents, Aunt Katherine, Georgina, and his sister Karie-Anne and her husband whom Joycelynn had met the night before at their combined family dinner. Behind each of their families, their nieces and nephews were chatting amongst themselves.

North Bay was Brandon's best man, and the two of them looked incredibly handsome standing side-by-side with their hands clasped in front of them, smirking as they repeatedly bumped shoulders.

Elizabeth's husband Mark, whom Brandon had asked to be an usher, was stealing admiring glances at his wife as she welcomed incoming guests. Dee was standing up front, too, and looked stylishly chic wearing a tuxedo. She had cried when Brandon asked her to be an usher in honor of Terry, but today she seemed peacefully happy. Both of Joycelynn's sisters were bridesmaids, and were whispering to each other as they waited for Elizabeth, her matron-of-honor, to join them up front, and for their wedding to begin.

When Cecilia began playing "The Rose," Joycelynn looped her arm through her father's, and asked, "Are you ready, Dad?" For reasons she didn't want to think about today, it was the first time her father would walk her down the aisle, making her marriage to Brandon feel even more blessed and right. Her father squeezed her hand as she inhaled a calming breath and then whispered, "Let's go."

The room filled with a spiritual tranquility as she locked eyes with Brandon and slowly walked toward the podium. His gaze tender, she melted when he mouthed, "You look beautiful." She felt beautiful wearing her off-the-shoulder cream sleeveless silk dress embossed with tiny flowers. The floor-length skirt swayed with her as she walked, making her feel very princess-like and graceful.

Taking Joycelynn's hand as she released her father's arm and stepped up on the podium, Brandon's heart swelled with love. From the day they met, when she'd perkily offered him cover under her huge yellow umbrella that she called her portable sunshine, he'd been mesmerized by her beauty, *joie de vivre* and kindliness. Noting the sparkle in her sapphire eyes, how lovely her copper hair looked falling in waves about her slight shoulders, and her quarter-smile begging to break into a full grin, he felt like the luckiest man alive. In a few minutes she'd be his wife, and the only thing that kept him from doing a jig across the stage and hollering *she's mine* was that it would embarrass her.

As the music faded, Barbara softly said, "Joycelynn," as her cue to begin her vows to Brandon.

"Brandon Ashton, until you, I walked in the love of Source, but ran from love on earth. Being with you freed my steeled heart. In your love, I've found the warmth of sunshine, the strength of the wind, and the serenity of stilled waters. In the comfortable silence of our love, I have found peace."

When their minister nodded at him, Brandon began, "Joycelynn Rose, my teacher, my friend, my confidante. I admire you for your love of people and animals, your courage and convictions, and for showing me that life is not a journey with an ending, but a journey of never-ending beginnings."

Holding each other's hands, eyes locked, they spoke their shared vows. "I ask you to partner with me in love and matrimony, and to grow and prosper by my side through this life and eternity. I believe in you, in the love you so willingly share, and in the guiding hands that brought us together. Our shared love for each other, our families and friends, are gifts that I will forever treasure, respect and honor. I entrust you with my heart, my life and my soul, for today and for always."

After slipping each other's rings onto their fingers, Joycelynn dabbed at her tears and Brandon grinned as Barbara proclaimed, "I now pronounce you husband and wife. You may kiss the bride."

"Finally!" Brandon hollered, scooping Joycelynn into his arms, dipping her backward and kissing her with abandon. When he raised her upright, Joycelynn lifted a hand to her brow and sighed passionately, which set everyone to laughing and clapping.

When the laughter subsided, Barbara announced the second half of the ceremony. "The first addition to Joycelynn and Brandon's new family will be their heart-chosen son, Michael Brown, who most of you know by his nickname, North Bay." She grinned before explaining, "I say *first addition,* because knowing how much our newlyweds love animals and people, I wouldn't put it past them to adopt an entire zoo or a village."

She paused while everyone chuckled and she motioned for North Bay to stand next to her. When he did, she continued, "What you might not know is that this is a very special young man. North Bay lived on the streets a while back. When the fall turned cold, fearing his pet would freeze to death over winter, he placed him in an animal shelter. Joycelynn adopted his dog, but Lightning wasn't having any part of being separated from his beloved guardian. The very first chance he found, Lightning ran for miles and across a bridge to a homeless shelter, where he somehow knew his master would be. Joycelynn and Brandon took North Bay and Lightning under their wings and fell in love with them both."

Barbara beamed at the self-conscious teenager before retrieving an official looking document from the podium. "North Bay and his natural father, Dylan Brown, worked together in drafting this 'Contract of Love' that the four of them are going to sign." After making eye contact with him, she asked, "Dylan, will you come up on stage with us?"

Barbara waited for Dylan to join them, then handing the paper to North Bay, she asked, "Would you like to read what it says?"

"Can I put it on the podium?" North Bay asked nervously. When Barbara nodded, he said, "Dad, come with me. You gotta read your part, too."

Dylan went to stand beside his son. Though he appeared somewhat ill at ease, he bobbed his head encouragingly as he urged, "Go ahead, Son."

"Okay, here goes." North Bay glanced at Joycelynn and Brandon, then began, *"Document of Love. I am officially agreeing to being your adopted son, provided that: one, my dog can always sleep in my room; two, that when I'm a hotshot like Brandon, you guys let me pay you back for all the nice stuff you've done for me; and, three, that whenever we get a new dog, I get to name him."* His head still down, he grinned. "I wanted to put in that I never have to clean my room or do the dishes, but Dad wouldn't let me."

Everyone laughed as North Bay moved aside and Dylan stepped in front of the podium. Glancing toward the newlyweds, he said, "When I first met these two, and the idea of their adopting my son came up, I admit I thought they were both a little kooky. However, the more I've come to know them, the more I've come to admire them. They're good people and Joycelynn reminds me a lot of North Bay's mother and my late wife, Amber. We lost Amber a few years back. It was incredibly hard on us. It's a blessing to have someone in our lives that reminds us of her loving and caring ways. So here's my part, *Joycelynn and Brandon, I entrust you with helping me to teach my son, Michael Brown, a.k.a. North Bay, to be a good man and to honor his mother, Amber Brown, by doing his best by people, no matter what. I officially give you permission to kick his butt when it needs kicking, to hold his hand when it needs holding, and to call me anytime your methods don't do the trick.*" He beamed at North Bay before grabbing him in a bear hug. "I'm proud of you son."

Everyone applauded as they stood to watch the newly formed family hugging and slapping each other on the back. When the commotion subsided, Barbara concluded the ceremonies. "As you can see, our chapel is small. Those of you invited today, were selected because you're the closest people to our newlyweds and new family. But as you know, there are many people Joycelynn and Brandon consider part of their extended family. We hope you'll stay today for coffee and cake, and join us again for their wedding reception, which will take place this Saturday, at Joycelynn's special singles reunion dance."

"I'll bet I can get you to sleep in my bed tonight," Brandon whispered in Joycelynn's ear, before reluctantly moving aside as well-wishers started approaching the stage.

"I think you might win that bet," she laughingly retorted as Elizabeth looped her arm through Joycelynn's and edged her toward the counseling room.

Closing the door, Elizabeth asked, "How are you?"

"Emotional," Joycelynn admitted. "The wedding was wonderful. North Bay and Dylan's 'Document of Love' was beautiful." She lightly laughed, her eyes misting. "Why being happy makes you want to cry, I'll never understand."

Nodding and smiling, Elizabeth walked over to a small bureau where she retrieved an envelope. Handing it to her best friend, she said, "Mark and I have a little surprise gift for you."

Inside the envelope was a brilliant white card embossed with two doves and a gift certificate for a weeklong stay at The Westin Bayshore hotel near Stanley Park in downtown Vancouver. Deeply touched, but certain that there was no way she and Brandon could stay in a hotel for a week, Joycelynn anxiously asked, "What about North Bay and the dogs, who's going to take care of them?"

"Dylan!" Elizabeth supplied gleefully. "His suitcase is in the trunk of our car. So are yours and Brandon's."

"They are?!" Joycelynn shrieked, wondering *how* and *when* Elizabeth had managed to pack both of their suitcases without her knowing.

"North Bay's been slowly packing Brandon's suitcase all week. When your husband left to come here today, your adopted son finished throwing in your new husband's toiletries and shoes." Laughing, she added, "You might want to check what he packed before you make any formal dinner plans."

"When did you pack my stuff?" Because they each had a key to the other's house, she didn't ask how Elizabeth gained entrance into her place.

"Today, after you left," she said triumphantly. "Packing for you was easy: purple pyjamas and slippers, two sweatshirts, a couple of pairs of jeans, sneakers, underwear, make-up, and toiletries."

Thinking of the alluring negligee she'd purchased for her first night with her husband, Joycelynn groaned. Purple pyjamas just weren't going to do the trick.

Knowing exactly what was on her best friend's mind, Elizabeth teasingly assured her, "Don't worry; that sexy little black number you bought for your honeymoon is in there, too.

Although, I hope you realize that seeing you wearing it will likely bolt Brandon into full cardiac arrest."

"Am I supposed to wear my wedding gown to the hotel?" Joycelynn cheekily asked in an attempt to quash the onslaught of belly butterflies accompanying her imaginings of making love with Brandon.

"I picked out a nice outfit for you. It's on a hanger in the car, along with your shoes, boots and winter coat." She grinned. "I thought this through, you know?"

"Of course, you did." Joycelynn hugged Elizabeth. "Why are you so nice to me?"

"So you won't whine," Elizabeth teased.

Joycelynn laughed. "Speaking of wine, I could use a glass of that expensive champagne Brandon brought for our wedding toast."

"Me, too," Elizabeth said, releasing her embrace. "That new husband of yours is probably wondering what happened to you."

"Oh, I think he's accustomed to sharing me," she said aloud, while recalling how worried she'd once been that Brandon might morph into a possessive freak. Although he sometimes seemed disappointed when she left his place early to work on her novel or *Heartmind Wisdom*, he never complained. When she was dragged out and sore following a marathon week, he rubbed her back or feet. At Christmas, he'd been a prince helping her to coordinate the inclusion of both of their families and North Bay's into their celebration. Their short courtship had been busy and eventful. If he were going to become demanding, jealous or possessive, she'd have seen signs of it by now. Mind, heart and soul, she knew that Brandon would always be there for her, as she would always be there for him.

Climbing into the limousine a few hours later, Joycelynn snuggled against Brandon and purred, "That was the nicest day of my life. Thank you."

"No, *thank you*." Brandon kissed the top of her head. "You were pretty emotional during the ceremony. How are you feeling now?"

"Excited," she exclaimed. "I can't believe that our good friends planned a week for us at The Westin Bayshore."

"I was hoping you'd say that you're excited that we're about to spend our first night together." He feigned a small pout, laughing when she gently elbowed his ribs.

"I'm nervous about that," she confessed, before teasingly asking, "What if you're a terrible lover; then, what'll I do?"

"Fake it," he retorted with a guffaw. "My ego is easily bruised."

"*Fake it*, I can do that!" she chirped. "But I'm sure it'll be wonderful." Closing her eyes, she leaned her head on Brandon's shoulders and silently thanked Source for the many gifts her life was unfolding.

As they both suspected, their lovemaking was tender and blissful. Brandon not only liked her new negligee, he insisted she wear it every night, telling her that he didn't care if it needed washing. Joycelynn *did* care, so each morning she washed it in the bathroom sink, before hanging it on the shower rod to dry. On their last night in the hotel, she hid the little black number beneath her purple pyjamas and showed up at their bedside in flannelette. When he grimaced, she laughingly removed her pj's, striptease style.

Though they missed the dogs and North Bay, their time alone sped by much too quickly. Every day, they walked the seawall around the park, holding hands and talking about their future. Evenings, they dined out in various restaurants, then went to their room and made love.

On the last morning of their honeymoon, Brandon teased her, "It's a good thing you quit running those singles dances, or I might have become a jealous man. I saw the way some of those men look at you."

"Really, I didn't notice anyone looking at me. I did, however, notice a tall blonde checking out your butt."

"What tall blonde?" Brandon played along. "You should have pointed her out right away. Having your butt checked out is quite a compliment for a guy."

"I'm sorry, I didn't know," Joycelynn apologized cheerily. "In the future, I'll be certain to immediately alert you of any butt-checking I observe." Quickly pecking his lips, she reached under her pillow. "I had this made for you. I hope you like it."

Brandon was pleasantly dumbfounded as he opened the small blue box and discovered a gold necklace looped through what appeared to be some kind of charm. When he inspected it further, his heart somersaulted—it was a wooden nickel encased in gold. Turning it over, he read the inscription: *Don't take any wooden nickels.* Stunned, for a long moment he just stared at his bride. He didn't wonder why she'd commissioned the jewelry; he knew that it was her way of honoring Terry's part in their having come together as husband and wife. "Thank you," he finally said, then softly kissed her.

"You're welcome," was all she got out before he again covered her lips with his and they made sweet, sensuous love until it was time to check out of their room and go home.

Laden with their bags and gifts they'd received at their wedding reception, as they stepped off of the elevator at home, they were thankful to be greeted by North Bay and two tail-wagging dogs.

Taking Joycelynn's bags, the teen explained, "I was out on the balcony and saw you pull up."

"You were watching for us like a nervous mother hen," Brandon teased. "You missed us; admit it." Dropping his bags just inside the door, he playfully tackled the teen.

"You missed me more," North Bay bantered, jumping up as he tried to hook Brandon's head.

Brandon dodged the hold, grabbed and twisted the teen's arm behind his back, then pulled him close against his own body. "Call me Daddy, North Bay. Say it now or I'll tickle you to death."

"You and whose army?" North Bay retorted, twisting free and again jumping for Brandon's neck.

"You need some help, Son?" Dylan stepped into the fun, startling Brandon, who had obviously forgotten that North Bay's father would be there.

"So you brought your own army," Brandon quipped, then ran to hide behind his wife. "Just so happens that I did, too." He winked at Dylan, as Joycelynn stepped sideways.

"I'm a lover, not a fighter," she joked, her cheeks flushing red as she realized she'd left herself wide open for teasing from all three of them.

Brandon was bright enough not to step into that one, but the sly grin that North Bay exchanged with his father, let her know exactly what they were thinking. Thankfully, her husband quickly rescued her.

"Look what Joycelynn had made for me," Brandon said, pulling his new necklace over his head and handing it to North Bay. *"Don't take any wooden nickels* was my best friend's and my childhood code." He glanced at Dylan and explained, "My friend Terry died this past fall. His sister Dee agreed to be an usher in his place."

Dylan nodded. "I spent some time talking with Dee and her husband at your reception. It sounds like you lost a good friend. I'm sorry."

"Is that a real wooden nickel?" North Bay asked as he studied the coin.

"It's authentic," Joycelynn assured him. "After the depression, some U.S. merchants and banks used wooden nickels in place of coins. I found that coin on EBay and had a friend of mine craft it into a medallion."

"Cool!" North Bay passed the necklace to his father, suddenly seeming a bit nervous as he said, "Dad and I made you something while you were away. We hope you like it."

Joycelynn and Brandon glanced around. Everything in the living-room appeared exactly as they'd last seen it. "What?" they asked in unison.

North Bay and his father exchanged slightly smug, conspiratorial glances, before Dylan said, "It's in your office."

The newlyweds headed down the hall, both shrugging their shoulders as they tried to imagine what they were going to find in Brandon's office. When they opened the door, they fell against one another. There in the center of the room was a huge oak table. On one side was Joycelynn's computer and papers, on the other, Brandon's. Against the wall was a matching bookcase complete with dropdown doors. Her books were neatly aligned on one side, his on the other.

"We thought you guys might have a hard time figuring out how to fit two desks into this room, so we designed and made the table," North Bay explained as he brushed past them, then reached under the table and opened a huge wooden drawer. "Brandon's side has a drawer, too. They both lock, so you don't have to worry about me running off with a sack full of your important papers."

Grinning, Brandon spiked his hand through his hair. "It's terrific! You two must have worked night and day to get this ready." He walked over and ran his hand along the glasslike finish, shaking his head as he glanced at Joycelynn, who felt like crying.

Coming to stand beside her, Brandon placed his arm around his wife's shoulders. A catch in his voice, he said, "Thank you Dylan and North Bay. It's perfect."

"A guy I met on a job interview let me have the wood for next to nothing," Dylan supplied. "He was asking for a lot more, but by the time he finished hearing about how you two were helping out me and my son, he practically gave it to me."

Brandon nodded.

Joycelynn was pleased that the two men had worked together on such a beautiful project. Whatever damage Dylan's gambling had done, was well on its way to be forgotten by North Bay.

"The next time you see that guy, please tell him how grateful we are," Brandon said, squeezing his wife close.

"I'll tell him tomorrow, when I show up for work," Dylan announced proudly.

"You got the job!" Joycelynn shrieked. "Congratulations!"

"He got a car, too," North Bay interjected. "That is, if you think a rusted-out old beater is a car."

"It has wheels and an engine. It'll do for now," Dylan defended his vehicle. "Besides, this way I don't have to worry about you asking to borrow it when you finally get the nerve up to ask the little cutie at the corner store for a date."

"There's a little cutie at the corner store?" Brandon joined in the fun. "Is she the reason you're always volunteering to fetch groceries?"

North Bay blushed as he glanced at Joycelynn, who asked, "Why would you need to borrow a car? You don't have a driver's license."

"I have a learner's permit." Taking out his wallet, North Bay pulled out the paper that proved it. "Dad took me. We've already been out driving three times."

"Which is another reason that I bought an old beater," Dylan said. "Parallel parking isn't your strong suit."

"It's nobody's strong suit," Joycelynn defended North Bay. "When I was learning to drive, I took out my fair share of garbage cans before I mastered that technique."

"I told you that everybody has trouble parking," North Bay said. "I got it right the last time."

"The last time I set the markers a mile apart. I could have manipulated a bloody airplane into that spot."

"Sure you could have," North Bay cheeked, pushing his wallet into his pocket.

His eyes on his son, Dylan jerked his head in the direction of the doorway. "How about I buy you lunch and we give these two lovebirds a chance to settle in?" was the last Joycelynn and Brandon could hear of their conversation.

"Dylan's a nice man," Joycelynn commented as she faced her husband. "He loves his son a lot."

"He loves *our* son a lot. You do remember that we unofficially adopted him?"

"I remember." Joycelynn smiled, kneeling down to pet Scruffy, who was glued to his master's side. "I think your dog missed you."

"I missed him, too." Brandon joined her on the floor, winking as he asked, "You happy?"

"Very," she answered, stifling a yawn as she smiled. "But I could definitely use a nap."

Brandon responded with a mischievous grin.

"I really mean a *nap*," she retorted.

"Spoil sport." Standing, he helped Joycelynn to her feet. "Don't tell me that the honeymoon is over already."

"The honeymoon better never be over," she countered as they walked toward the master bedroom. "I'm still worried that once you've lived with me for a week, you're going to think that I'm a slob and demand a divorce."

Opening the door to their bedroom, Brandon asked, "Do you want me to carry you over the threshold for good luck?"

"My nursing skills are less accomplished than my housekeeping skills," she teased as she walked into the room and stopped dead in her tracks. The throw pillows from her bed were scattered across Brandon's. The closet doors were wide open, and her clothes and shoes were as neatly aligned as his. Walking into the en-suite bathroom, she saw that another vanity had been added. "When did all this happen?"

"I have a small confession," Brandon answered, grinning as he took her hand and led her out of the bathroom. "I was in on the hotel room and our week away. Elizabeth and Mark gave us the room as their treat, but the new vanity and your clothes being here are my doing. I wanted you to feel comfortable on your first night in your new home."

Stunned and amazed, Joycelynn didn't know whether to laugh or cry. "How?" she asked, flabbergasted and unable to form a complete sentence.

"Elizabeth and her housekeeper brought your clothes and things over. Dylan and North Bay installed the vanity."

"Did you know about the desk, too?"

"No, that was entirely Dylan's and North Bay's doing." He shook his head. "It's an amazing gift. I know how much work it took for them to achieve a fine finish like that." His expression changed to worry. "I hope Dylan was telling the truth about getting a good deal on the wood."

"The desk is his way of repaying us for taking care of North Bay. I hope he didn't spend too much of his savings, too. But I understand his need to regain his pride by doing something special for us."

"I guess," Brandon agreed.

"I *guess* that I am officially moved in," Joycelynn said, flopping backward on the bed, delighted when Fat Cat came to put his nose next to hers. "Dylan's keeping my furnishings and dishes. My clothes and office things are here. I guess all that's left for me to do is begin my life of luxury."

"Aren't you streaming a live *Heartmind Wisdom* book signing tomorrow afternoon, and then teaching a writing class tomorrow night?"

"Yes."

"So that's not exactly a life of luxury."

"I think it is," she retorted seriously. "I love my work!"

"I'm kind of new at this napping thing," Brandon teased her. "Does it take place dressed, or naked?"

"Naked!" She laughed as she jumped up, tossed the decorative pillows off of the bed and crawled under the covers.

Brandon hurriedly locked the door, and then climbed in with her as Fat Cat bee-lined it off of the bed. "You're still dressed."

"You're still talking." She closed her eyes. "How am I going to sleep, if you keep talking?"

"I think the bigger question is how you're going to sleep if you're laughing?" he retorted as he attempted to tickle her.

Joycelynn responded by lifting her arm over her head and pretending to snore.

"I forgot that you're not ticklish. That's not fair."

"No, but you are *very* ticklish." She opened one eye and smiled. "And if you don't let me take my nap, I'll be obliged to demonstrate just how unfair the life of a ticklish person can be."

"I love you." Brandon dropped his head onto his pillow and chuckled.

"I love you, too," she whispered as she thought about her new home, their wedding, and the lovely gifts they'd received. Each present had been amazingly thoughtful—Elizabeth and Mark's gift of a week at The Westin Bayshore hotel, Dylan and North Bay's lovely office furniture, and her new husband's bathroom-vanity.

Feeling incredibly grateful, she recalled one of her favorite Wayne Dyer quotes: *"There is no way to prosperity, prosperity is the way."* When she lost her house and savings to her gambling addiction, she'd hung onto Dr. Dyer's wise words, interpreting them as meaning that prosperity was more about having a grateful state of mind, than the accumulation of things. No matter what she once owned, or would one day own or not own, *true* prosperity came from an abundant appreciation of earth's natural treasures.

Because of her prosperous attitude, at the beach she found abundant solace in the soothing sounds of the gulls and lapping water, and in the staggering splendor of sunsets and sunrises. Sometimes when she feared she'd never recover financially, she'd meander through the forest, finding peace in the greenery and singing birds. At Maggie's shelter, she found the unconditional love of the animals, eagerly greeting her without caring as to whether she was a pauper or queen. When human contact seemed the tonic she needed to lift her spirits, she turned to Elizabeth and Mark, her family, and to the open arms of the people at the chapel.

In addition to her Kindness is Key aha moment, her emotional healing was largely due to the shame she shed when she realized that, aside from losing things she'd once owned, nothing had really changed. If she'd given up on the future, or caved in to her après gaming financial and emotional despair, her life circumstances would never have played out into her lying next to the most wonderful man she'd ever known. Because without gratitude, she wouldn't have had the *insight, will, self-worth,* or *confidence* necessary to uncover the inherent gifts in *challenge* and *adversity*—gifts that led her toward her life purpose of seeding global kindness, one heart at a time.

Snuggling up to her new husband, she smiled. Wayne Dyer was right: *"There is no way to prosperity, prosperity is the way."* It was wisdom she'd share with her newly adopted son the next time he complained about his father's dilapidated car. Though she suspected North Bay already appreciated that, what mattered most, was that his dad loved him enough to take the time to teach him how to drive.

PURPOSE

> "Everything in the universe has a purpose.
> Indeed, the invisible intelligence that flows
> through everything in a purposeful fashion
> is also flowing through you."
> Dr. Wayne Dyer
> Spiritual Teacher, Author and Speaker

Her hectic schedule and the fact that she and Brandon spent way too many nights talking into the wee hours, was what Joycelynn reasoned explained why she seemed to be incessantly tired. That and the fact that she was writing her next novel, while still in the midst of the whirlwind promotion of her last one. In addition, she and Elizabeth had begun coaching a new group of writers for their next *Heartmind Wisdom* inspirational anthology. As much as she loved her life, sometimes it was difficult to maintain a balanced pace.

Brandon seemed more tired than usual, too. The only household members with an abundant supply of energy were the dogs and North Bay. Fat Cat was as lethargic as Joycelynn, purring wildly whenever she curled up with him in the king-size bed, and then falling asleep for however long that she did. On the third day that her afternoon nap stretched into three hours, she booked an appointment with her doctor.

After examining her, Dr. Nolte smiled pleasantly as he set about writing on a pad of forms. "I don't see anything wrong, but I'd like you to have a few blood tests."

Getting dressed, Joycelynn asked, "Do you think that I might be anemic? We order in dinner more often than we should, but we always have salad, and I eat a couple of pieces of fruit every day."

"Anemia is a possibility, and I'm having your iron levels checked. There are a few other blood tests I'd like to run, as well."

"What other blood tests?" she asked, buttoning her blouse.

"For starters: diabetes, liver function, and cholesterol." A Cheshire cat grin leapt across his face as he added, "And pregnancy."

"Why would you test me for pregnancy?" she screeched. "I'm fifty-six years old and I haven't had a period for nearly a year."

"Which means you're *in* menopause, not *post*-menopausal," he explained. "Although it's rare for women your age to conceive, it's not impossible."

"This would have been good to know when I got married," Joycelynn said, sounding harsher than intended. "We're a little old to be thinking about a having a baby." Imagining Brandon's response, she wondered if he'd be thrilled or worried. Since marrying him, she'd learned that he had a habit of researching everything on the Internet. If she announced she was pregnant, it would undoubtedly be his first line of action.

"Lots of people have babies later in life," Dr. Nolte reassured her. "You're healthy and I assume your husband is, too."

Joycelynn didn't answer as to the state of Brandon's health. Besides having the diet of a teenager and being tired of late, he seemed healthy. "How soon can we find out if I'm pregnant?" she asked, already planning on purchasing an over-the-counter test on the way home.

"If you go next door to the clinic right now, I'll have your pregnancy test results back by this afternoon. The rest will take a few days."

Bending forward to tie her sneakers, she noticed that her jeans did feel tighter, and immediately thought of the fetus she'd lost. "What are the chances of someone my age carrying full term?"

"Age is less of a determining factor for a healthy pregnancy and delivery than it once was." Dr. Nolte leaned back in his chair, his clasped hands resting on his abdomen. "Of course, older expectant mothers have higher incidents of associated complications such as diabetes and high blood pressure. They're also more likely to require a caesarean section, or deliver prematurely. As well, they have an increased occurrence of fetal chromosome abnormalities, which we would test for around four months."

The doctor handed her two medical requisition sheets, which Joycelynn folded neatly and placed in her purse. Standing and shaking his hand, she asked, "What time should I come back?"

"Four o'clock," he warmly answered. "In the meantime, try not to worry. If you're pregnant, you have options."

Try not to worry, Joycelynn mused as a young pretty nurse took her blood. She had two and a half hours to *try not to worry* and the only way that was going to happen was if someone were to knock her unconscious. Leaving the clinic, she went to sit in her car and called Brandon's mobile. Perhaps if she heard his voice she'd feel calmer, instead of feeling as though her life had just tumbled crazily out of control.

"What's up, angel? Is something wrong?" Brandon asked, obviously having checked to see who was calling before he answered.

"Nothing," she replied, trying to sound cheerful. "I just wanted to hear your voice." She wasn't really lying, nothing was truly *wrong*.

Quickly putting two-and-two together, Brandon asked, "Didn't you have an appointment with your doctor today?"

"I just left there." She smiled, hoping her sunny facial expression would somehow reach her voice. "He sent me for a couple of tests to try and figure out why I'm so tired lately."

"Spill it, Joycelynn," Brandon said. "I know you well. You're about as good at hiding your emotions as a nine months pregnant woman is at hiding her belly." He chortled, before teasingly asking, "You're not pregnant, are you?"

"Maybe," Joycelynn whispered.

"*Maybe!*" Brandon's voice shot up. "I was kidding."

Imagining him nervously pacing and spiking his hand through his hair, she felt guilty for worrying him.

"You're kidding, too...right?" Brandon asked, his tone somewhat more controlled.

"I'm afraid not." Joycelynn watched as a young woman fastened a squiggling toddler into a car safety seat. "I'm supposed to try not to worry until I see the doctor again at four."

"You shouldn't worry," Brandon agreed. "You're possibly pregnant, not dying." He paused, before adding. "We'll figure this out together. If you're pregnant, then it's a gift from Source."

"Every time you want me to see things your way, you claim that *whatever* is a gift from Source." She laughed, thinking of how often her husband used *her* beliefs to manipulate situations to *his* advantage.

"My docket is clear for the rest of the day. Would you feel better if I came with you at four?"

"I would," Joycelynn answered, somewhat relieved. At least she wouldn't be alone when she found out whether she was pregnant.

"Have no fear. Stay where you are and I'll be right there," Brandon cheerfully exclaimed in his best Superman voice.

"You don't have a clue where I am." Joycelynn laughed lightly.

"Yes, I do," Brandon fibbed. "You're at...."

"I know you're waiting for the address to come up on your computer," she teased him. "Why don't you just let me give it to you?"

"It's a guy thing," he mumbled, two seconds later shouting, "I've got it. I'll be there within half an hour."

"I love you," she whispered, but he had already hung up the phone.

At Dr. Nolte's office, Brandon took the chair next to Joycelynn's, then reached for and held her hand. "Pregnant or not, we're a team. You're not in this alone." He smiled boyishly. "It might be fun to have a kid brother or sister for North Bay."

"It might be," Joycelynn agreed as she noticed that the circles under Brandon's eyes seemed darker in the bright office light. Maybe he needed glasses.

When the doctor came into the room, she introduced him to Brandon as she clung onto her husband's hand.

"You're definitely pregnant," Dr. Nolte said, glancing up from the paper on his desk. "About three months."

"Three months," Joycelynn exclaimed. "We must have conceived on our honeymoon!"

"You wouldn't be the first," Dr. Nolte replied cheerfully before becoming serious. "You have options...."

Before he finished what he was about to say, Brandon raised his hand to cut him off. "We need to know what the possible complications might be, and what we can do to ensure that both Joycelynn and our baby are fine. Obviously, our take-out food diet is a thing of the past. She's going to have cut way back on her workload, and...." He'd have kept listing his developing action plan, but when Joycelynn tightly squeezed his hand, he shut up.

"Do you have anything we can read?" she asked, looking at the doctor. "I'm certain my husband will be on the computer all night, but I'd feel better reading something from you."

Dr. Nolte smiled. "Your age is reason for caution, not concern." He squared off with Joycelynn. "You're more healthy and fit than many of my younger expectant moms, so stop worrying." He glanced back at Brandon. "You're right. You might want to cut back on take-out foods; too much salt and too many empty calories. And I want to start Joycelynn on a special vitamin regime. As for her work schedule, it should be fine for the next while. If she starts to feel run down, or too tired, we'll look at her activity level. Right now, I think the two of you should forget about your age and concentrate on what a blessed event this really is. Plan a nursery, start a college fund... whatever makes you happy. But stop worrying."

The doctor rummaged through his bookshelf, came up with a couple of pamphlets and handed them to Joycelynn. "I'm going to schedule you for an ultrasound next week, followed by an amniocentesis test. Outside of that, what I recommend is a nice dinner out to celebrate." Smiling at Joycelynn, he added, "No champagne for you."

Walking them toward the door, Dr. Nolte placed his hand on Brandon's arm and asked, "When's the last time you had a physical?"

"Drumming up business, are you?" Brandon cheeked back, then shrugged. "I don't know, two or three years. Why?"

"Nothing, I just like to make certain that my expectant fathers are as fit as my expectant mothers. It isn't fair to the ladies if we prod and poke them, while their men get off scot-free."

"I'll make an appointment with your receptionist." Brandon shook Dr. Nolte's hand. "We might as well have the same family doctor. Perhaps we should send our adopted son in, too. Though I imagine he won't be too happy about the idea." He winked at Joycelynn, before glancing back at the doctor. "Any chance you take dogs and cats for patients? Our vet bill sometimes gets a little out of hand."

Dr. Nolte chuckled and shook his head. "I've often told my own wife that I should have either become a veterinarian, or married one."

"I'll take that under advisement in case this wife doesn't work out," Brandon joked as he dodged Joycelynn's arm punch. "Is becoming violent a pregnancy symptom?" he continued teasing her as they made their way to her car.

"Thank you," Joycelynn said as she fished her car keys out of her purse, and then standing tiptoe, kissed his cheek.

"Thank you, for what? A few seconds ago you were trying to punch me."

"For coming with me. For your dumb jokes. For making being pregnant at this age seem fun and normal."

"If it weren't meant to be fun and normal, nature would never have let it happen." He pulled her close and hugged her. "If there was anything to worry about, Dr. Nolte would have told us."

"Thank you, just the same." She leaned into his broad chest and inhaled his familiar smell. "You're a good husband."

"You're a *good little woman*," he teased, "*pretty, kind and a fine cook.*"

"I'll see you at home." Stepping out of his embrace, she gently poked his ribs. "You're cooking."

"If I'm cooking, you and North Bay are suffering."

"Then you're buying," she chirped as she slid into her car and closed the door. After rolling down the window, she finished with, "Dr. Nolte told us to celebrate. After we walk the dogs, let's take North Bay somewhere special for dinner."

"Maybe we should call Dylan, too," Brandon suggested. "He's as much a part of this family as the rest of us."

Joycelynn nodded, put her car into gear and headed for home. With one hand on the steering wheel and the other on her belly, she mused that what had a few hours ago seemed like a freakish mistake, now felt like a blessing. She was going to be a mom.

In her fourth month, the amniotic fluid sample showed that their baby was healthy. To celebrate, Brandon purchased a crib and changing table, which North Bay and his father assembled. When they were done, and it became obvious that the master bedroom was too crowded, Dylan suggested they all switch residences. As the renovations were mostly completed, he argued that it made more sense if Joycelynn and Brandon lived in the house, rather than the condominium.

For many reasons, Joycelynn agreed. The dogs would at least have a small yard, so she wouldn't have to worry about taking them outdoors to do their business when the guys weren't home to help her. The house had five bedrooms, which meant that there was enough room for two offices, a nursery for the baby, and North Bay would still have his room.

On the weekend that they finished switching residences, Joycelynn was excited about living in a bigger place. However, it saddened her that they were leaving their first matrimonial home. Brandon responded to her tears by teasing her that the more her pregnancy progressed, the more her emotions fluctuated. In his usual flippant manner, he also suggested that she might want to hurry up the production process.

During her last trimester, after delightfully accepting Joycelynn's request that she and Mark be the baby's godparents, Elizabeth broadsided her by suggesting that they continue with their *Heartmind Wisdom* writing classes, but place their *KiK* seminars on hold. Joycelynn had long forgotten about finishing her latest novel, knowing that when she was ready, it would be waiting to be written. Though it sometimes felt as if her life were being peeled away one activity at a time, she agreed with her partner's part-time business plan.

With less time spent working on Kindness Is Key, Joycelynn's days naturally became maternally centered. With the guys' help, she finished decorating the nursery. With Elizabeth's help, she shopped for baby clothes. With Brandon's back and foot massages, she survived the weight gain and the aches and pains.

Pregnancy, she concluded during her ninth month, was not a middle-aged woman's game.

On the day that their daughter was born, Joycelynn felt like the luckiest woman alive. *Alma Amber Margaret Ashton* came into the world at seven pounds, three ounces and with the lungs of an opera singer; although, Brandon suggested it sounded more as though her fan belt were broken. They had chosen the baby's first name after Joycelynn's mother, her second name after North Bay's mother, and her third after Brandon's mother.

Much to her surprise, when Joycelynn came home from the hospital with the baby, Brandon announced he had taken paternal leave, and would be staying home with his wife and daughter. Happy to have the company and help, Joycelynn didn't question his decision. Their finances were such that they didn't have to worry, and she was thrilled that her husband was taking fatherhood seriously. Everything seemed perfect, until the day that Brandon fainted and their lives unraveled with the spinning fury of a tightly wound golf ball unleashed from its dimpled casing.

Sitting at her husband's bedside, Joycelynn tried to ignore the tubes and machines as she waited for him to regain consciousness. All the hospital doctors would say was that he was very sick, so she called Dr. Nolte. When he arrived, he explained that when Brandon went for his physical, his blood tests showed abnormalities. Further testing revealed acute myeloid leukemia, or AML. Past that Caucasian men over fifty were more prone to the disease, there was no explanation as to why he had developed the cancer that overrode his system with the massive production of abnormal blood cells. Brandon had refused all treatments including chemotherapy, radiation and a bone marrow transplant. He'd also refused medication that might retard the disease. Dr. Nolte had spent hours trying to educate and reason with him, but beside improving his diet and taking mega vitamins, Brandon insisted he had a better plan and wouldn't budge.

"Hey, sleepyhead." Joycelynn smiled as her husband's hand twitched in hers, and she turned to see him open his eyes. "How are you feeling?"

"Tired," Brandon said, alternating between opening and closing his left eye, then his right.

As a nurse entered the room and checked Brandon's vitals, sounding far calmer and braver than she felt, Joycelynn said, "I think he's having trouble focusing his eyes."

"I'll call the doctor," the plumpish, middle-aged nurse said, and then hollered, "Welcome back," as she scurried from the room.

Her emotions a nightmarish mishmash, Joycelynn didn't know where to begin with her list of worries and regrets: she felt guilty for not taking his continuous bouts of flu-like symptoms more seriously; was terrified that he might die; and, angry at him for suffering alone, shutting her out and refusing treatment. Half of her wanted to scream at him until she was hoarse; the other half wanted to curl up in his arms and cry.

"I'm thirsty," Brandon said in a weak voice that broke her heart.

"The doctor will be in shortly," she answered, fearful of giving him liquids without first checking. Leaning forward, she ran her hand along his cheek. "You scared me half to death."

"Where's the baby?" Brandon asked through parched lips.

"Elizabeth is with her." She smiled reassuringly. "Alma's fine. I've already called home about a half dozen times. At the moment, she's sleeping."

"You should go to her." Brandon squeezed her hand. "The little monkey is probably hungry."

"There's freshly expressed milk in the refrigerator," Joycelynn said, attempting to sound cheerful. "Our daughter is fine. It's her father I'm worried about."

"I should've told you," Brandon said, trying to lift his head off of his pillow and failing. "I'm sick."

"Dr. Nolte was here. He told me everything." The doctor hadn't really told her everything, just the medical portion. Only Brandon knew why he had refused treatment for his disease. But now wasn't the time to grill him about his motives for signing his own death certificate.

"Are you mad?"

"Mad, confused...scared," she admitted, her tone flat, her expression blank.

"I'm not going to die," Brandon stated with as much conviction as his strength permitted. "I have a plan."

"Dr. Nolte mentioned that, but didn't seem to know what your plan might entail."

Before Brandon could respond, one of the hospital doctors entered the room, and Joycelynn moved away from her husband's bed. As he finished examining Brandon, he glanced at her before addressing his patient. "Mr. Ashton, I hope that this little scare has put some commonsense into your head. You can't beat *aml* without treatment."

Brandon didn't respond, so the doctor turned toward Joycelynn.

"Depending on how far the disease has progressed, with chemotherapy followed with radiation, or a bone marrow transplant and drug therapy, your husband has up to a seventy percent chance of a full remission. Without treatment, it doesn't look good." He hung his head, as if wishing he had better news. "I'm waiting to hear from his specialist, but my preliminary recommendation is to immediately start him on chemo." He stopped talking while he made notes in Brandon's chart. "Dr. Nolte tells me that your husband has his own plans, but wasn't able to elaborate on what those might be." He shook his head. "I've seen many miracles in my years as a doctor. Should your husband continue to refuse treatment, I'm hoping that I see one more." He patted Brandon's leg. "Let me know what you decide."

"He's thirsty," Joycelynn said, her eyes pleading with the doctor for some indication of what she could do to help.

"He can have a few sips of water or gingerale. He's on intravenous fluids, so there's no danger of him being dehydrated." He turned to face Brandon. "If you start feeling nauseated, ask the nurse for Gravol."

"Up to a seventy percent chance of survival, sounds good," Joycelynn said, lifting her husband's head so he could drink the water she was holding. He took a sip through the plastic straw, and when he didn't seem to want anymore, she guided his head back onto the pillow.

Peering into her eyes, Brandon explained, "I've been sick for a long time. My cancer has metastasized and I have a small tumor on my spleen. Even with treatment, my specialist estimates that my chances are much lower than the average—only about twenty or thirty percent."

"People can live without a spleen," Joycelynn responded hopefully, ignoring the dismal prognosis. Again sitting on his bed and taking his hand, she continued, "All kinds of people have survived cancer. You're a healthy fit man. You'll beat this. I know you will!" The more she spoke, the harder it became for her not to start blubbering like a baby, so she became quiet.

Brandon gave her a few moments, and then with his eyes tenderly locked on hers, he explained, "My entire system is compromised. Yes, I could have a splenectomy and undergo cancer treatment. Put us both through a hellish nightmare that won't save my life, or even prolong it for years."

"But you have to try," Joycelynn begged through streaming tears.

"I watched Terry suffer through cancer treatment. Witnessed my best friend die without dignity or grace. It's not what I want for me, or you. I know it seems unfair, angel. But I just can't."

"It's unfair and *stupid*," Joycelynn retorted as her anger took lead.

"Don't be mad at me, Joycelynn," Brandon pleaded, his eyes cloudy with regret and worry. "I'm sorry that we didn't have this conversation when I was feeling stronger. I didn't' think that my disease would advance this quickly. But it did." Squeezing her hand, he said, "Please let me explain why I didn't immediately tell you. It's important to me that you understand."

When Joycelynn nodded, he began, "When I first found out that I had leukemia, I was hopeful that it would be a non-aggressive blood cancer, so I didn't immediately share the prognosis with you. I wanted to be able to deliver some good news with the bad. Plus, you were so incredibly happy caring for Alma, I couldn't tell you that I was sick and might die. Switch your attention to me and away from our precious baby."

After resting for a second, he continued, "Sometimes, I'd think it was time to tell you, then I'd watch you sitting in the nursery breastfeeding her, and couldn't bring myself to interfere with something so serenely beautiful. The early months of life are a precious time between a mother and her child, and I wanted my wife and daughter to have as much of that peaceful bonding time as humanly possible."

"So what is your plan?" she softly asked, curious and scared.

"I want to try cryogenics."

"You want to be frozen like a Popsicle!" Joycelynn shrieked, fervently shaking her head as she dropped his hand. "Too experimental; it's not going to happen." Leaping up, she fisted her hands on her hips and paced. "We'll figure this out, Brandon. But not that! Not cryogenics!"

"Why not?" Brandon asked, trying to lift his head from the pillow and failing.

"Cryogenics is ridiculous and crazy!" Calming herself, Joycelynn sat on the end of the bed and placed her hand on his leg. "No one has ever been revived from a cryogenic state. Science just isn't that advanced and likely never will be." Her mind whirling, she tried to recall what she'd read a couple months ago, when she happened upon an advertisement on Brandon's computer for an institution in the United States who vitrified people in liquid nitrogen and then stored them in cryostats. The idea seemed ghoulish to her, so she'd never mentioned reading about it to Brandon. Seeing the advertiser's website on Brandon's computer hadn't alarmed her. She simply assumed it was one more topic he was researching, along with bee farming, flower propagation and a zillion other subjects.

Brandon's insatiable thirst for knowledge was one of the many things she loved about him.

"It's no more ridiculous or crazy than cloning living beings seemed a decade ago," Brandon calmly countered.

"It's not the same," Joycelynn argued. "You're asking me to agree to letting you die so that you can be preserved, on the off-chance that you can be resuscitated years from now, when I'll likely already be dead." She shook her head. "Brandon, you have a wife and daughter. We need you to fight this thing so you can be with us as long as possible." Crying uncontrollably, she finished with, "We need you now."

When she regained her composure, Brandon spoke slowly and softly as he rationalized, "I know you want me to fight, Joycelynn. But you didn't watch Terry suffering in agony for months, praying and waiting for the mercy of death. I want your memories of our life together to be about the good times. Maybe within a decade or two, they'll find a cure for leukemia, and cryogenics will evolve to the point where I can be resuscitated." Smiling faintly, he added, "You're the one who believes that divine intervention is rapidly propelling science, so don't be too angry with me for putting my faith in future medicine, not current."

"I'll be a wrinkled old prune by then," Joycelynn said, interjecting humor she didn't feel.

"You'll be gorgeous and vibrant until you're a hundred years old," Brandon assured her. "Maybe by the time I come back, they'll be able to retard or reverse the aging process."

"You won't be around to see our daughter growing up," Joycelynn argued, panic setting her stomach ablaze. "Who's going to help me make decisions about what's right and wrong for Alma and North Bay?"

"You'll have Dylan, Elizabeth and your family to help you," Brandon answered logically. "With luck, I'll be revived in time to spoil our grandchildren."

"No," Joycelynn mouthed, numbly rocking her head from side-to-side. This couldn't be happening. It had taken her half of her life to find this intelligent caring man. Now, she was losing him. How could it be part of Brandon's purpose-path to suffer such a cruel fate? It didn't make sense. She needed him. Alma and North Bay needed him.

"Can you sit closer so that I can touch you?" Brandon asked, and she did. Holding her hand, he shared the rest of his burdens, "I need to be preserved while there is minimum damage to my body, and before the cancer metastasizes into my brain. Cryogenics is illegal in Canada, so I've made arrangements in the United States. I found a local funeral home willing to refrigerate me as soon as my heart stops, and they'll ensure that my body is properly cooled and transported. My lawyer has the instructions, so you won't have to…."

"Shush." Joycelynn pressed her fingers to his lips. She couldn't bear to hear more, and she knew her husband well enough to know that his mind was set. Maybe she'd broach the subject in a few days, when he was feeling better.

Taking her hand and holding it against his heart, Brandon softly said, "A very wise woman once told me that, *once felt, love connects souls through all time and space and can never be erased.*"

Recognizing the quote from her novel, Joycelynn pursed her lips and fought back tears. She believed that love was eternal, but at the moment her beliefs gave nil comfort.

"Repeat our wedding vows with me," Brandon urged, smiling through his tears.

"That's silly," she protested, but when he squeezed her hand and began, she joined in, their eyes tenderly locked as they repeated the promises they'd exchanged one short year earlier. "I ask you to partner with me in love and matrimony, and to grow and prosper by my side through this life and eternity. I believe in you, in the love you so willingly share, and in the guiding hands that brought us together. Our shared love for each other, our families and friends, are gifts that I will forever treasure, respect and honor. I entrust you with my heart, my life and my soul, for today and for always."

Leaning forward and brushing his lips, Joycelynn whispered, "I will always love you."

"I will always love you, too, angel." Brandon held her gaze for a long moment, before wrapping her in his arms and kissing the top of her head.

Four weeks later, sitting at her kitchen table with Elizabeth, Joycelynn began to plan her husband's memorial. "Brandon made me promise to hold a celebration of life at the Inner Garden Chapel." Fighting tears, she bent forward and stared at the little angel fast asleep in her baby chair. There was nothing to celebrate. Brandon was gone and had taken her heart with him.

"Who'd you like to officiate, Barbara or me?" Elizabeth asked, as she stood and went to put the kettle on for tea.

"*You*, if you're up to it," she answered, knowing it was a lot to ask. Elizabeth and Brandon had become good friends. Officiating his celebration would likely unlock the flood of emotion her best friend kept tucked inside for Joycelynn's sake.

"Did Brandon request anything else?" Elizabeth enquired softly.

"He made me promise to keep a daily journal and take tons of pictures," Joycelynn answered. "He tried everything to convince me that science will soon be able to resuscitate cryogenic patients, just as they do drowning victims." She wiped at her tears with the back of her hand. It was a gigantic leap to compare reviving a drowning victim who'd been brain dead for minutes, to resuscitating someone whose body fluids have been replaced with *cryoprotectants*, and then vitrified at liquid nitrogen temperatures for years.

"Perhaps they will be able to revive him one day," Elizabeth said as she placed teabags into a porcelain pot. "All we can do is hope and pray."

Joycelynn had read everything written on cryogenics, and had spent numerous hours consulting with the directors of the institute where her husband's body was now sealed in a cryostat. As far as she could see, there wasn't much *hope* Brandon would ever be revived, so she changed the subject. "Brandon came to me last night."

"That doesn't surprise me," Elizabeth responded cheerfully. "Did he come to you in a dream, or did you actually see him?"

"It was around four a.m. I thought that I heard Alma fussing, so went into the nursery to check on her. She was sleeping peacefully, but I had a feeling I should stay with her, so I sat in the rocking chair next to her crib. When I looked up, Brandon was standing by the window."

Elizabeth poured the boiled water into the pot, retrieved two cups from the cupboard, and placed them on the table before sitting down. Reaching for Joycelynn's hand, she asked, "Did he say anything?"

"He said, *I'll wait for you on the other side.*'" Staring at Elizabeth, she added, "I don't know what that means."

"I imagine it means that he's crossed over and is waiting for you," her best friend replied. "It's not like you to question what happens when someone dies. You know that life is eternal and that we all return to the lovingness of Source." Gently squeezing Joycelynn's hand, she finished with, "I'm not certain what you're asking."

"How can Brandon wait for me at Source when he might come back to earth?" Once voiced, she realized that her question was ridiculous.

"I'd guess that his telling you that he's *waiting for you...* means that souls reunite at Source. If he'd gained some insight into future cryogenic advancements, he'd likely have said something such as *I'll be back soon.*"

"I suppose that's what he meant," Joycelynn agreed, "but as illogical as it is, I'm still wishing that he *will* come back to me in this lifetime. It makes me feel a little crazy."

Elizabeth nodded. "Losing a loved one is never easy. Holding onto hope that Brandon might be back is bound to make you feel a little crazy."

"Unfortunately, it's what I'm going to being thinking about for the rest of my life," Joycelynn confessed. "I can't bring myself to totally abandon the idea that my husband might eventually be resuscitated, because it would feel as though I were betraying him."

"I imagined it's a little like having someone declared missing and presumed dead."

"I suppose it is," Joycelynn agreed, pouring cream into her tea and taking a sip. "Lucky me! I now have a *spirit*-husband to go with my *spirit*-dog." Just as she believed she'd one day be reunited with her golden retriever, she knew she'd also one day be reunited with Brandon. Especially now that her husband's soul had come to tell her that he was waiting for her.

"I'm sorry," Elizabeth offered, her eyes misty. "You know that I'm always here for you."

"I do know that." Joycelynn held her best friend's caring glance. "And I still have Alma, North Bay, Dylan, the dogs, and a very fat cat to keep me company on earth. But as truly grateful as I am for your love and theirs, sometimes…."

"*Sometimes*, it's not enough," Elizabeth finished her sentence.

Joycelynn only nodded, unsure if she'd ever fully appreciate Brandon's argument that, beginning with losing Terry, his life purpose included being cryogenically preserved. But it wasn't her place to question her husband's, or anyone else's, interpretation of their soul-chosen reason for coming to earth. Though she suspected Brandon's theorizing had more to do with wanting her to accept his decision, rather than being beliefs he'd actually adopted as his own.

"Are you going to be okay?" Elizabeth asked worriedly.

"I'll probably be sad forever," Joycelynn admitted. "I know he's always close by, because every so often I catch a whiff of his cologne or hear him softly calling my name. He's definitely watching over us." Trying not to cry, she twisted her wedding ring as she added, "But I miss having him here in human form."

"If you think in scientific terms, he's still physically here in his daughter's DNA," Elizabeth offered as Alma started fussing.

Picking up the baby, Joycelynn said, "If our daughter turns out to be half the person her daddy *was*, or *is,* she'll be our crowning glory." She turned to face Elizabeth. "Sometimes late at night when the house is creaky quiet, and I'm sitting in the nursery peacefully holding Alma, I feel closer to Source. It's as though we are both being basked in the purest, most gentle love. It's an indescribably beautiful and serene feeling."

For a moment Elizabeth remained quiet, totally surprising Joycelynn when she finally said, "I'm certain that Source holds wee children and their mothers in love's palm."

"Why did you say that?" Joycelynn demanded more than asked, the hairs standing straight on her arms and neck.

"I don't know, it just came into my head and I said it." Tucking her chin closer to her chest and squinting curiously, she studied Joycelynn for a moment, before asking, "Why?"

"Brandon used to say those exact words," Joycelynn exclaimed as she clutched her daughter to her breast. "Think! Did you ever hear Brandon say those words to me?"

"The phrase just popped into my head. I thought it sounded comforting." Elizabeth laughed nervously. "I don't know if I could even repeat what I said."

Settling back in her chair, Joycelynn felt peaceful, almost happy, as she cooed to her daughter, "Daddy talked to us through Auntie Elizabeth. What do you think about that?"

Three months later, as Joycelynn was snuggling Alma into her carriage on a glorious sunny day, the doorbell rang. When she answered it, the postman had her sign for a registered parcel. She recognized the handwriting—it was Brandon's.

Closing the door, she sat at the kitchen table and stared at the package. After a few minutes, her hands trembling, she slowly removed the brown wrapping and opened the box. On top was a card with her name on it and a note that said *Read first*.

Dearest Joycelynn,

By now you've had time to adjust to life as a single mom. I know it was never what you wanted, but I also know that you are a strong and capable woman. Just as you were and will always remain the perfect wife for me, you are the perfect mother for our daughter.

I hope that you've gotten over being angry with me for choosing cryogenics. However, you more than anyone, realize that we sometimes just know things without being able to explain how or why we know them. I knew that I wouldn't be able to win the battle with cancer. That even if I underwent treatment, I'd still die. I chose what I believed was the quickest and most humane way to exit earth. Maybe science will advance and we will be together again in this lifetime. But I doubt it. I've paid to keep my body preserved until Alma's twenty-fifth birthday, and arranged with my lawyer as to where to bury my body when that time comes. (You'll find his card taped to the bottom of this box.)

By now, my lawyer should also have processed my life insurance policy with you named as the beneficiary. I asked him to wait until you contacted him before dispensing you the money. I'm hoping that you'll use your unexpected windfall to open that retreat in Costa Rica that you and Elizabeth always dreamed about. I've also set aside enough money for a down-payment on a house for North Bay. My lawyer has the details. You will know when it is the right time to give the funds to our adopted son.

You'll also find nineteen birthday cards for Alma and three for North Bay. You see, I was paying attention when you bought all the gifts for North Bay under the guise of having missed his birthdays. (If North Bay squawks about Alma getting more cards than him, put him in a headlock and tell him that it's not my fault that he was older when I croaked.)

Joycelynn, my sweet, sweet angel, it's time to stop grieving for me and get back to the work that is your life purpose—encouraging others to be kind to themselves as a way of seeding global kindness. In your latest novel, there's a quote by Wayne Dyer: *"Everything in the universe has a purpose. Indeed, the invisible intelligence that flows through everything in a purposeful fashion is also flowing through you."* From the day that you and I met, you often talked about life purpose and how everything in the universe is connected and interconnected through all time and space. The *invisible intelligence* to which Wayne refers, is the love you call Source. We can never truly be separate, for the invisible love of Source flows through us all—you, me, our daughter and son, our pets, families, and friends. Stay strong in your beliefs, sweet angel. I love you with all my heart and soul for today and for always.

I'll wait for you on the other side.

With love, Brandon xo xo xo

P.S. I've enclosed the wooden nickel charm and chain that was your wedding gift to me. I wanted to ensure that it wasn't destroyed, or lost, before we meet again.

Before going through the box Brandon had sent, Joycelynn reread his letter three times, repeatedly staring at the line *I'll wait for you on the other side.* They were the exact words her husband had said when he appeared by the nursery window.

A preview into the continuing journey
of Joycelynn and Elizabeth

THE WOODEN NICKEL
WELLNESS RETREAT AND SPA

THE WOODEN NICKEL WELLNESS RETREAT AND SPA

Where Kindness is Key and Health Golden.

An Inspirational Novel about
Life Here and at Source

Coauthored by
JOYCE M. ROSS and E. PATRICIA CONNOR

Co-founders of Kindness is Key Training Inc.

13 Keys to *Living the Life* YOU ARE MEANT TO LOVE Personally, Professionally and Spiritually.

Kindness Key # 1

HARMONY

❧

"Happiness is when what you think, what you
say, and what you do are in harmony."
Mahatma Gandhi

Alma burst through the swinging retreat doors carrying a
gigantic bundle of white roses interspersed with purple
irises. "Aunt Elizabeth, some man just dropped these off. Where
should I put them?" she asked, her freckled pixy nose curled
curiously as she studied the card accompanying the bouquet.
"They're from someone I don't remember, but likely should,
because they knew to send Mom's favorite flowers."

Pulling off her gardening gloves and walking toward her
goddaughter, Elizabeth shouted planting instructions over her
shoulder, "North Bay, that hole needs to be at least a foot deep,
and make certain you pour the bucket of stones in before you
plant the tree; Jatrophas need good drainage. You know how
rainy it gets here in southern Costa Rica; especially, during the
green season."

Ignoring North Bay's exaggerated grunts as he hoisted the
gallon bucket of rocks, Elizabeth put on the reading glasses
she kept on a string around her neck, and read the card aloud,
*"Recordando a nuestra embajadora de paz y bondad. Manuel
Quesada."* Taking off her glasses and letting them dangle again,

she handed the small card back to Alma. "Do you remember the day trip we took to the Guanacaste Region?"

"That's where Mom fell in love with the Jatropha tree," Alma said, staring at the card again.

Brushing a shiny amber bang back from her goddaughter's pretty face, she smiled. Though she had her father's eyes, Alma looked so much like her mother, Elizabeth sometimes mistakenly called her Joycelynn. "Manuel Quesada was the man who chartered the helicopter."

"I remember him," Alma said. "He and his wife came here for our anti-stress treatment after their son died. He spent most of his time on the boat with Mark trying to hook a sailfish. She spent most of her stay learning about Bach flower remedies and local herbs from you."

"I remember getting caught in the thunderstorm and having to wait out the rain for hours," Elizabeth said as North Bay joined them.

"I painfully remember having Mom's fingerprints on my leg for weeks," North Bay interjected. "She hated helicopters, but she still went with us."

Smiling reminiscently, Elizabeth retrieved her gardening gloves from her apron. "Your mom was a true trooper, which is why we should finish planting the Jatropha tree in her honor."

"I can't believe she's been gone for a whole year," North Bay mumbled as he shuffled alongside of Elizabeth and Alma. "I miss her."

"I miss her, too." Elizabeth looked out at the Pacific Ocean, warmly recalling how excited she and Joycelynn had been when they opened the *Wooden Nickel Wellness Retreat and Spa*. Brandon had been gone for about a year, when Joycelynn announced that she was finally ready to use his life insurance money for the purpose her husband intended. Within weeks, they flew to Costa Rica, rented a four-wheel drive, and spent days touring the mountainside looking for a suitable location. Two months later, Dylan, North Bay and a team of local carpenters started building. Their first guest walked through the doors of their thirteen-bed retreat on the second anniversary of Brandon's passing.

"Why did Mom love this kind of tree so much?" Alma asked as North Bay lowered the tree into the rock-bottomed hole.

"Because it's a less polluting form of biofuel, was the main reason. Although she also loved that its broad leaves have medicinal purposes, and that the tree's latex contains *jatrophine*, an alkaloid with anti-carcinogen properties. The tree also helps to purify the soil, so it's an all-around biogeological saint." She laughed as North Bay rolled his eyes. "What?" she asked, knowing full-well he wasn't interested in hearing about herbal healing remedies.

"Alma, when are you going to learn *not* to ask Aunt Elizabeth questions about plants, trees or flowers?" He bent for the shovel, picked up a scoop of dirt and spread it around the tree.

"I like learning about the healing properties of the plants and trees. Sometimes the kids in my English class ask about the local vegetation, and I don't want to appear ignorant." She fisted her hands to her hips the way her mother used to do. "Do you have a problem with that, because if you do...." Then, as if suddenly deciding it was futile explaining anything to her older brother, she stopped talking, did an about face and headed back toward the spa, tossing her hands into the air as she walked away.

"She's moody," North Bay muttered, dropping to his knees and patting the dirt around the tree.

"Today is the anniversary of the car crash that killed your mother," Elizabeth said softly. "Alma is entitled to be as moody as she pleases." Tousling his hair, she added, "You're entitled to be grumpy, too."

"I'd rather just work." Standing, he brushed the dirt off of his hands. "I'm going to fix the hinge on the *Integrity* room door." He picked up the shovel and pail and plunked them into the wheelbarrow.

"The guest in the *Dream* Room complained that her showerhead isn't supplying enough water. Would you mind taking a look at it?"

"I'll look at it, but Dad's better at plumbing. Maybe he can fix it when he gets back from town."

"As long as someone fixes it," she said, wiping her beaded forehead. "Thank you for helping plant your mom's tree. You're a great kid!"

"*De nada.*" North Bay stooped for the wheelbarrow, mumbling, "I'm not a kid."

"You are to me!" Elizabeth laughingly retorted as North Bay headed toward the tool shed. *Everyone under fifty seems like a kid when you're as close to Source as I am,* she mused. Alma was nearing twenty-two. North Bay was thirty-nine, married and had an expectant wife. Recalling how horrified Joycelynn had been when her daughter turned twenty, Elizabeth's heart ached. She missed her best friend every second of every hour. Feeling more melancholic than she cared to be, she checked her watch. Mark and the hotel guests wouldn't start returning from their various adventures for another two hours, and she had four hours before she needed to get ready for her evening meditation class. It was time to stop making excuses and start the writing project that had been nagging at her, or more accurately—haunting her.

Joycelynn had authored the majority of the inspirational novels for their Kindness is Key mission, but there was one more that had to be written. For weeks now, Elizabeth had been having the same dream, over and over. Each night it seemed to last longer and become more vivid. It was as though Joycelynn were trying to write from Source and was downloading her life on the other side into Elizabeth's dreams.

After making and pouring herself a cup of green tea, Elizabeth opened her laptop and began typing.

Chapter One

Recordando a Nuestra Embajadora de Paz y Bondad!
In Memory of our Peace and Kindness Ambassador!

I awoke feeling as though I was dreaming, and with my feet moving forward in directions of their own intention. Now and then, I would make them stop so that I could gaze upon something that seemed familiar—a mailbox covered with colorful graffiti, a swing in an old oak tree, or a young person whose eyes I seemed to know from somewhere long ago. I walked for hours, down streets that were oddly familiar, yet strange. No one seemed to notice me, though I was noticing them. That is, unless I include the elderly gentleman that threatened me with his walking stick when I tripped over it. He noticed me. I wish that he hadn't.

At dusk, when the sinking sun dimmed the world to the grayish hue of an old black and white movie, my two feet—which I knew belonged to me because they were on the end of my legs—walked me right up the stairs of the home I'd shared with Brandon. My arms seemed to have their own independent mind, too; for though I was afraid to knock on the door, I did anyway. I wanted to scream at my arms. Tell them that I didn't want to know who was living in my house. The house Dylan and North Bay had renovated and where my baby girl had her first birthday party. Especially, I didn't want to know who slept in the room where I'd last made love with my dying husband. And why were there dogs on the other side of the door, barking their heads off and sounding exactly like Robin, Lightning and Scruffy?

"You should answer the door, Brandon…she's your wife," Steve argued, checking his appearance in the mirror.

Why Joycelynn's first husband bothered glancing in the mirror, Brandon would never know. He always looked exactly the same, minus the change in outfits. "You were married to her, too! Plus, you've been waiting for her longer than I have, so you should have the honor of answering her arrival."

"She doesn't know that I'm dead!" Steve countered.

"She doesn't know that she's dead!" Brandon rebutted huffily. She thinks that she's dreaming, and it's our job to welcome her back to Source in as kind and gentle a manner as possible.

"It will be more kind and gentle if you talk to her first!" Steve said, stretching his height as tall as he could, seemingly vexed that he still measured two or three inches shorter than Brandon.

"She thinks that you're still alive." Brandon spiked his fingers through his hair and paced. "She'll just assume that you bought her old house."

"What about Robin, Lightning and Scruffy?" he asked with a smirk, knowing he had a good point. "She'll recognize the dogs! Heck, she designed an entire greeting card line in Robin's honor! He thought for a moment before filling in the name, *"Purple Pyjama Cards."*

"Oh, all right!" Brandon sucked in a whopping big breath to steel his nerves. "If she faints, it's on you!" he grumbled, placing his hand on the doorknob.

"People don't faint here—or get sick or die. We're at Source, remember?"

"Apparently people don't get any more cooperative at Source either," Brandon mumbled, tucking in his chin and opening the door. "Hello, angel."

Recommended Reading

Braden, Gregg. *Deep Truth: Igniting the Memory of Our Origin, History, Destiny and Fate.* USA: HayHouse, Inc., 2011.

Braden, Gregg. *The Divine Matrix: Awakening the Power of Spiritual Technology.* USA: Hay House   Inc., 2007.

Burchard, Brendon. *Life's Golden Ticket: An Inspirational Novel.* New York: HarperCollins, 2007.

Cameron, Julia. *The Artist's Way.* New York: Penguin Putman, 2002.

Dyer, Wayne W. *Change Your Thoughts, Change Your Life – Living The Wisdom of the Tao.* USA: Hay House Inc., 2007.

Dyer, Wayne W. *Wishes Fulfilled: Mastering the Art of Manifestation.* USA: Hay House Inc., 2012.

Hay, Louise L. *You Can Heal Your Life.* USA: Hay House Inc., 2004.

Kindness is Key Training Inc. *Heartmind Wisdom – An anthology of inspiring wisdom from those who have been there.* USA: Balboa Press, 2012

Kuntz, Ted. *Peace Begins With Me.* Coquitlam: Ted Kuntz, 2005.

Leonard, Barbara. *Don't Just Stand There Sucking Your Thumb*
.... New Westminster: Balance Point – Inner Garden Awareness
Institute, 2003.

Tully, Brock. *Reflections – for someone special*. Vancouver: B.
Tully, 1983.

Wieder, Marcia. *Making Your Dreams Come True*. New York:
Harmony, 1999.

Recommended Music

Hagan, Denise. *For Those Who Hear*. Rosa Records, Sneezer
Publishing, 2006.

Recommended Websites

www.kindnessiskey.com
www.heartmindwisdom.com
www.humanpeacesign.com
www.innergarden.com
www.worldkindnessconcert.com
www.mooncoinproductions.com (Kindness Rocks)
www.denisehagan.com
www.peacebeginswithme.ca
www.brocktully.com
www.mercyships.ca
www.mercyships.org